Managing Archives

CHANDOS
INFORMATION PROFESSIONAL SERIES

Series Editor: Ruth Rikowski
(email: Rikowskigr@aol.com)

Chandos' new series of books are aimed at the busy information professional. They have been specially commissioned to provide the reader with an authoritative view of current thinking. They are designed to provide easy-to-read and (most importantly) practical coverage of topics that are of interest to librarians and other information professionals. If you would like a full listing of current and forthcoming titles, please visit our web site **www.chandospublishing.com** or contact Hannah Grace-Williams on email info@chandospublishing.com or telephone number +44 (0) 1865 884447.

New authors: we are always pleased to receive ideas for new titles; if you would like to write a book for Chandos, please contact Dr Glyn Jones on email gjones@chandospublishing.com or telephone number +44 (0) 1865 884447.

Bulk orders: some organisations buy a number of copies of our books. If you are interested in doing this, we would be pleased to discuss a discount. Please contact Hannah Grace-Williams on email info@chandospublishing.com or telephone number +44 (0) 1865 884447.

Managing Archives

Foundations, Principles and Practice

CAROLINE WILLIAMS

Chandos Publishing

Oxford · England

Chandos Publishing (Oxford) Limited
Chandos House
5 & 6 Steadys Lane
Stanton Harcourt
Oxford OX29 5RL
UK
Tel: +44 (0) 1865 884447 Fax: +44 (0) 1865 884448
Email: info@chandospublishing.com
www.chandospublishing.com

First published in Great Britain in 2006

ISBN:
1 84334 112 3 (paperback)
1 84334 113 1 (hardback)

© C. Williams, 2006

British Library Cataloguing-in-Publication Data.
A catalogue record for this book is available from the British Library.

Typeset by Domex e-Data Pvt. Ltd.
Printed in the UK and USA.

To Jonathan and James

Contents

List of figures

List of tables

Acknowledgements

There are many people to thank for their contribution to this publication, not least current and former students and colleagues both at home and abroad who have in different ways influenced my thoughts and informed my understanding. In particular, I am indebted to Margaret Procter and Michael Cook of LUCAS for reading and commenting extensively on the text and for their ongoing advice and support. Thanks are due also to Carl Newton and Jonathan Pepler for their useful and constructive comments and to Christopher Williams for creating the index.

For permission to reproduce screen shots I gratefully acknowledge: The National Archives (Figures 4.10, 5.2, 5.3, 5.4, 5.6, 6.1); DS Ltd (Figures 3.1, 4.7, 4.8); The University Archives, The University of Iowa Libraries, Iowa City, Iowa (Figure 5.5); the School of Library, Archive and Information Studies, University College London, and the George Orwell Estate (Figure 5.1); University of London Computer Centre (Figure 4.11); The Sainsbury Archive, now The Sainsbury Archive at the Museum in Docklands (Figure 5.7); HSBC Group Archives (Figure 5.8). Many of the examples used throughout the text are drawn from sources held at the Cheshire and Chester Archives and Local Studies. I am indebted to the County Archivist Jonathan Pepler for his permission to use them.

About the author

Caroline Williams worked in archives and records management in local government before joining the University of Liverpool in 1996. She was instrumental in the establishment of the Liverpool University Centre for Archives Studies (LUCAS) in the same year: LUCAS is the university's centre for research, education, and training in archives and records management and its Executive Committee comprises academics, practitioners and users of archives. She became director of the Master's programme in Archives and Records Management in 1997. She has been Chair of FARMER, the Forum for Archives and Records Management Education and Research in the UK since 2003 and a member of the International Council on Archives Section on Education and Training since 2001. Current areas of research interest and publication include the history and diplomatic analysis of the record, and the interface between theory and practice.

The author may be contacted by:

E-mail: *C.M.Williams@liverpool.ac.uk*

Introduction

Records are indispensable for the efficient management of our lives, of organisations and of government but are often undervalued, ignored or misunderstood. Yet they help support the rights and responsibilities of every individual and enable the smooth running of all organisations – from governments to golf clubs and multi-nationals to mosques. At the same time archives, the small subset of records selected for permanent preservation, provide individuals with a sense of identity and preserve the culture and history of a people.

Between them, archives and records provide an infrastructure for both personal and public activity. But for the real potential of archives and records to be realised they need to be managed in a professional manner. Records managers are concerned with the administration of the current records of an organisation and archivists with those records that have been selected to be kept permanently. Both groups have principles and practices in common and have close ties with other disciplines, both in the information sector – knowledge, document and information management – and in the cultural sector – museums and library management.

The purpose of this book is first to provide an introduction to the common theory and principles that underpin both records and archives management. Secondly, it offers practical guidance to those working specifically with archives. It is aimed at those who are starting out as archive professionals and need a basic handbook; at students on archives, records, museums, library and information programmes who are seeking an introduction to the discipline; and to anyone who has taken responsibility for archives but without any prior experience.

Chapter 2 looks at general principles and approaches. Chapters 3–6 focus on specific aspects of archive work. These chapters briefly describe the underlying theory, principles and standards upon which practice is founded, suggesting possible techniques, and using real-life examples alongside suggested reading and websites for further study. The final chapter introduces some of the management techniques necessary for running an archive service. Although the guidance is aimed primarily at a UK audience it draws on examples of international practice when appropriate.

Principles and purposes of records and archives

Before you can get down to practical work on archives you need have some appreciation of the concepts and principles that underpin all basic archival practices. Knowledge and understanding of these will give you the confidence to use the appropriate procedures and techniques in specific situations. This chapter aims to set the context for archives; subsequent chapters give more detailed practical guidance.

This chapter:

- defines records and archives and principles and concepts;
- identifies their similarities to and differences from other information sources;
- explains how people and organisations use records and archives;
- describes the core functions of archives management;
- describes the role of the archivist and records manager; and
- identifies the historical and institutional environments in which archives are found

Defining archives. What is the difference between records and archives?

Definitions are often vexing, and nuances of language can lead to a number of interpretations. We need to be clear about definitions, however, in order to:

- explain precisely and confidently to colleagues, managers, customers and friends what it is we do;

- recognise the boundaries of our professional activity as well as commonalities with other disciplines; and

- understand our own professional roles and carry out our responsibilities.

An understanding of archives cannot be separated from an understanding of records: although processes for dealing with them might vary, they are inextricably linked. However the words 'archives' and 'records' mean different things to different people. Anything that is old and/or needs saving can be 'archived'. A random search of the term reveals the University of Virginia's hypertext archive of British poetry and a weather archive at the National Climatic Data Center in north Colorado; the University of Liverpool's library catalogue includes such titles as the *Archives of Mathematics* and *Archives of the Peat Bogs*. And 'records' are not just written – they might be musical, criminal or broken!

Archivists and records managers must work to more specific definitions than these. For them *records* comprise information generated by organisations and individuals in their daily business and personal transactions. *Archives* are a subset of these: they are those records kept for their continuing value. Archivists and records managers might also use the word 'archives' to refer to a building where archives are stored or as part of the title of the service or agency that manages them.

The generally accepted difference between records and archives, at least for most anglophones, is that the term

- 'records' has been applied to the products of current and ongoing activity, whereas

- 'archives' has been defined as referring to any records with long-term continuing value that have been kept either because they may be necessary for ongoing organisational purposes to their creating body or because they have additional research value.

However, in many European languages the word 'archives' is taken to mean both records in use for current purposes and those maintained for their continuing long-term value: in France last week's email and a ninth-century Carolingian charter may both be 'archives'. In England the first archival theorist, Sir Hilary Jenkinson, did not differentiate either: to him archives were created as part of any transaction, and subsequently preserved. To Sir Hilary a 'record' was a transaction resulting in a legal document produced by a court 'of record'.

In America in the mid-twentieth century Theodore Schellenberg, of the National Archives and Records Service in Washington, was the first person to articulate a difference and division between records and archives. He perceived 'records' as created and maintained for current organisational purposes and 'archives' as records set aside and used for purposes *other* than those they had been created for, such as historical research. (Americans also identify a distinction between 'archives' as being generated by organisations or institutions and 'manuscripts' as being generated by individuals or families.)

Australian archivists were early critics of the idea of a rigid division between records and archives. They developed a holistic, 'continuum-based' approach that argues that there is no one point when a record suddenly becomes an archive in some sort of linear progression; and that in any case it is possible to use records/archives as a record or archive at the same time. Yesterday's 'archive', for example a nineteenth-century map used by the local historian to trace field boundaries, can become today's 'record' when it is required as evidence of public rights of way, in current court proceedings.

These diverse approaches are reflected in the different national and international definitions of archives shown below. The most recent and most authoritative is that provided by an international standard, published in 2001.

Definitions of records and archives

United Kingdom

Archives (including records)

'A document which may be said to belong to the class of Archives is one which was drawn up or used in the course of an administrative or executive transaction ... of which itself formed a part; and subsequently preserved in their own custody ... by the person or persons responsible for that transaction and their legitimate successors.' Sir Hilary Jenkinson, *Manual of Archive Administration*, 1st edn, 1922.

United States

Records

All books, papers, maps ... made or received by any ... institution in pursuance of its legal obligations or in the transaction of its proper business and preserved ... by that institution or its legitimate successor as

---

evidence of its functions, policies, decisions, procedures, operations or other activities or because of the informational value of the data contained therein.

Archives

Those records ... adjudged worthy of preservation for reference and research purposes and which have been deposited or have been selected for deposit in an archival institution. T. R Schellenberg, *Modern Archives*, 1956, p. 56.

Australia

Records

Recorded information, in any form, including data in computer systems, created or received and maintained by an organisation or person in the transaction of business or the conduct of affairs and kept as evidence of such activity.

Archives

The whole body of records of continuing value of an organisation or individual ... sometimes called the 'corporate memory'. Australian Standard AS 4390:1996.

International definition

Records (and archives?)

Information created, received and maintained as evidence and information by an organisation or person, in pursuance of legal obligations or in the transaction of business. ISO 15489:2001.
(The international standard does not explicitly define archives.)

I shall return to the practical effects of these definitions later. Increasingly the distinction in definition between records and archives is blurring, and the term 'record-keeping' is increasingly being used to describe and encompass the complementary disciplines of records and archives management. But whether you think of records/archives as two parts of a whole, as part of a record-keeping continuum or as two distinct areas, it is still the case that when jobs are advertised they are either for an archivist, whose main role is looking after non-current archival records, or for a records manager, whose job is to maintain records for current purposes. However, an archivist with no knowledge of records management, or a records manager who had no understanding of archival practice would not be very employable. You will need to bear this discussion in mind when I consider two current theories, the records life cycle and the records continuum, in more detail.

For practical purposes I am here defining archives as those records that need to be kept for the long term: you might envisage archives as a 'subset' of records.

The qualities of records (and archives)

Evidence of a transaction

What really distinguishes a record from any other kind of information is that it is produced as a result of a unique activity or transaction and can therefore provide evidence of that activity or transaction. A set of minutes is evidence that a meeting was held and certain subjects discussed; an email is evidence that a message containing information has passed between two or more people. If you go into a shop and buy a cabbage, what is the record: the cabbage, the paper bag with the greengrocer's name, the till receipt? Not the cabbage – we cannot derive information from it; nor the paper bag – the greengrocer has hundreds with the shop's name on so it is not, on its own, going to help provide evidence of this particular sale. However, the till receipt supplies evidence of the transaction – the proof of purchase – because it identifies the shop, the item sold, the amount paid and the date. You may be able to take the cabbage back and swap it for a cucumber, provided you keep the receipt. The receipt is the record: it provides the evidence of the transaction and of the circumstances, the context in which it took place (Figure 2.1).

This is an example of a record of a fairly low-level transaction. More broadly, organisations produce records of the transactions that underpin their functions and activities – their 'mission', if you like. So, if business *functions* are what an organisation is responsible and accountable for doing to fulfil its stated role and its responsibilities to its stakeholders, and business *activities* are what an organisation does to carry out its business functions,[1] then *transactions* are associated with the accomplishment of each individual activity. Functions are *what* they do, and activities are *how* they do them.[2]

Figure 2.1 A record

```
              MARKS &
              SPENCER
            22 Foregate Street.
                  Chester.
            TEL 01244 348441.

         VAT No: 232 1288 92

                                     £
    00847254     CABBAGE HEARTS      1.29

    Balance to pay 1 item           1.29

    Cash tendered                   5.00

    Cash due                        3.71
    03/02/05 13:09 13728916 0438 358 124
```

Any organisation has two types of function: those that are specific to its core business, its *substantive* functions, and those that support the core business, the *facilitative* functions, those which all organisations have to engage in, such as administration, managing finance and human resources. This is more easily understood if we look at an example.

Three of the substantive *functions* of a university might be identified as research, teaching and learning, and student administration and support. One of the *activities* that occur as part of the teaching and learning function is examination setting and marking. One of the *transactions* associated with this particular activity might be giving written feedback to students. The written feedback is then the record resulting from this transaction, and is evidence that I have undertaken the activity required.

Content, context and structure

It is accepted theory that an authentic and reliable record should have three attributes:

- Content – the information or subject matter contained in the record.
- Context – relating to the process of which the record is a part; the environment and web of relationships in which the document was created and used.
- Structure – the format and medium of the record.[3]

Let us apply these attributes to the written feedback given to Bart Simpson for his essay on 'How study at secondary school helps the college student to contribute to community life'.

The *content* of this record comprises my comments on why he failed: plagiarised content, failure to focus on the question, below-standard grammar and general presentation, inappropriate comments about teaching staff.

The *context* is demonstrated by the fact that the feedback is from me, a university lecturer (I signed it), addressed to Bart, an enrolled student of the university, as part of a required activity. Bart may keep a copy (or more likely bin it), the university will keep a copy, where it will stay with other pieces of feedback resulting from similar processes or transactions until it is no longer needed and is destroyed. There is a web of relationships here too. There is a relationship between the university, Bart and me. There is another between me, as creator of the record, and the record itself. There is also a relationship between this piece of feedback and Bart's written essay: neither can be fully understood without the other. And the context of the business process is supplying feedback as part of the examination setting and marking activity within the teaching and learning function.

The *structure* of the feedback relates to its appearance and format – on university headed paper, for example, in a format that is specifically created for the purpose. Fields for completion include the student's name and/or number, date and details of performance against stated assessment criteria, and a final mark. If the feedback merely comprised notes on the back of a shopping list, for example, Bart might reasonably query its authenticity and reliability.

Although the feedback carries the essential elements that make it a record, the records management service will have ensured that, because of its lack of long-term value it is not likely to reach the archives. It will have had a retention period (a date for its destruction) attached to it (well, to the whole series of feedback forms for the students in Bart's year) and may be kept for a couple of years. Higher-level documentation of Bart's overall performance will be kept for longer, and a decision about what to transfer to the archives, if anything, will be made by the records manager and archivist.

Authenticity, integrity, usability, reliability

In addition to these attributes, the International Standard requires authoritative records to have the qualities of authenticity, integrity, usability and reliability.[4] It is these characteristics that set them apart from other forms of information. *Authentic* records are what they claim to be, created or sent by the person claiming to have created them and at the time claimed. *Reliable* records are those that can be trusted to be full and accurate representations of the business transaction in hand. Records that are authentic and reliable will have *integrity* and to be *useable* people must be able to locate, retrieve, present and interpret them.

The medium and format of records and archives

Individuals and organisations have always used whatever technology is to hand for making records. So media (the physical carrier or support) and format (how they are presented) can vary enormously. From the media of clay tablets, papyrus, parchment and paper to microform, film, video, audio, magnetic, optical and digital media – all are capable of receiving, storing and transmitting recorded information.

How records are presented is often determined by their medium. Parchment can be rolled but photographic paper cannot, for example. Rolls, volumes, files or dossiers, single pages, maps, microfiche, photographs, audio and videocassettes, disks, DVDs, databases, spreadsheets and e-mail are some of the many formats in which records may be met with.

Archival principles and concepts

Life cycle

Two concepts currently used by archivists and records managers when considering how to manage records and archives are those of the life cycle and the continuum. These provide a framework for conceptualising the goals and tasks associated with records management and archives management.

The life-cycle concept is based on the notion that any record has a life, and that like an organic being once it has been generated it has an active life in maturity, a less active life in old age, and in the end is discarded (it 'dies') and either destroyed (hell) or transferred to the archives (heaven). (The process of deciding on its long-term future has sometimes been described as purgatory.) We can think of it as the lifespan or time period from the creation or receipt of a record through its useful life to its final disposition. Most records do progress from being current, to semi-current, to non-current (or -active if you prefer).

The model is useful because it enables us to track, in a sequential process, the progress of a record and to ensure that the right processes are undertaken at each phase of its life (Figure 2.2 and Table 2.1).

But not all records follow a similar path. Some records are born archival: you would not consider destroying the instrument of abdication statement made by the English King Edward VIII in 1936 or Abraham Lincoln's Emancipation Proclamation of 1863 just because they had fulfilled their immediate role. Other records are born ephemeral: unless you have a particular interest in cabbages or receipts you are not going to keep a cabbage receipt longer than it takes to clear your bank account (if you did not pay cash). And a record's life can last a week or less, 10 years or longer – and a record created in 1850 can be as current as one created last year if it is still being used. We have already discussed cases where archival records are once more required for current purposes – so records can go in and out of 'currency', or backwards and forwards around the life cycle.

The life cycle represents Schellenberg's view of a clear division between records and archives. In practice, records managers have traditionally been responsible for managing the current and semi-current records and archivists have taken over responsibility at the archival stage. At the end of the records life cycle those records selected for their continuing value as archives become subject to a further series of *archival* processes that are fully described below. This division between the two aspects can lead to disjointed practice: the records manager describes (through file plans, classification schemes, for example) the current/semi-current records for one set of processes; the archivist then re-describes them when they are transferred to the archives for a different set. Would it not be easier if they only had to be described once?

Figure 2.2 The life-cycle

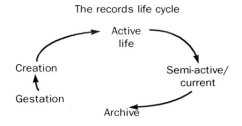

The records life cycle

Table 2.1   Life cycle processes

Phase	Considerations	Processes
Gestation	Does this activity need recording?	Decisions about its form, content, life span – before it is created
Creation and capture	Record is created/ received and captured in a record-keeping system	Application of appropriate metadata (descriptive information about the record's context); systematic capture
Active life	Record is referred to frequently	Appropriate access, storage, retrieval, security, preservation, appraisal, some destruction
Semi-active life	Record is referred to infrequently	Less access, retrieval, off-site storage, appraisal, some destruction
Archive	Records accessed as archives, for non-current purposes	Archival standard storage and access: a further cycle of processes

The other issue that the life cycle, because it is based on linear progression, cannot encompass is that of electronic records. In a paper environment, where the record is a physical item, it is possible to capture and file it, take it out and review it, store it in acid-free boxes, conserve it and so on as the need arises. In a paper record the message (writing) is inextricably attached to the medium (paper), but electronic records (e-recs) are virtual – they only exist as binary digits randomly stored in a computer until you call them up. The medium is separate from the message. Unless you plan all the necessary maintenance processes at the time of their creation and capture they simply will not survive to become archives. Issues such as technological obsolescence, the need to migrate data to new platforms, the safeguarding of the authenticity of a record as it undergoes updates, and decisions on precisely how long its life span will be all have to be dealt with at the outset.

Continuum

The records continuum, developed in Australia, is an indicator of the increasingly 'holistic' approach to records discussed earlier. It is '... a consistent and coherent regime of management processes from the time of creation of records (and before creation, in the design of recordkeeping systems), through the preservation and use of records as archives.'[5] It recognises that the processes carried out (separately) in the traditional records management domain and in the traditional archival domain are basically similar: we create or receive records, we classify, appraise, control and maintain them, and we make them accessible. It argues that these processes are so interrelated, overlapping and integrated – especially, but not only, in the electronic environment – that it is counterproductive to maintain any distinction.

When presented as a theory, the continuum model represents record keeping-based activity as an ongoing movement in and through four dimensions and four axes. The axes represent the general elements for demonstrating accountability: 'who [identity] did what [transactionality], what evidence exists about this [evidentiality], and how it can be recalled from documents and archives [record keeping containers].'[6] These elements occur within four dimensions or layers representing actions taken and documents created: Create, Capture, Organise (i.e. maintain documents and archives) and Pluralize (i.e. make available as evidence of collective memory).

Thus, whereas the life-cycle approach perceives each stage as linear with and independent of the other stages, the continuum perceives record keeping as multidimensional. It suggests that the management of records is not time-based or sequential, and that actions on the record are seamless and may be simultaneous: a record may at one and the same time be accessed for current organisational and archival purposes especially if it is in electronic form.

All this can be quite hard to grasp. It would, I think, be a mistake to try rigidly to relate the theory to practice, but much more useful to allow it to insinuate itself into your consciousness and enhance your understanding of records and archives and the actions that are performed around them.

Provenance

The term provenance is familiar to anybody who watches antiques programmes. In archival terms it refers to the administrative origin of a record or of an archival collection and is concerned with determining how the individual or organisation accumulated, organised and used its records.

According to the principle of provenance the link between archives and their creator should be maintained in order to preserve the quality and context of the evidence that is contained implicitly or explicitly in the archive. Nor should archives from different creators be intermingled. As Sue McKemmish says, provenance:

relates to the preservation of the context of the records, that is, their links to purpose, function and activity, to the individual or parts of an organisation which created them, and to other records created by that individual or that organisation.[7]

Not only is the provenance of a collection of archives itself, of who created and maintained it, important to an understanding of its context, so is the relationship of its constituent parts (the interrelationship of the documents in it). Joe Soap's admission to Parkfield's Primary School in 1980 is noted in its admissions register; the fact of his being caught smoking behind the bike shed in 1985 is noted in the daily log book, and his punishment for doing so in the punishment book. Photographs of him as captain of the school football team for three years show the numerous trophies of which he was so proud. Separation of these records, or viewing any in isolation, might lead to a very partial picture of Joe's progress at school: to retain their full evidential value they need to be managed as a unit.

Original order

Like the principle of provenance, that of original order is another with a long history in archival literature. It requires that records should be maintained in the order in which they were placed by the creating organisation or individual where it can be discerned. The idea is that archivists restore this 'original order' to present to the user an unaltered view of how the records were managed in current use. It ties in with notions of the objectivity of the record, the role of the archivist being to avoid putting on 'spin' when interpreting them. However, it is sometimes difficult to tell how records were maintained while in use, and so schemes of arrangement or classification have to be devised, usually based on the administrative structure or functions of the creator. This is discussed further in Chapter 4.

The document, knowledge and information management disciplines

Records and archives need to be considered within the wider 'information' context. Just as the distinction between records and archives is often blurred in practice, so it is between information, documents and knowledge, and thus of information management, document management and knowledge management. It is highly likely that some of the products managed by these disciplines will be viewed and used as archives.

Here are some working definitions. Doubtless there are others (e.g. the words 'document' and 'archive' to a computer programmer may mean something quite different) but I hope they will help you to see the *differences*. However, there are few strict boundaries, and it is important to realise that in practice there is fluidity and flexibility (Tables 2.2. and 2.3).

Table 2.2   The information spectrum: from knowledge to archives

	Description	Example
Knowledge	What's in our heads: 'tacit' (not easily expressed) and 'explicit' (can be communicated)	Tacit: we know what coffee smells like; explicit: can describe how a photocopier works
Information	Knowledge becomes information when people communicate it	Photocopier manual
Document	A single item, with information content and structure but lacking context; not part of a 'transaction'	Photocopier manual; newspaper; list of opening hours; shopping list, etc.
Records	Recorded information, created or received and maintained as part of a business or personal activity: contextual and transactional	Letter(s); invoice(s); file or dossier etc.; must have evidence of a transaction. A list of shop opening hours included in a letter (a record) becomes part of that record.
Archives	Records with continuing value	In theory, records of continuing value: in practice any of the above which retain an interest

Table 2.3 The 'knowledge' disciplines

Discipline	Definition
Knowledge management	Managing knowledge from all sources within an organisation (e.g. employees' knowledge), including records, and exploiting it for the benefit of that organisation or business[8]
Information management	The management of information products of any kind which support business activities (e.g. technical manuals, journals) beyond that supplying evidence of those activities (records)
Document management	Deals primarily with individual documents; but electronic document management systems (edms) can have similar functionality to electronic records management systems (erms)
Records management	The efficient and systematic control of the creation, receipt, maintenance, use and disposition of records in any format throughout their life cycle[9]
Archives management	The selection, preservation, maintenance, arrangement description and access to materials of continuing value for the long term

How people and organisations use records and archives

Individuals and organisations create, use and keep records in the course of their lives and their work: indeed, records provide the infrastructure for life and for business. Without records you would find it difficult to claim your rights as a citizen (passport, birth certificate); provide evidence (of exams passed); be able to account for your actions (you *did* pay your phone bill) or recall life's events (postcards of those sunlit holidays on the beach in Tobago; the last letter your grandmother wrote before she died). These records accumulate, and those that you decide to keep will form your personal archive.

Organisations, too, create and keep records for similar purposes: to enable them to carry out their current business functions and activities; to demonstrate compliance with legal requirements; to account for their actions; as evidence of transactions undertaken; and to provide information about their activities. *Every* organisation, from governments to primary schools and from multi-nationals to your local convenience store, keeps records of its activities in order to:

- provide it with the body of information necessary to continue or further to develop or revise those activities;

- protect itself in case of legal or other challenges, i.e. to enable it to produce evidence to show that it has acted appropriately on a matter and has met its obligations; and

- meet the accountability requirements imposed on it by the regulatory environment in which it operates.

For example, a pharmaceutical company will maintain records of its research and development into its cosmetic product 'Bright Eyes' so that the information will be available for reference when planning the newer and better version 'Brighter Eyes'. It will retain them also for purposes of product liability. If challenged in court by a customer that the product had damaged her eyes, referring to its records should enable the company to demonstrate that it had rigorously followed all requisite industry procedures, and conducted exhaustive pre-launch trials. It might also choose to demonstrate its accountability to regulators and stakeholders by publishing results in a more open way than any of its competitors.

So there are clear benefits to good records management. Describing what can happen in the absence of good records management can make a more compelling scenario. Here are some high-profile examples.

Record keeping: the big picture

In apartheid South Africa, the destruction of records as government policy demonstrated that government's denial of any notion of democratic accountability to a majority of its citizens.

The opening of the files of the Stasi, the East German secret police, after the fall of the Berlin Wall shattered many lives when they revealed that many ordinary citizens had informed against friends, neighbours and relations.

The failure of some banks in the UK and elsewhere to maintain proper archives and records systems has led to the inability of the descendants of many Holocaust victims exterminated in death camps to claim their inheritances.

Lack of resources in post-colonial Africa has led to a loss of knowledge about its countries' infrastructure and people. Records of bridges, drains, railways and roads, and those relating to people's health, voting, land and pension rights have been lost.

Records are created and kept because they enable individuals and organisations to operate effectively and provide evidence of their actions. *Archives* are also kept for these reasons, but as a subset of records selected for permanent preservation – and they have an added cultural and societal dimension, too.

The Council of Europe says:

> Archives form a basic and irreplaceable part of the cultural heritage. They preserve the memory of nations and the survival of human memory in large part depends on them.[10]

Archives, like records:

- permit continuity and consistency in administration;
- document, in a democracy, governmental responsibility and accountability to the people over time;
- provide us with a sense of national, regional or civic identity;
- educate, entertain and enrich our lives by providing appealing and tangible manifestations of our history, as well as useful information.

Some of the scenarios described above show that the 'big' records and archives management issues centre on the necessity for transparent record keeping for accountability and the protection of human rights. They demonstrate that access to archives is a democratic necessity for cultural and 'identity' reasons, and that the maintenance of proper records is fundamental for good governance and the maintenance of infrastructures. People working with records on a daily basis, whether or not with records of this kind of sensitivity and importance, should realise that how they manage them matters.

Those managing archives are concerned with the cultural, social and historical value of these archives in addition to their legal and business value. They provide equality of access to researchers with a wide range of interests and competences: from economists and environmental scientists to geographers and genealogists; from school children and students and their teachers to the retired; and those with a range of abilities and disabilities.

> Records have multiple purposes in terms of their value to an individual, organization or society. They are vehicles of communication and interaction, facilitators of decision-making,

enablers of continuity, consistency and effectiveness in human action, memory stores, repositories of experience, evidence of rights and obligations. On a darker note, they can also be instruments of repression and abuse of power.[11]

Introducing the core functions of archives management

The life-cycle description in Table 2.1 refers to archives and a 'further cycle of processes'. If we were operating in an entirely holistic and 'continuum-compliant' environment such processes would have been undertaken on behalf of the archives at the time of their creation and capture. Some in-house archives, where the purpose of the service is to care solely for the archives of its parent body, do operate systems that encompass current record and archival processes. However, many archival collections will have long been orphaned from any parent body conceivably interested in incorporating at an early stage any archival processes, and they have been acquired, as archives, by collecting repositories. Indeed, one of the premises upon which this book is based is that there remains a need for guidance precisely for those archives that are now coming in from the cold. Although some processes mirror those undertaken by records managers, there are some significant differences, not least in approaches determining the content of 'collections' and methodologies for making them accessible to users.

The basic mission of an archival organisation is to select, preserve and make available the collections in its care. In order to do this a range of substantive functions needs to be carried out. Some of these relate to the administrative control of material through physical processes, and others to intellectual control, the exploitation of the information contained in the archival and other resources.[12]

These substantive functions, described in detail in later chapters, are:

- acquisition, selection and appraisal;
- arrangement and description;
- provision of access and reference services;
- storage and maintenance of archives;
- preservation and conservation;
- advocacy and outreach.

Facilitative functions, described in Chapter 7, are:

- setting and implementing goals, aims and objectives;
- managing establishment, financial and human resources;
- evaluating strengths and weaknesses;
- measuring performance.

The role of the archivist and records manager

Students gaining archival qualifications from universities will usually have been equipped to act as both records manager and as archivist: this is important if they are to be able to bring a proper perspective to bear on their professional practice. Other courses prepare students for careers in information and library management, where there is more emphasis on the broader field of information than on the 'record'; others that impact on the cultural and artefactual aspects of the archivist's work are cultural heritage and museum programmes.

Both records managers and archivists are involved in managing the records of organisational and individual activity. They are concerned with the proper appraisal, arrangement, and access and retrieval of information, and the protection of their holdings with appropriate equipment and environmentally sound storage areas. Both are concerned with security issues, with business continuity planning in case of disaster and with the use of technology to support their functions. However, differences do result from the different immediate objectives of records management and archival programmes.

Records managers are primarily concerned with what the International Standard describes as supporting the organisation's business functions by helping to 'create and maintain authentic, reliable and usable records, and protect the integrity of those records for as long as required' for example in public administration or corporate business environments.[13] Their first duty is, therefore, to the record-creating organisation. However, when that organisation has an interest in maintaining its archives in the long term the records manager can assist in identifying records of potential archival value.

The chief mission of the archivist is to select, preserve and make available the archives in his or her care. They consider the cultural and social value of records alongside their business and legal value. They work in a range of contexts. In one model the archivist maintains the archives of his or her parent body ('in-house model'), whether a government, organisation or institution, firstly for their administrative usefulness to the creators or their successors. Records that have been identified by the records manager (in discussion with the archivist) as having archival value will become the archivist's responsibility and members of the organisation his or her prime clients. As already discussed 'archives' can still be called upon for use for 'current' purposes. In small organisations the archivist and records manager may well be one and the same.

Archivists also work in environments where the link with their employer is tied in less with the management of the organisation's own records than with managing collections taken in from external sources, in line with a specific acquisition or collections policy ('collecting model'). Here the archivist will select, preserve, arrange, describe and make accessible these to a wider client group and for a wider range of research purposes.

Whether archivist, records manager or both, it is important to view ourselves as operating within an overarching record-keeping profession in which records managers and archivists work alongside each other in designing and managing systems that ensure the capture of those records that may have continuing value. Although the roles of records manager and archivist may require different skills, they are to some extent mutually dependent, sharing a common concern for the identification and preservation of records and archives of relevance to their organisations.

Archives and organisations in context

(Not the) History of archives

Archival institutions develop naturally as cultures develop a written from an oral tradition and adopt the practice of recording information by 'writing' on any receptive material. They originate from:

- the need of rulers and governments to operate efficiently supported by appropriate administrative infrastructures;
- a realisation of the value of archives as encapsulating precedent and recording rights; and

■ an appreciation of archives as cultural artefacts and as an expression and reflection of 'nationhood'.

Some discussions about the history of archival institutions start by describing their likely origins in the ninth millennium BCE when the Sumerians, in what is now Iraq, recorded financial transactions on clay.[14] Others start in ancient Greece where it is known that the fifth century BCE Athenians cared for their records in the Metroon, a temple next to the court house in Athens; or with the Romans: in the sixth century Justinian ordered the construction of public buildings for the safe storage of archives in order to preserve public faith in them and to perpetuate memory.[15] In 'modern' Europe the Church, in the form of the papacy and the monasteries, as well as the monarchies maintained rudimentary and often peripatetic archives; that of the Simancas is recognised as the first distinct European archives repository when it was established by Charles I of Spain in 1543. The establishment of the *Archives Nationales* in Paris in 1794 is arguably the moment of recognition in modern times of the state's responsibility to preserve and care for the records of its people.

Although it is not the purpose of this book to explore archival history in detail, an examination of the literature is a useful way of reminding us about the enduring connection between records and the processes of business and social life. It also enables us to appreciate some of the continuities of practice: that then and now records were created for current use and future reference and used as evidence; stored in purpose-built containers and buildings and classified for purposes of retrieval.[16]

National models

National archival traditions are founded on a country's individual legal, administrative, cultural and social practices. The way governments govern has led to different administrative infrastructures being developed, and the way they manage their archives has led to the application of different archival principles and practices on a national basis.

In countries with highly centralised systems of government, for example in China and former communist countries, state control has led to a regularisation of practices from the centre. By contrast, in countries with a federal structure such as the USA and Australia (where the individual states together form a united nation, but remain independent in internal affairs) the national archives have archival organisations in each state, responsible for the records of federal functions (defence, foreign policy), but individual states have a great degree of independence over the management of their own archives, in state archives, state libraries and historical societies as we shall see below. Switzerland's model is even less centralised than that: each canton manages its archival organisations independently, with no central requirements for standard legislation, procedures or practices. In the UK, England, Wales, Scotland and Northern Ireland have also developed their respective archives broadly independently.

Differences in different countries' legal, administrative, cultural and social traditions reflect on the 'collecting' mission of their national archives, too. The mission of the English National Archives, the National Archives of Australia and the Bundsarchiv in Germany is to take in the official records of governments and the courts of law as part of an ongoing administrative process; they do not as a rule accept non-official records. The National Archives of Scotland and the Public Record Office of Northern Ireland do the same, but will in some circumstances take in non-official and private and personal papers. By contrast, in Canada the concept of 'total archives' led the national archives to collect records from any source at all provided they contained information about that country.

Library and manuscript materials

Unlike archives, libraries are mainly concerned with information products, books, magazines, and so on, rather than raw data generated by a business or personal activity. Thus, unlike the outputs of most record transactions, most library materials are not unique; they are usually published for multiple distribution and – most importantly – are single, discrete items. Manuscript means, literally, written by hand. The term is often used to indicate original individual manuscript documents which are not born of a transaction or business process and do not depend on associated documents for their meaning. Thus, a poem by Wordsworth, a nineteenth-century recipe book, an autograph of Orson Welles, the draft of a Virginia Woolf novel fulfil the criteria. Books, lone items and discrete manuscripts may be catalogued using bibliographic standards and systems such as the Anglo-American cataloguing rules (AACR) and guidance in *Archives, Personal Papers and Manuscripts*.[17]

By contrast, records and archives are aggregates of interrelated items: numbers of documents strongly linked by provenance to their creator and which gain significance and meaning from their relationships with other records (e.g. like Joe Soap's school records and Bart Simpson's essay feedback) in the same 'collection'. They need different treatment, too:

archives are traditionally arranged and described as aggregates, preserving their provenance, structure and function, and specific archival standards give guidance on how to do so. Secondary finding aids are subsequently compiled to enable access to specific subjects.

But it is difficult, and not always helpful, to maintain such distinctions: the archive of Winston Churchill will include drafts and published versions of his speeches and histories, diaries, photographs and portraits. Would you separate these out from his correspondence with Roosevelt or the minutes of meetings held at Chartwell or Downing Street because they are not strictly archives? Would you put the original draft and diaries in a manuscript collection, the published speeches, histories and diaries in a library, the photographs and portraits in a museum and the rest in an archive? There are certainly issues about the physical preservation of different types of material that might lead to their deposit where the relevant expertise can be found, but the provenance of such material should always be carefully recorded.

National archives and libraries

For historical and practical reasons libraries may contain archives and manuscripts, and archives may have book material and are likely also to hold manuscripts. Different models in the relationship between archives, libraries and manuscripts are evident at national and state levels. In Europe archives developed independently of libraries, and their origin, as part of an administrative process, led them to being identified at first more with their evidential than their cultural attributes. Similarly, the first archivists were administrators – neither historians nor librarians. National libraries – the British Library or the Bibliotheque Nationale for example, remained distinct from the outset.

In Australia and North America the situation developed differently, with the cultural and historical aspects of archives being the prime driver towards the establishment of archival institutions, with many having their beginnings in the manuscript divisions of libraries. In early twentieth-century Australia the Commonwealth National Library was responsible for government archives (other than those of the World War I, which went to a museum, the Australian War Memorial) until the Archives Division gained its independence in 1961.[18] In Canada the influence of librarians led the Public Archives Act of 1912 to favour the 'historical' attributes of archives over the administrative and evidential. Although the balance has long been redressed, the relationship is still strong and in 2002 the National Archives of Canada and the National Library of Canada united to form Library and Archives Canada. In the US the Library of Congress collected the archives of the federal government before the National Archives was established.

Museum archives

Museums, too, have always taken in archives. In their early days, before appropriate archival repositories had been established, they were fairly indiscriminate in their collections policies. Today these will include ongoing organisational records as well as archives that support their object collections. This statement from the Science Museum in London is typical of how some of today's museums view their role in relation to their archive collections:

> Both the Museum and the Library have acquired archival material throughout their history, especially manuscripts, and frequently in the form of large collections. Such material, often collected in the past simultaneously with related objects, has effectively complemented the many object-based collections. Today, material is acquired in the areas of the history of science, technology, medicine and industry, and of physical science and technology for which there is no local or specialist repository.[19]

'Public archives' and 'historical manuscripts'

One environment where the influence of a library culture has had a lasting effect on archival infrastructures is in the US. Here the terms 'public archives tradition' and 'historical manuscripts tradition' have very specific meanings. These were originally derived from a perceived distinction in the way written materials should be defined and handled depending on where and how they were managed. If they were managed by a body whose main function was to service the archives generated by its employing body (e.g. the state) then they belonged to the public archives tradition and in state archives. If they were managed by an institution whose remit was to collect materials from the world outside and to foster research then they belonged to the historical manuscripts tradition, and went to the state libraries. Libraries were the original bodies for taking in the latter type of material – which whether it was 'archival' or not was considered as 'manuscripts'. In-house State archival institutions developed later and many actually grew out of the manuscript rooms of State libraries.[20] For example, the Minnesota State Archives, managing the records generated by the State, is just a department of the Minnesota Historical Society, which collects 'historical manuscripts' – even though in reality these may include the genuinely archival, organisational, records of, say, the Northern Pacific Railroad.[21] Thus, a public archives service may well hold items acquired originally from outside the organisation, and manuscripts acquired by a library may well exhibit archival characteristics.[22]

A recent American textbook says 'while archives are generated by organizations or institutions, manuscripts are generated by individuals or families' and 'the holdings of an archival repository are called "records" ... [and] the holdings of a manuscript repository are called "papers" ... the custodian of organizational records is called an archivist, while the custodian of personal papers is called a manuscript curator.'[23] This seems to create a tension where none need exist. Fellow American Richard Cox of the University of Pittsburgh says: 'There is really no room for disagreement. Archivists are archivists. Archives are archives. Archives are composed of records. Historical manuscripts are composed of records, and they constitute archives. Manuscript curators are responsible for records *and* archives.'[24] So that's all right then.

The relevance of identifying differences

I have spent time on these issues for the reason that whatever you *call* them (and we never will agree on terminology) it is important to recognise the particular *attributes* of the information source you have to hand and manage it according to the recognised professional and technical processes for that source. If you do not, you will fail in your professional job of managing the resource properly and your clients and users will not be able to exploit it to its full potential. As noted above, library materials and other single, discrete items are described according to library standards and practice, whereas archival material, because of its interrelatedness, has to be described (catalogued) in line with archival standards such as the International Standard Archival Description (ISAD(G)), or the Canadian Rules for Archival Description, to take a national example.

Different traditions lead to different practices and methodologies. This makes it difficult, and dangerous, to make generalisations about what is the ideal way of doing anything. It all depends on your circumstances.

But, as Eric Ketelaar says, differences are interesting and should be investigated and understood – and trying to force uniform practice in disparate environments would be counterproductive.[25] Once comparative practices are understood within their specific professional contexts, you can start to tease out common elements in theory and practice. The archival profession is developing both national and international standards that support the commonalities and differences in practice, and which I shall look at later.

Organisational models of archive repositories

I have cited as examples of agencies or repositories those of central and state governments. There is, of course a need for every organisation to care for its records if it is to fulfil its stated mission satisfactorily; and although not all of them do so, and even fewer consciously maintain an archive, you can imagine what a broad spectrum of archives potentially need to be catered for. These include the records of publicly funded public-sector bodies such as central, regional and local government; of universities, colleges and schools; of the private sector such as businesses, families, individuals, religious dominations and churches; and of institutions of all kinds such as societies and charities.

It is quite difficult, and perhaps not always helpful, to categorise archives in terms of 'public' and 'private' because these terms can mean different things to different people and in different countries. In the UK, for example, 'Public Records' are defined in legislation as solely those produced by departments of central government, courts and tribunals and include records of some such bodies produced locally (such as by local Courts of Quarter Sessions).[26] To others the phrase might apply to any official records produced by a public authority[27] but this, too, becomes misleading for example when public authorities become privatised. Public archives often have different status and access rights from private archives.

Table 2.4 demonstrates the main distinctions in the operation of publicly funded and private archives services. In order to understand fully the different models of archival organisations and the archives they hold we need to take account of the nature of their:

| Table 2.4 | Remit and role of publicly and privately funded archives |

	Publicly funded institutions	Private and commercial
Source of authority	Statutory legislation, royal charter; decision formally recorded in minutes of central council, board, committee, etc., of governing body.	Private trust, board of directors
Legislative environment	Access and privacy; human rights, health and safety, and public records sector specific	Companies Acts; industry and sector-specific regulations
Source of funding	Central/local government; external grants	Commercial, profits of business, charitable, etc.
Goal or mission	To select records for long-term safekeeping, to preserve, store, manage them and make them available	To promote commercial, business or other organisational objectives
Stakeholders	Employers, tax payers, members of the general public requiring access, 'non-users'	Shareholders, directors, management board, internal clients
Acquisitions remit	In-house, collecting and combined (see below)	Usually in-house only
Access remit	Open access	Internal clients and users take priority

- *Source of authority*: from where does the archival organisation receive its remit to act?
- *Legislative and regulatory environment*: what kinds of legislation and industry regulations are applicable in this environment?
- *Source of funding*: where does the capital and revenue income come from?
- *Goal or mission*: what is the strategic aim of this body?
- *Stakeholders*: who has an active or passive interest in the performance of this organisation?
- *Acquisitions remit*: what is the archival collection policy of this organisation?
- *Access remit*: who is eligible to access the archives of this body?

Table 2.5   Acquisition models

Model	Archives acquisitions remit	Examples
In-house	Dedicated to the management of records and archives of its parent-body and thus derived from a single creating organisation, and its predecessors. No external collecting	National governments: UK National Archives; National Archives of Australia Universities: Oxford University Businesses: Coca Cola, HSBC, Rothschild
Collecting	Primarily dedicated to collecting archival material generated by bodies external to their parent-body in line with an acquisitions policy, for purposes of research	National libraries and museums: British Library, Australian War Memorial Specialist collections: The Wordsworth Library
Combined	Manages own organisations' archives and records: collects from external sources in line with an acquisition policy	National governments: Libraries and Archives Canada, National Archives of Scotland Universities: Glasgow University UK local authorities: in-house and collect within geographical area US State Historical Societies: state archives and manuscript collections

There is obviously a wider variation of situations than can be illustrated here. But Table 2.4 does provide a useful analytical model: certainly wherever you work you will need to be aware of which is the specific profile of your own environment.

Breaking down one aspect in a little more detail, repositories caring for archives broadly fall into one of three main acquisitions models. At one end of the acquisition spectrum an archival body may maintain the records and archives solely of its own parent body, and, on the other, it may seek to collect 'orphaned' archives from external bodies who for one reason or another do not maintain them themselves. The first is known as the 'in-house' model and the second as the 'collecting' model. A third, fairly common model is where repositories combine both functions (Table 2.5).

The type of model chosen does not derive from the nature of the organisation: governments, states, local authorities, universities, business and specialist collections, and so on, may follow any one of the three, depending on their specific business remit.

Archives in the UK and Ireland

England and Wales

There are four main areas of responsibility for archives: central and local government, and education in the public sectors, and business and specialist, largely but not entirely in the private sector. At government level ministerial responsibility for each of these varies, as does their source of funding and the type of archival repository or record office that in the main takes responsibility for their archives. Central government (i.e. 'public' records) and the National Archives are the responsibility of the Lord Chancellor and the Department for Constitutional Affairs. The responsibility for locating and advising those holding private archives now also falls to the National Archives.

The Office of the Deputy Prime Minister funds local government and hence local authority record offices and archives. However, substantial funding for the cultural exploitation of archives is derived via the Department for Culture Media and Sport, which is responsible for the Heritage Lottery Fund and other grant-awarding bodies. Local authority record offices developed in the first half of the twentieth century in response to the need to save historical 'orphaned' archives within their geographical areas; however, today most also offer a records management service to their parent body too, providing a 'combined service'. Currently the only formal link between central government and local authority archive services is where the latter have the role of a 'Place of Deposit' for 'public' records generated locally, such as those of local courts, hospitals, etc., under the 1958 Public Records Act.

The National Library of Wales in Aberystwyth is the principal repository in Wales, and is funded by the National Assembly for Wales. Each of the Welsh counties has its own record office.

Scotland

The National Archives of Scotland has a greater oversight of Scottish repositories than does its counterpart in England. It is funded by the Scottish Office and receives both public and private archives. The regional authorities of Scotland provide archives and records management services for their areas: these are mostly quite recent.

Northern Ireland

The Public Record Office of Northern Ireland is the only record office in the province and receives material from both public and private sources.

Universities

Higher education is the responsibility of the Department for Education and Skills, with much of the funding being channelled through the Higher Education Funding Councils and other funding bodies. University Special Collections and Archives often combine responsibility for manuscripts, early printed books and artefacts, and archives taken in from external bodies for research purposes with an in-house records management service to the university's departments.

Business and specialist

There is a wide range of business and specialist archival repositories in the UK, most of which do not fall within the public sector. A number of these have well-established archives services, and although their main priority has to be fulfilling the needs and requirements of their parent body, many welcome researchers from outside too. Details of these are available from the ARCHON directory housed on the website of the National Archives.[28]

Notes

1. Joint Information Systems Sub-Committee HEI Business Function & Activity Model, *http://www.jisc.ac.uk/index.cfm?name=srl_intro*
2. McLeod, J. (2002) *Effective Records Management – Part 2: Practical Implementation of BS ISO 15489–1*, BSI DISC PD0025–2. London: British Standards Institute, p. 13.
3. Erlandssohn, A. (1997) *Electronic records management: a literature review*. Paris: International Council on Archives, Committee on Electronic Records, p. 19.
4. International Organization for Standardization ISO 15489: 2001 (E) *Information and documentation: records management, Part 1 General*, 7.2.2–7.2.5, p. 7.

5. Standards Australia, Australian Standard AS 4390, *Records Management*, Homebush, NSW, Part 1, General Clause 4.22.

6. Upward, F. (2005) 'The records continuum', In *Archives: recordkeeping in society*. Edited by McKemmish, S., Piggott, M., Reed, B. and Upward. F. Wagga Wagga, NSW: Centre for Information Studies, Charles Sturt University, p. 202.

7. McKemmish, S. (1993) 'Introducing archives and archival programs', In *Keeping archives*. Edited by Ellis, J. Port Melbourne, Australia: Australian Society of Archivists, p. 10.

8. Best, D. (2002) *Effective records management – Part 1: a management guide to BS ISO 15489–1*, BSI DISC PD0025–1: 2002. London: British Standards Institute, pp. 6–8.

9. Shepherd, E. and Yeo, G. (2003) *Managing records: a handbook of principles and practice*. London: Facet Publishing, pp. 17–18; *International Standard: Records Management ISO 15489–1:2001*; Parker, E. (1999) *Managing your organization's records*. London: Library Association.

10. Council of Europe Committee of Ministers (Recommendation No. R (2000) 13 of the Committee of Ministers to Member States on a European Policy on Access to Archives), 2000. Available at: *http://www.archives.gov.ua/Eng/Law-base/Recommendations.php* [accessed 2 January 2006].

11. McKemmish, S. (2005) 'Traces: document, record, archive, archives', In *Archives: recordkeeping in society*. Edited by McKemmish, S., Piggott, M., Reed, B. and Upward. F. Wagga Wagga, NSW: Centre for Information Studies, Charles Sturt University, pp. 1–20.

12. Cook, M. (1999) *The management of information from archives*, 2nd edn. Aldershot: Gower, pp. 39–40.

13. ISO 15489–1:2001(E), p. 4.

14. Posner, E. (1972) *Archives in the ancient world*. Reprinted (2003). Chicago: Society of American Archivists; O'Toole, J. (2002) *Understanding archives and manuscripts*. Chicago: Society of American Archivists.

15. MacNeil, H. (2000) *Trusting records*. Dordrecht: Kluwer.

16. Duchein, M. (1992) 'The history of European archives and the development of the archival profession in Europe', *American Archivist* 55: winter, 14–25; Mackenzie, G. (1999) 'Archives: the global picture', *Archives* XXIV:101, 2–15.

17. Gorman, M. (ed.) (1989) *Anglo-American cataloguing rules*. ALA Editions, US; Hensen, S.L. (1989) *Archives, personal papers and*

manuscripts: a cataloguing manual for archival repositories, historical societies and manuscript libraries. Chicago: Society of American Archivists.

18. Golder, H. (1994) *Documenting a nation: Australian archives: the first fifty years*, Canberra: Australian Archives, p. 26.

19. Science Museum's homepage, *http://www.sciencemuseum.org .uk/library/index.asp* [accessed 14 February 2005].

20. Schellenberg, T. R. (1956) *Modern archives.* Chicago: University of Chicago Press, p. 20.

21. 'The Minnesota Historical Society is a private, non-profit educational and cultural institution established in 1849 to preserve and share Minnesota history. The Society collects, preserves and tells the story of Minnesota's past through interactive and engaging museum exhibits, extensive libraries and collections, 25 historic sites, educational programs and book publishing.' *http://www .mnhs.org/about/index.html* [accessed 8 February 2005].

22. Cook, *op. cit.*, pp. 8–9.

23. Hunter, G. S. (2004) *Developing and maintaining practical archives.* New York: Neil-Schumann Publishers, p. 3.

24. Cox, R. (2001) *Managing records as evidence and information.* Westport: Quorum Books, p. 24.

25. Ketelaar, E. (1997) 'The difference best postponed', *Archivaria* 44: Fall, 142–8.

26. *Public Records Act, 1958,* (c.51). London: HMSO.

27. A Canadian interpretation says the domain '... extends beyond the realm of actions taken by governments and the direct agents of government to include all actions that affect the public interest and thus fall within the public arena.' Nesmith, T. (1999) 'Still fuzzy, but more accurate', *Archivaria* 47: Spring, 147.

28. National Archives: Services for Professionals, *http://www.archon .nationalarchives.gov.uk/archon/* [accessed 25 August 2005].

3

Selection, appraisal and acquisition

The three core functions of an archive service are the selection, preservation and provision of access to the records and archives in its care.

Selection is a key function: deciding what you propose to keep of your own organisation's records and/or to acquire from elsewhere is fundamental not only to how the service will develop, but in contributing to shaping the written and cultural heritage.

This chapter considers the theories, systems and processes surrounding archival selection, appraisal and acquisition. It will help you to:

- differentiate between selection, appraisal, acquisition, collection, accession and documentation;
- develop an awareness of current archival appraisal theory;
- write an archival acquisitions/collections policy;
- develop an acquisitions strategy;
- establish processes for the systematic acquisition and accessioning of material;
- apply appropriate methodologies in the appraisal of records and archives;
- negotiate successfully the donation or deposit of material.

Much has been written about both the theory and the practice of appraisal. Theorists seek the ideal theory to guide professionals' thoughts and actions and practitioners seek explicit instructions about what to keep and what to discard. In describing current ideas and practices we should acknowledge that:

> No single textbook discussion of appraisal or standard of practice, or agreed benchmarks can be used as a technical manual to guide

mechanical tasks or for rote application. Appraisal must be a live procedure which recognises the nuances of situation and timing, and caters for the constraints of resources.[1]

In other words there is no single appraisal solution. However, decisions bearing on the retention or disposal of current or archival records have to be made, and these can happen at any point during their life cycle. All records professionals need to be aware of the processes involved in appraisal across the spectrum, even if their particular role does not require expertise in all of them.

Records managers help records creators decide how long series of records should be kept for operational purposes, using retention schedules or disposal authorities to define the retention periods and consequent disposal actions. They deal with hybrid systems, with paper and electronic media, but the principles are the same. Electronic records will not survive to become archives unless early decisions are made about how to maintain their authenticity, reliability and accessibility throughout their current and archival lives. Making decisions as early as possible in the life of the record also means that electronic record-keeping systems as well as physical storage areas are not cluttered with unnecessary material. It also makes it easier to ensure a seamless flow of material of continuing value to the archives section of the organisation. There is plenty of advice available elsewhere for those involved more specifically in records management.[2]

The archivist who takes in archives from his or her employing body may be less involved in developing retention schedules for current record series, but will discuss those for potentially archival records with the records manager, and subsequently receive these records as corporate archives. An archivist or manuscript curator whose main task is to collect archives for research purposes from external sources will do so in accordance with a stated acquisitions or collections policy. Only acquisitions that fall within its remit will be acquired.

Definitions

Definitions in this area can be confusing because they tend to have different meanings for different writers and are sometimes loosely applied. A holistic definition of *appraisal* comes from Australia. Appraisal is 'the process of evaluating business activities to determine which records need to be captured and how long the records need to be kept, to meet business needs, the requirements of organizational accountability and community expectations.'[3]

This high-level inclusive definition concentrates on current rather than archival records: the reference to 'community expectations' refers to archival provision and use. A more traditional definition (again Australian) says: 'Determining which of the records will become archives and which shall be discarded is the archival skill of appraisal.'[4]

'*Selection*' is used also to refer to the act of determining which records are of sufficient 'continuing value' to be acquired by an archival repository either from the parent body or externally. Top-level selection decisions should comply with an *acquisition* or collection policy that has been drawn up in line with the organisation's mission and goals: an in-house archive will have a different acquisitions remit from its collecting counterpart. The document that defines an archives' acquisition focus is an 'acquisition policy'. Those in the historical manuscripts tradition and other collecting archives may use the term '*collection* policy' instead because they collect material that may include personal and other non-organisational material, but in reality terminology is fairly fluid. *Documentation*, when applied to appraisal, is a proactive strategy that aims to ensure the retention of core documentation relating to defined areas of human activity that might not otherwise be properly recorded. An *acquisition strategy* (or collection strategy) is a proactive and systematic plan for enhancing collections. This involves evaluating current holdings against the acquisition policy and setting appropriate, measurable targets.

Selection might be undertaken at the 'collection' level – for example, the few surviving archives of the Paperclip Collectors' Club fall within your acquisitions remit but after appraisal you might decide that they are not worth acquiring. Selection might take place at lower levels. You might select the archive of the Northern Gas Board for retention, but on appraising its content decide to discard the chequebook stubs and duplicate copies of printed material, and keep the board minutes and annual reports. Or again the series of files on the project to sanitise litterbins in Ramsey Street might be worth considering for selection as might that relating to the industrial poisoning of the water supply of 4000 inhabitants of Gotham City. After appraisal the former will probably be found to have no continuing value, judged not worthy of retention and destroyed. The latter may well be selected for transfer to the archives. (This is a value judgement with which you might disagree – I will discuss this later.)

Thus, whereas '*appraisal*' is the process of evaluating actual or potential acquisitions, the skill of judging – by understanding what values records have – what should be kept, the word 'appraisal' is also commonly (and loosely) used when discussing the various theories and practices surrounding the decision-making process.

Appraisal theory

Appraisal is a core skill of the records professional, whether records manager or archivist. It is important because whether you are appraising for current operational or archival research purposes you are involved in making a judgement about what should be retained – and in the long term defining the future research resource and contributing to moulding the historical record. As one writer put it, 'our most important and intellectually demanding task as archivists is to make an informed selection of information that will provide the future with a representative record of human experience in our time.'[5]

This is quite a responsibility and has given rise to much debate. This debate involves:

- whether archivists *should* in fact make appraisal decisions at all, and, if so,
- *why*, and for what purpose, they should do so,
- *what* should they appraise and
- *how* such decisions should be reached.

The first two of these issues, the 'whether' and 'why' questions, are often centred on an intellectual enquiry about the wider purpose of keeping archives. One could say that it generates 'ideas-based' theory, allowing interesting speculation – for example whether archives should 'aim at shaping as true as possible an image of society' – that is not necessarily intended for practical application.[6] The last two issues, about *what* we appraise and *how* we go about it, have given rise to a range of standards and methodologies of direct use in the work place, from national to local and specialist archives. These then are more 'practice-based' approaches.

Should archivists be involved in appraisal?

Hilary Jenkinson, Deputy Keeper of the UK Public Record Office in the middle of the twentieth century, argued that if the archivist decides which archives should be kept and which discarded, he or she is distorting history and compromising the impartiality of the record because any appraisal decision will be subjective. He thought that record creators or administrators should be the only people who should appraise – because their decisions would be based on administrative need and not some external value judgement: the archivist was simply a custodian. More recently, too, Luciana Duranti, an Italian academic working at the University of British Columbia, argued that making judgements based on the potential 'value' of the document is to 'renounce impartiality, endorse ideology, and consciously and arbitrarily alter the societal record.'[7]

Most people take a more pragmatic line, however. Other theorists contend that there is no point in aiming at objectivity in the historical record because all documents are the product of a particular time and context, and bear the biases of these.[8] Archivists should therefore, it is argued, based on their understanding of records' context, content and use, be prepared to appraise, and are indeed better equipped than most to make appraisal judgements. Practitioners, often overwhelmed by a mass of material offered to them for which they have too little storage space, readily select and appraise archives, supported by appropriate practice-based methodologies, standards and guidelines. It is my view that archivists *should* be prepared to make appraisal judgements, and to be able to justify and document their decisions.

Why should archivists select and appraise archives?

Opinions on the purpose of appraisal, identifying what archivists are actually trying to achieve through selection and appraisal processes, again vary widely. Some argue for the simple preservation of evidence of functions and activities as created, without making any judgements regarding the value of their content; others argue that archivists need to seek out secondary research value from the content or information contained in the archives; and the most radical seek to document all of society's actions.[9]

A survey of UK practitioners in a wide variety of repositories in 2003 showed more modest, but more realistic, ambitions – and I suspect these are typical. Purposes included:

- to select records that will have a permanent value for the business;
- to build a comprehensive but compact picture of the organisation over time;

- to continue to supply the historical record;
- to record the business of government;
- to comply with appropriate collections policies;
- to make sure records are accessible;
- to make it easier for researchers;
- to maintain maximum information in minimum space;
- to make the best use of space.[10]

Archivists based in working environments, therefore, are likely to see their appraisal function as derived from the mission and goals of their organisation, supported by a finite amount of resources.

What and how should archivists select and appraise?

Perhaps the question here should relate not only to the kinds of archives that archivists will be required to evaluate, but also what methodologies they might use. This section, and the next, will concentrate on the methods that are currently available and how to use them effectively.

Acquisitions/collections policies

Archivists should only appraise material that falls within the scope of an acquisitions policy. The first task is therefore to develop an organisational acquisition/collection policy in order to give direction to the selection function. This is done by harnessing it to the mission and aims/goals already identified. An acquisition policy:

- overtly supports the aims and objectives of the organisation;
- provides an objective conceptual framework for rational and consistent decision-making;
- focuses resources in selected areas;
- supports the proactive development of holdings;
- defines the scope and content of the collection;
- guides staff, users and potential donors in what may be acquired;
- suggests criteria for the refusal of unwanted material;

- prevents the overlap of collecting areas between repositories;
- brings continuity to the acquisition function in times of organizational or staff change.

It:

- stipulates the nature of the acquisition focus in terms of creating organisations and/or individuals: geographical or territorial limits, thematic and subject based;
- identifies which media and formats can be managed.

Thus, an in-house archive, for example of central government or a business, will acquire the archives of its parent-body and its predecessors whereas a collecting archive will focus on material generated externally. An archive service that combines these two functions will need to construct its acquisition policy accordingly.

Here are some examples.

In-house

The first example that of the National Archives (TNA), formerly the Public Record Office (PRO). TNA states strategic acquisition objectives, beneath which are identified eight selection themes that indicate how the strategic objectives can be fulfilled. Individual departments of government consider the themes, highlighting from these those that are specifically tied in with their own operational functions, which functions they will therefore document.

UK TNA strategic acquisition objectives

'Our objectives are to record the principal policies and actions of the UK central government and to document the state's interactions with its citizens and with the physical environment. In doing so, we will seek to provide a research resource for our generation and for future generations.'

The eight selection themes within this, identified under two headings are

2.1 Policy and administrative processes of the state

    2.1.1. Formulation of policy and management of public resources by the core executive

    2.1.2. Management of the economy

2.1.3 External relations and defence policy

2.1.4 Administration of justice and the maintenance of security

2.1.5 Formulation and delivery of social policies

2.1.6 Cultural policy

2.2 Interaction of the state with its citizens and its impact on the physical environment

2.2.1. The economic, social and demographic condition of the UK, as documented by the state's dealings with individuals, communities and organisations outside its own formal boundaries

2.2.2. Impact of the state on the physical environment[11]

Individual departments and agencies across government then develop operational selection policies derived from their operational functions. It is through these more detailed policies that the collection themes are applied by departments in the selection and appraisal of their records. Thus, the Civil Aviation Authority and the Department for Transport make the following statement:[12]

OPERATIONAL SELECTION POLICY OSP26
THE REGULATION OF CIVIL AVIATION
1972–2002
THE RECORDS OF THE CIVIL AVIATION AUTHORITY AND THE DEPARTMENT FOR TRANSPORT AND ITS PREDECESSORS
Records will be selected under the following collection themes of PRO's Acquisition Policy:

2.1.1 Formulation of policy and management of public resources by the core executive;

2.1.2 Management of the economy;

2.2.2 Impact of the state on the physical environment.

This high-level, top-down approach signals government's aim to apply rational and consistent policies that will produce a reliable record of its activities over time.

Corporate archives also develop in-house acquisition policies, although these are often less formal as their remit is internal and publication less of a requirement. For example, the Rothschild Archive statement says:

> The records of the London firm, N M Rothschild & Sons, form the core of the Archive, reflecting the activities of the other banks through many series of correspondence and accounts that circulated between them. Records of many of the Rothschild family's activities were maintained by the bank, including accounts for the management of their estates and some correspondence.[13]

Collecting archives

Collecting archives take records, regardless of their provenance, that are relevant to their chosen theme. This may relate to a particular geographical area – national, regional, local – within a specific time frame, and/or centred on a particular subject. They often collect a range of material, including artwork and artefacts, that relate to their theme.

Two examples are described here, one centred on a famous individual and his circle, the other on a theme. I have paraphrased the descriptions provided on each of the respective websites.

Collecting archives acquisition policies

1. The **Wordsworth Trust** collections relate to the poet, William Wordsworth and his circle and are based at his home, Dove Cottage, in the Lake District. Begun in 1891, it includes a selection of his furniture and memorabilia and a collection of books. The Trust became a major archive in 1935 when Gordon Graham Wordsworth, the poet's grandson, bequeathed his collection of some 90% of the poet's working manuscripts.

   The collections constitute the major holding of material relating to Wordsworth and his circle, which included Coleridge, Southey, De Quincey and their families. It is in the sheer range of cultural interconnection that the collection provides the opportunity for studying and interpreting a major period in the history of this country and, indeed, the western world.[14]

2. The **Labour History Archive and Study Centre** (LHASC) in Manchester is the only specialist repository for the political wing of the Labour movement. It holds records for working-class political organisations from

---

the Chartists to New Labour and the archives of the Labour Party and the Communist Party of Great Britain. It also collects the personal papers of radical politicians, writers and left-wing organisations. The archives are managed by the John Rylands University Library of Manchester and are housed at the People's History Museum. The archive collection complements the objects, photographs and banners found in the museum's collections and researchers may well find material of interest in both.[15]

It is important that a collecting archive define clearly its acquisition remit and that the document that articulates this is made publicly available. As a public statement of intent, the policy gives notice that the repository intends proactively to develop its holdings in a specific way. However, there are one or two issues worth considering. First you should ensure that you are not setting yourself up to compete with the acquisitions policy of another organisation. New archives, for obvious reasons, are hungry for material but it is in the interest neither of the records nor of the user to have fragmented subject areas. It is even more important not to split individual collections between different repositories, unless their media (e.g. sound archives) need special storage. The dictates of provenance should be followed here: additional deposits to collections should follow the earlier ones. It is rarely sound to split archives: a split archive can result in the loss of evidence and the confusion of the user.

Secondly, it is important to settle a theme around creating organisations or individuals if possible, and take in the material of that creator intact in order to preserve evidence of context as well as content. If you decide to collect around a particular subject, e.g. farm machinery 1870–1970, you need to ensure that you are not going to be in the business of pirating. You might legitimately take in the organisational records of Massey Ferguson, but it would be less sociable to cherry-pick the 1900–1910 machinery purchasing accounts of a farmer in Saskatchewan leaving the remainder of his archives, of the timber and animal husbandry management, and so on, for the repository whose long-held policy had been to take in the records of state agriculture. Collaboration is more productive than competition between archives: indeed, if you are offered something which falls outside your collecting policy and within some one else's you are duty bound (it is an ethical issue) to pass it over. Sadly 'some institutions regard manuscript collecting as a branch of intercollegiate athletics and vigorously strive to beat the competition' has been one writer's lament.[16]

As far as UK collecting archives are concerned, TNA's *Standard for Record Repositories* states:

> The archivist in charge should draw up, and the governing body should approve, a clearly defined statement of collecting policy which indicates the subject areas within which records are sought and acquired, any geographical restrictions affecting the scope of material collected, and the various media for which appropriate storage and access facilities are provided.[17]

The following are TNA recommendations of what might be included in a collecting archives acquisition/collection policy statement. It provides a very useful framework, and a more detailed version is available, if you want to use it as a model in your own environment.[18]

Model acquisitions/collection policy framework

1. Information which identifies the repository and the governing body

Name of the repository
Address
Identity of the governing body/authority

2. Information about the legal status of the repository or other source of its authority to collect

Statutory position/obligations
Official external recognition of the repository
Other constitutional foundation for the collection policy
Standards

3. Information about the scope of, or limitations to, policy

Overall policy and priorities/mission statement
Geographical area
Subject area
Chronological period
Genre or media of records held

Co-operation/demarcation with other repositories whose collection policy overlaps

4. Information about the process of collection

Methods of acquisition
Conditions associated with accessions
Selection/de-accessioning policy

Unlike an in-house archive, which acquires its holdings by means of an internal transfer from the parent body, a collecting archive may receive material in a number of ways. This might be by donation or gift, by deposit on loan or by purchase.

Combined: in-house and collecting

Many archives services function on behalf of their parent body and as a collecting archive. The acquisition policy for each needs to be clear and might open with the following statement:

Borsetshire County Council

The service's objective is to select, preserve and make available for research:

(a) archives and records of Borsetshire County Council and its predecessors and other authorities whose powers and duties have been transferred to the Council; and

(b) archives and records from other public and private sources relating to all aspects of the history and development of the geographical County of Borsetshire and its inhabitants.

I will come back to point (b) later.

Developing an acquisitions strategy

Once your organisation's acquisition policy is in place you should evaluate each new accession against the policy to ensure it complies. If you have the resources you need to develop a proactive and systematic plan for enhancing collections – an acquisitions strategy. As noted above, this involves evaluating current holdings against the acquisition policy and setting appropriate, measurable acquisition targets.

Acquisition strategies typically include 'deciding which records creators to solicit ... whether to accept records when unsolicited offers are made ... determining how many of the records are taken when a collection is acquired.'[19] It is desirable to do so, however, not in some kind of splendid institutional isolation, but with an awareness of the collecting agenda of other institutions and cultural domains (such as museums). We need to bear in mind that 'the activities of one institution are linked to those in another, so too the records of those activities are linked':[20] records created in one court of law around an individual's criminal activity may have a connection with those created in another, and legitimately held in different archives. While accepting that we cannot achieve the 'perfect' archive, comprehensive, objective and likely to suit all possible requirements, archivists often adopt a pragmatic method of selection that aims to satisfy both organisational and other stakeholder needs within the recognised constraints.

How will you develop your acquisition strategy?

Deciding aims and outcomes

There are two levels to this. Your long-term aim may be articulated as 'increasing the quality and variety of our research resource to attract a wider audience' or 'increasing representation of minority groups in our archival collections'. Medium- or short-term objectives will be easier to set once you have evaluated your existing holdings and identified available resources.

Allocate appropriate resources

A proactive acquisition strategy will require the commitment of substantial resources. Storage and conservation costs will include housing, packaging materials and provision for special media; costs for seeking out and initial processing of newly acquired collections will include producing advertising leaflets to inform potential donors and depositors, considerable staff time – some at quite a senior level – transport and materials; the generation of finding aids needs to be costed in too.

Check appropriateness of acquisition policy

This involves judging how relevant, realistic and useful your acquisition policy is in practice. Some, particularly in-house, archives may have no choice about what they are expected to acquire, while collecting archives may be able to define a specific focus. Consider Borsetshire's statement above that says that it collects 'archives and records from other public and private sources relating to all aspects of the history and development of the geographical County of Borsetshire and its inhabitants'. This is a very broad statement, necessary because this archive service is the official repository for the county. However, although it reflects an ideal to be aimed at it is unlikely to do more than scratch the surface of what is potentially available within this remit. Because it enables the service to take in just about anything, the temptation is to be reactive – to accept what is offered – and as there is plenty offered, mainly from groups representing the well-established (and so well-documented) in society, to keep staff occupied, there is no incentive to seek material from those minority groups, occupations or communities that are harder to penetrate. Furthermore, it is all too easy to go on collecting more of the same: the accounts of every non-conformist chapel, for example, without necessarily judging the value of the evidence and information each contains (they may be unique, but are they really worth keeping?).[21]

If you cannot re-focus your overall acquisition policy statement, then consider developing a 3- or 5-year operational plan, setting targets for specific topics to document or organisations to approach. In doing so you might consider consulting your stakeholders – particularly your researchers. TNA, for example, aims 'to include researchers in the development of our selection priorities. Thus our policy documents and guidance are the subject of public consultation ...'[22]

Evaluate your holdings

How far have you established a collection that reflects the aims of your acquisition policy? What are the strengths? Where are the obvious gaps, in terms of either organisations or themes not represented? Has there been a coherent attempt to achieve a quality resource, or is there a quantity of low-level material using up valuable resources? How far do records accurately fulfil the collecting themes? If, for example, 'sport' is a theme do collections represent individual sportsmen and women as well as clubs? Veterans as well as children? Tiddleywinks as well as football? Finally, what do you have that can be disposed of? 'De-accessioning', or discarding material previously judged worthy of retention, can be fraught with difficulty but be a last resort.

Complementary collections

Strategic thinking could bring dividends for your users. There is no reason why you should have in your institution's custody all the data available on a particular theme or collecting area, and indeed it is likely that you do not. You may not have either the expertise or the appropriate facilities for dealing with material other than standard written texts, and possibly photographs. Gathering information together *about* complementary materials – artefacts, film, textiles, library materials, for example – and creating multi-institutional finding aids at an intellectual level will also broaden your own knowledge and understanding of a specific area.

How do archivists appraise?

This takes us on to *how* you are going to implement selection and appraisal on the ground. There are a number of available approaches, including:

- proactive multi-institutional documentation strategy;
- macro-appraisal and functional analysis: the top-down approach;
- pragmatic focused acquisition strategy – the Minnesota method;
- record-based analysis: the bottom-up approach;
- appraisal policies and guidelines.

Documentation strategy

This developed from the realisation firstly that a vast 'universe of documentation' existed beyond the remit of the archivist, and secondly that the typical institutional approach to appraisal was not sufficient to produce an adequate representation of what society was actually like. It also acknowledged that society does not leave evidence of its actions just in written form and that it was therefore necessary to work with specialists in other forms of material culture, such as artefacts. It assumes that it is possible to define what a proper and adequate documentation of society might be, and that such an end is possible. It requires the definition of specific themes – e.g. the documentation of localities – to be established as steps towards its achievement. It is perceived as a collaborative and co-operative process and assumes cross-disciplinary collaboration and far wider responsibility for the archivist than merely considering the records of his or her own authority.[23]

A number of projects have been undertaken to test the validity of this theory in practice. These have had some measure of success, and some problems too, such as the difficulty of establishing inter-institutional co-operation, due to institutions prioritising their own needs.[24] One practitioner found it far too resource-intensive to undertake: 'the universe is too vast, the would-be co-operators each have their own agenda, the eyes of the funding agencies eventually glaze over.'[25] It seems that the jury is still out as far as practitioners are concerned, but the idea of proactively documenting should not be dismissed: it is a useful conceptual tool to bear in mind when planning any acquisition strategy. Do not reject it before considering how this approach might be useful to you: what has your local museum or library got that relates to your collections? Networking with other professionals can be valuable for you, and particularly so for your users – who are not interested in *where* material comes from, just that it is accessible.

Macro-appraisal and functional analysis

A number of national governments, notably the UK, Australia, Canada and the Netherlands, have led the way in changing the approach to and methods of appraisal. This has been in response to elements in the changing record-keeping environment, such as the need to accommodate digital records, to streamline techniques for the selection of bulky paper records, and to enable consistent selection decisions to be made across different media and disparate creating departments and bodies. Macro-appraisal is being adopted in a range of organisations, both public and private. It is of immediate concern to records managers, but archivists, too, need to understand how it will affect the shape of the archive of the future.

The methodology is underpinned by the principles of macro-appraisal and functional analysis. It differs from the traditional record-based, bottom-up methods by being a top-down approach. Macro-appraisal assesses the value of records at an organisational level – government, business, department or unit – rather than at an individual file of document level. It is a strategic approach, analysing the functions of the organisation and identifying the most significant: records supporting those functions will be retained. Because it is the functions that are being evaluated there is no automatic need to review the records themselves. The records of 'insignificant' functions are automatically de-selected.[26] It is also seen as a way of documenting the relationship between three interrelated entities: (1) the creators of records, (2) the functions and processes documented by the records, and (3) the citizens or clients upon whom the functions impinge and who in turn can influence both (1) and (2).[27]

The strengths of this approach are its strategic vision and coherence. Because it looks at functions across the whole organization rather than department by department it avoids redundancy (duplication) and inconsistency. It also accommodates the needs for efficiency savings – taking away all that labour-intensive file-by-file work – and accommodates the needs of digital records. Some argue that functional appraisal rejects research values because it is directed towards key functions rather than records. National archives such as those in the UK and Canada are overtly involved in consulting stakeholders in order to mitigate the possible dangers inherent in the approach: in TNA the eight collection themes, for example, have been determined in consultation with users. Archivists in collecting archives, faced with a large accumulation of records for which they have little external contextual information, may find it useful both to appraise and to arrange and describe collections by function.

Pragmatic acquisition strategy

Frequently repositories do not have the resources to take in the totality of records stated in their acquisition policies and have to seek methods to deal with the problem. One methodology developed in the 1990s by the Minnesota Historical Society aimed to prioritise which and what quantity of business records generated within the State of Minnesota it would accommodate. With two members of staff dealing with acquisitions, and a state whose historical industries were milling, lumber and the railroad, and current ones banking, computing and medical technology, choices had to be set if the future business archive of the state was not to be dictated entirely by chance. The archivists took a macro-appraisal approach, analysed their current holdings of business archives and consulted a number of scholars in the discipline before appraising business records creators across the state.

In brief, the method they chose involved ranking businesses by economic impact, extant documentation, identification with the state and the degree to which the industry was unique to Minnesota, and then creating four levels from Level A (seek to document thoroughly) to

Level D (preserve minimal evidence) with a fifth level 'Do not collect'. Archivists were intent on a utilitarian approach, based on the notion that what should be acquired is 'that body of material that will provide the most use for the widest variety of users through preservation of the smallest quantity of records possible.'[28]

The advantages of this method are that it enables archivists to take a degree of control in a situation of archival abundance and limited resources. It does not pretend to be objective, but decisions are clearly documented so that future archivists and users can understand the context of the appraisal decision-making process. Level of 'use' as a criterion for decision-making seems sensible, but should not be the sole criterion: past use is not necessarily an accurate indicator of what future use will be. It implies that you should discard unused archives – including perhaps those of primary evidential value (the articles of association; the committee minutes) that no one wants to see but that must be kept; those for which there are no finding aids to make the archives accessible in the first place; those that are subject to temporary closure periods for reasons of privacy, and so on. However, an analysis of use can inform us about research trends and discussions with researchers and remains an important part of the selection process.

A range of business archives have investigated this methodology, attracted by the notion of a solution to issues of bulk. However, it has not been widely adopted because it remains very costly in terms of staff time and other resources.

Record-based analysis

Macro- or top-down functional methods of appraisal do not depend on looking at the records themselves, both for practical and for strategic reasons. They are useful when quantities of archives or ongoing records systems are being analysed.

Many archivists, however, continue to appraise records by looking at them. Appraising in this way is often described as a micro- or bottom-up approach, and can be suitably applied to many small- or medium-sized archives received by repositories. In making appraisal decisions by physically examining the record, a set of values and criteria will be applied. These will relate to:

- the identification of such attributes as evidential and informational value;

- an appropriate understanding of the context of the records' creation;
- the overall quality of the collection and its constituent parts in terms of completeness, density of information, contribution to knowledge and physical condition.

Guidance in selection should be supplied by the retention/disposal schedules, appraisal checklists and guidelines already in place in house or collecting archival repository.

Sadly there is no one 'right' answer to appraisal. Once you accept that appraisal is a necessary activity for the archivist you are faced with the knowledge that no appraisal can be objective or value-free. Records themselves carry the biases of their creators and contexts, and the appraisal process itself is undertaken by archivists who bring their own particular set of interests and values. However many sets of guidelines or established techniques you might have you will find that two archivists left to appraise the same collection will come up with two different solutions. I have known archivists who hesitate to discard anything and others whose guiding principle is 'if in doubt, chuck it out'!

Archivists start from the premise that records are unique, and have some intrinsic value, and that destruction inevitably means loss. Against this, records managers aim to select for continuing value usually no more than 2 per cent of what is created across the board, and archivists may need to be equally rigorous with accessioned collections. How can we ensure a balanced approach? In practical terms, in order to select and appraise we need to consider the provenance or context of archives, the functions they were created to support, and the nature and 'value' of the information they contain.

Determining evidential and informational values

Hilary Jenkinson argued that archives were kept as evidence of the transactions of which they formed a part. That historians or others used them subsequently for the value of the information they contained was incidental. Archives, he said, were not 'drawn up in the interest or for the information of Posterity.'[29] It was therefore no part of the archivist's work to select or appraise archives for purposes of research. As noted earlier, only the administrator should be empowered to do this.

Jenkinson's younger contemporary Theodore Schellenberg, who ill-advisedly referred to Jenkinson as 'an old fossil', worked at the newly established National Archives and Records Service in Washington during a period of administrative growth during World War II. He saw that selection and appraisal could not be avoided, and were indeed desirable, and that the *content* of the records and its value for research needed to be evaluated alongside their values as evidence that certain activities and transactions had taken place. As well as differentiating records from archives he also defined a new set of values: primary and secondary.[30]

- Primary values are those in records that support the business needs and administrative requirements of the creating organization. Primary use is by the organization.

- Secondary values are those values that records/archives have which support activities *other* than those for which they were created – thus, for research and other 'secondary' uses – and can form the basis of appraisal decisions. There are two aspects to secondary values:

  - Evidential values: these are the attributes of records that articulate how the creating body conducted its business and carried out its functions at all levels of the organisation. These are contained in records that show legal status and decisions; financial activity and accounting; and administrative and operational business structures and conduct. They provide *evidence* of how the organisation worked and depend on an understanding of context and provenance.

  - Informational values: these are the attributes concerned with the content of the records in terms of its uniqueness; the degree to which the information is concentrated (relating to its 'quality'); and the importance of the information contained. It may occur at very low levels of administration as well as higher and is judged not on the importance of its context but on its value as *information*. Pertinence, not provenance.

Preston Dock: seeking records with evidential and informational values

Some years ago I was asked to appraise the records of Preston Dock, in Lancashire, which was closing. Based on research I had done in advance I expected to find a range of evidential and informational data. Prime evidential records should provide me with clear evidence of how the organisation had worked and was structured and how the docks were operated over time. So I wanted laws, bye-laws and regulations, board and committee minutes, annual financial statements, details of the range and hierarchy of officials and employees and their roles and responsibilities – high-level documentation showing the corporate governance, structure and functions of the dock. I found none of these. In their absence I had to think again. I learned that much had been lost due to flooding, but more usefully that some of the corporate records remained with the Borough Council, which had run the dock since 1883.

Operational records remaining at the dock, such as the daily sailings and arrivals books dating from 1881, and the engineers' reports and dredging records, helped to confirm that the two main structural entities were the Dock Manager's Office and the Ribble Engineer's Office. Not the top-level 'evidential' material I was looking for (because these were dealing with repetitive daily/weekly/monthly activities) but useful for an understanding of the basic structure and regular functions and activities of the dock.

Scattered all over the floor and tied in parcels, mostly damp and illegible were the bills of lading. There were hundreds of them. They contained the details of the cargo that each ship carried – timber from Norway, silks and textiles from India, etc. In order to establish what evidence these contributed to how Preston Dock worked I would only need to keep a handful: they were all in the same form, so it was clear what role they played in evidential and administrative terms. They might be 'low-level' documentation in terms of corporate evidence about the dock, but the information in each (when legible) was unique – of great value to historians, economists, statisticians and social historians.

It is misleading to think that archives have *either* evidential value *or* informational value. The example from Preston Dock shows that these values are inherent in all types of record but to a different degree, depending on what they were created and intended for. But I think the notion provides a useful 'rule of thumb' to use when analysing records and determining their value: evidential value is more likely to reside in records produced at the higher levels of management and informational value in those generated by repetitive operational activities, such as case files. You could also use a range of functional categories in determining evidential and informational values, for example (Table 3.1):

- Legal records – for corporate and individual rights and responsibilities, authorities to act, precedents: these are often the foundation and support for action in an organization.

Table 3.1	Examples of series of records within functional categories		
Legal	**Fiscal**	**Administrative**	**Operational**
Statutory orders	Published balance sheets	Minutes of boards and committees	Industry or organisation-specific production records
Bye-laws, rules, regulations	Financial statements	Business plans	Correspondence
Compliance records	Ledgers and other records of transactions	Mission statements	Case files
Agreements, contracts	External and internal audit papers	Employment, health and safety	Manufacturing or other processes
Evidences of title	Business plans	Personnel records	Research and development
Licences	Salaries records		

- Fiscal records – for financial transactions, accountability and performance: these demonstrate the competence of the organisation in meeting economic targets.

- Administrative records – for policy, planning, systems and procedures in implementing the business of the organisation: these enable the organisation to work and include management of facilitative functions.

- Operational records – for the substantive functions of the organisation and relate to its productive output and outcomes: these are central to understanding the unique nature of *this* organisation.

Material with informational value can comprise just about anything including any of the above. Useful information is contained in an organisation's telephone directories (about its structure) and its filing plans (about how records were administered and related to functions). Ephemeral material – publicity leaflets, company brochures, advertising material – provide important data for the researcher.

Archivists tend to make a beeline for archives with evidential value: their training is in extrapolating information about administrations and institutional context and development. Historians are more likely to be interested in the *content* of records, allocating less importance to how they were generated than to what they are *about*. Whereas the archivist might want to take a small sample of 2000 extant case files of inspections for factory pollutants, 1930–1970, in order to establish what they contribute to knowledge about how the organization *functioned*, the historian might want to keep the lot because each file contributes unique *content*, data ideal for offering quantitative statistical data across a broad geographical and/or time span. Case files like these, and the bills of lading at Preston Dock, sometimes called particular instance papers, need a specific appraisal approach.

Understanding context

As Michael Cook says, 'Archival appraisal ... should be done with impartiality [and] with expert knowledge. The knowledge required is that of someone who can represent the interests of research to the world of administration; and who can represent the needs of administration to the world of research.'[31]

It is only possible to make informed appraisal decisions once you understand the context in which the individual or organisation whose records you are appraising operated. Information regarding the external contexts, the political, legal and social, can be gained from a range of sources, before you even start to look at the records themselves. Initial preparation will enable you to form a series of questions about a particular collection: you will develop expectations about it, and your later analysis will tell you how far the records you find satisfy these.

Background to the organisation

What can I find out about Preston Dock, its history, goals and functions, before looking at its records? I check the Internet and library sources: histories of Preston; trade directories; newspapers. I learn that the River Ribble on which the dock is situated has been a navigable waterway since 1806, administered by various navigation companies until it was taken over by the borough council in 1883. Are there any extant records of these companies? What references are there to the dock in borough council records? What laws, bye-laws and regulations govern its constitution and activity? Is there a relevant act of parliament? What evidence is there of its internal organisation? What evidence might there be of links to other organisations? What other collections have been received in the past about this kind of organisation? Are there existing appraisal guidelines for the records of other public utilities? There is no point re-inventing the wheel if this route has been taken before.

Anticipated content

I discover that traffic through the dock reached a peak in 1968, when 500 dockers were employed and 16% of the UK's trade imports came through it. Latterly, cotton and wood pulp were the main imports, but as the cost of dredging increased and other docks provided faster turnaround times, the dock declined in importance, finally closing in 1980. Based on this knowledge I should look for evidence of the following functions: activity at policy and management level by companies and borough council; incoming and outgoing shipping traffic; goods import and export; maintenance of ships and the dock fabric; data on dredging activity; financial records of profit and loss and other accounts; records of employment of dockers, and maintenance and administrative staff. I should try to identify the organisational structure of the dock management, too. Finally, I maintain useful notes about the dock's context because they will be needed (either by me or by someone else) when the administrative history is written as an introduction to any subsequent catalogue, inventory or other finding aid.

I also need to make myself aware of likely research significance. What level of interest is there in the history of docks and ports? What do economic and social historians look for? What has been written nationally and locally? Which expert can I ask in order clarify what researchers are likely to be interested in? Is there likely to be data of genealogical interest (any wage books?).

As it turned out, and as noted above, I found less than I had anticipated of the high-level evidential material, but a mass of records supplying information about ongoing day-to-day activity. It taught me to ask questions about what to expect, and also to query what had happened to material that surely must have existed.

The appraisal process

The records themselves will supply the answers to many of these questions. Once you start the process of appraisal *in situ* there are three sets of questions to consider.

About the archival collection itself:

1. Does this collection come within the remit of the office's acquisition policy? Beware of taking in material that does not conform.

2. How far will it help to fulfil the office acquisition strategy? Does it add to new areas of knowledge or come from a type of creator not

previously represented? Or is it just more of the same? Remember that if you take *this* collection, you are denying a place to another, possibly more deserving.

3. On what terms is the office taking custody of it? Gift; purchase; deposit on loan? The answer will affect subsequent management processes: you have greater control over donated and purchased items.

4. Is it *the* archive? Not just circulated copies or drafts, but core records created and received by the organisation in the course of its business? If so it is what is known as the 'fonds', the technical term for the entire, uniquely created and accumulated 'collection'.

5. Is this archive complete? Or is it partial, perhaps because the rest has been deposited somewhere else, or been lost or destroyed? If incomplete is this 'rump' worth expending resources on? There is no point in keeping something merely because it is the only surviving item.

6. Is the material duplicated, either internally or externally? Internal duplication occurs through the existence of multiple copies – of meeting minutes or publications; also where low-level information has been summarized at a higher level (entries in cash books into journals or ledgers; information in personnel files into databases). Take information from the highest-level documentation available, merely sampling the lower. External duplication can occur where there are links with other organisations (such as when employees sit on other bodies and develop files about these). Do you need to keep these, or does the 'record' copy exist in the parent organisation?

7. Are there existing internal finding aids – correspondence indexes, file plans and classification schemes, phone directories? These are useful for understanding how the organisation was structured and the way it accessed its records. Was there a central registry or a more dispersed record-keeping system? Are the most useful in digital or paper form?

8. What are the form and media of the material: are data in digital form retrievable, is the physical condition of material adequate? Organisations operating since the 1980s are likely to have some records in digital or magnetic media: there are quite likely to be gaps where these have not survived.

9. Are there access restrictions to any part of the collection?

10. What resources will be needed to incorporate it with other holdings? What will be its priority for cataloguing?

About the content of the records:

1. Which records demonstrate evidential values:

    (i) about origins, structure, mission, policy, functions, activities;

    (ii) resulting from legal and regulatory environment and functions;

    (iii) reflecting financial performance and activities;

    (iv) demonstrating operation of substantive functions;

    (v) related to facilitative functions – personnel and administrative?

2. Are there quantities of particular instance papers, e.g. case files? You might need to sample these (see below).

3. What is the quality and quantity of informational data in the records?

4. How likely is the content to satisfy the current research agenda?

About the appraisal process:

1. Did I prepare myself appropriately to appraise this collection?

2. Does the evidential and informational value contained in the records selected justify its bulk?

3. Have I selected in the most concise form?

4. Have I adequately documented all my appraisal decisions for future reference?

5. Have I adopted a reasoned approach in making subjective judgements?

6. Have I taken adequate expert advice?

7. Have I acknowledged known research trends?

Appraisal guidelines

All archives are 'one-off', generated by unique organisations and individuals and appraisal of these has to be undertaken on a case-by-case basis. But similar organisations operate under specific legislation, undertaking similar functions and setting up similar administrations that produce predictable series of records (although unique in content). The records created by Preston Dock will have similarities to those of other docks and to other public utilities. Retention of such records for current purposes may be governed by legislation, by statutory order, or by internal guidelines and retention schedules. Businesses operating under the UK Companies Acts, for example, must create and maintain such corporate records as memoranda and articles of association, minutes of directors' meetings and annual reports.

In order to manage *archival* appraisal, repositories also produce internal guidelines for 'predictable' archival series and set up archival appraisal schedules that determine which of such series should be kept, which discarded and which sampled. Thus, a repository regularly receiving business records may recommend retention in all cases of memoranda and articles of association, partnership agreements, minute books, agenda and working papers for board and committee meetings, registers of shareholders and other substantive material, retention of ledgers or journals depending on which is the more detailed, sample and destruction in the case of petty-cash books and invoices, and review of correspondence to assess what is purely routine.

It is useful to review recurrent types of accessions received and to develop appropriate appraisal guidelines – or use those created by others – in order to rationalise the appraisal process.

Sampling

One of the most difficult types of records to appraise are 'particular instance papers' or case files. These are series of records each of which documents a particular instance of a general policy or activity: the cause of their existence is the same but the content of each relates to a specific case. Thus, hospital patient files, created for all patients and resulting from the same activity, carry unique data about a specific person; and the bills of lading at Preston Dock were issued by all carriers to serve as a receipt for the goods to be delivered, but are each unique in content. The evidential value of these is less than their informational value, and their large quantity, although a problem for the archivist, provides an opportunity for the researcher to extrapolate large-scale statistical data about the relationship between client and service-provider and gain real insight into the interface between the two. Such data today will be generated electronically and maintained in datasets. The archivist who has no input into the creation and maintenance stages of these may have difficulty in accessing and retaining them.

There are serious cost implications involved in keeping large collections of data whether in electronic or paper form. Archivists might decide that the bulk in relation to informational value does not justify the cost of retention and destroy the lot. Others will take the time to keep at least a sample of the data: the problem here, of course, lies in how to define the sample to be kept. There are a number of ways of sampling, and the choice of method depends on the required outcome. If you have a range of personal files, some of which relate to prominent people who you are keen to document, you might take a qualitative, subjective approach: because random sampling will not ensure that their files survive. If you are concerned to get an objective sample for statistical or quantitative analysis, a systematic or random sampling solution will be preferable. Table 3.2 shows available methods of sampling: before adopting one (or a combination) of these you might consult an expert in statistics to ensure you will get the required outcome.

Practical issues

If you have done your homework about the organisational context you will be able to make informed decisions: but there will always be instances where you need to take advice, from personnel in the creating organisation, from those experienced in research in the area and from colleagues. It is preferable to reach appraisal decisions in discussion with others and to document the decisions you make. Left to your own devices you become unaccountable; and although increasing experience will develop your expertise you should be open to challenge.

Table 3.2   Methods of sampling

Method	Purpose	Value
Keep typical examples	To show general nature and content of series	Illustrative: demonstrates evidential qualities
Purposive sampling	To highlight items relating to specific subjects or individuals	Qualitative: based on subjective decisions of value of subjects or individuals
Systematic	To select according to a stated pattern: numerical, chronological, topographical (depending on how data are arranged)	Consistent application of chosen pattern, although qualitative data may be lost
Random	To achieve a scientific, unbiased approach to data selection through computer-generated random numbered samples	Objective: each item has the same chance of being selected or discarded

All guidance will suggest that you take in records in their most concise form: for example, if you have annual balance sheets you may well not need to keep the series of accounts from which the data for them were compiled. However, this assumes that when they were created, records – particularly files – were classified in a way that enables this to be done relatively easily. Classification schemes or filing plans, where they survive, can be used as a basis for your appraisal decisions, and you may be able, on the basis of functional analysis, to ignore the file content completely. However, two problems frequently come to light: the first is that the file title bears no relation to its content (the 'General File' is the worst offender); the second is that files with some high-level information are often bulked out by masses of trivial material only worthy of destruction. Each of these issues can result in lengthy file-by-file analysis: ideally you should be able to discard the file merely by seeing its title. Although the usual recommendation is to keep or discard an entire file, there may be times when you find yourself stripping files of ephemera. This is recommended only in exceptional circumstances.

Finally, when appraising, bear in mind your long-term aims: it is only too easy to get caught up in the detail. Ensure you are appraising:

- in support of the strategic objectives and collection themes outlined in your acquisition policy;
- to develop consistent archival appraisal decisions within and across collections;
- to select archives that show the evidence, significance and contribution of organisations, their policies, processes, functions and activities, and that provide quality information;
- to select archives that illustrate the work and contribution of individuals to your specific political, environmental and cultural landscape;
- to facilitate the process of historical and cognate interpretation for the purposes of research.

Acquisition

The acquisition process enables the transmission of each new collection of archives into a repository. It results in the creation of core information about each individual accession and must be assiduously and meticulously carried out. I well recall a visit to a repository some years ago which had a fine leather-bound register with 'Accessions' stamped in gold on the spine – but which had no entries in it. Apparently the staff were so busy taking stuff in they did not have the time to document it. I also recall an instance where material held on deposit in an archive was sold to a new owner who, although agreeing to leave it on deposit, wanted (understandably enough) to see what he had bought. However, the accession details were so scanty that the record office concerned was unable to give more than an approximation of what he now owned. Poor practice can lead to enormous legal difficulties, and reflects badly on the service concerned.

Material can be received in an archives repository by different means. Repositories may acquire material *by statutory deposit* in accordance with specific legislation. An in-house repository will receive records by means of *transfer* from the parent body. Collecting archives may *purchase* collections from owners or salerooms or receive them as a *gift, bequest* or *donation*. In these cases ownership of the material is transferred to the collecting repository. Another method, which is still the usual method of receipt in many UK repositories, is *deposit on loan*, in which the depositor retains ownership but allows the record office to make the archives available for research. It is best to avoid this method if possible, as difficulties can arise in establishing ownership after the death of a depositor and when an owner decides to withdraw material (possibly for sale) in which office resources have been invested. Gift and purchase methods avoid these problems and enable the repository to operate freely. Some offices operate a system of 'permanent loan' but this can lead to misunderstanding about ownership and should be avoided.

Deposit on loan agreements

Each of these methods of transmission requires careful documenting. The deposit on loan needs additional attention because it takes the form of a negotiation between office and owner in which the rights and responsibilities of each need to be clearly articulated. Signed copies of the deposit (or loan) agreement should be exchanged at the time the deposit takes place, and you should ensure that the person depositing is either the owner or his or her agent. General guidelines are available on what such deposit agreements might comprise: suggested content is shown in Table 3.3.[32]

All repositories will capture details of each accession received whatever the method of its acquisition. Details need to be recorded in an accessions

Table 3.3   Particulars for inclusion in deposit/loan agreements

Date	Of deposit agreement Of periodic revision
Contact details	Of owner (and depositor, if agent) Of repository and parent body
Material to be deposited	Details of creators, content and covering dates Details of extent and condition; arrangements for destruction or return of unwanted material
Period of loan	Often indefinite A minimum number of years may be agreed
Storage and maintenance	State if in compliance with specific standards State type of storage offered
Conservation	State how prioritised (usually 'at discretion of repository') Specify responsibility for cost
Surrogates	State whether copies to be made for preservation or security reasons Specify likely format and responsibility for cost
Insurance	State provision (repositories may offer repair, not replacement costs) Specify whether at owner's or repository's cost
Finding aids	Detail lists, catalogues likely to be made State whether these will be placed on Internet
Access	State conditions for public access, subject to any agreed (stated) restrictions on use Whether charges for access may be made Conditions under which the material may be copied, published, exhibited (Copyright may not lie with depositor)
Withdrawal	Specify arrangements for any temporary withdrawal by depositor or other bodies (e.g. for exhibition or research elsewhere) Arrangements in the event of permanent withdrawal: whether period of notice required; whether office should be offered first refusal in case of sale; whether depositor is liable for any part of costs of care incurred to date
Changes	Require notification of changes of address; depositor's next of kin; probable heir to the material on death (if possible)

log that registers all receipts. In addition, it is necessary to generate an accessions file recording transactions with each depositor/donor, including copies of any agreements; and data relating to actions taken on the material, such as appraisal decisions, box and draft lists, temporary loans elsewhere, correspondence relating to publication, and copyright.

Details that need to be captured for each include the following:

- Date of accession.

- Unique accession identifier (usually next in numerical sequence).

- Associated accession file reference.

- Status of accession – purchase (include price, grants received), gift, bequest, deposit on loan.

- Contact details of vendor, donor, depositor (and agent if appropriate). Accessions from public bodies should include the position in the organisation of the depositor, as it might be necessary to contact his or her successor in the future.

- Description of material accessioned. Sufficient detail is required for identification and should include names of creators, material content, covering dates, extent, media and format; information on provenance, context and extant finding aids.

- Unwanted material – may be destroyed or required to return?

- Conditions of access – note conditions applied to sensitive material.

This is best done through entry into a database, which is easily updateable and is easily searched. It is now common for repositories to use a proprietary software system that will integrate the functions that represent the workflow of a repository.

The kind of functionality that these offer might include:

- a link from the accessions database to the depositor's database enables regular depositors to be entered from the depositor's database and linked to the accessions database without having to rekey the data;

- a link from the accessions database to the catalogue database enables a collection-level catalogue entry to be automatically created at the point of accession, and preliminary cataloguing information can be input at this stage;

- a link from the catalogue database to the location database means that a location can be allocated to show where the record is stored and used as a basis for ordering and retrieval;

Figure 3.1 Accession entry using DS Calm proprietary software

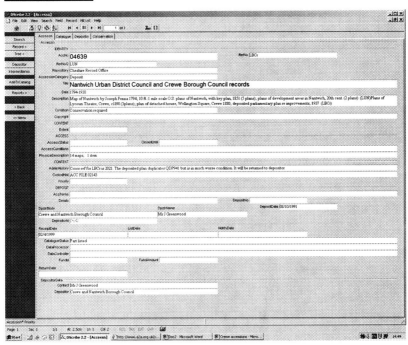

- a link from the catalogue database to the user database means you can input an order for items attached to a catalogue record. The user inputs a request for specific items to be produced.

Later chapters will continue the theme of management functions in relation to storage, conservation, cataloguing and retrieval. These functions follow on from and depend on robust acquisition policies and procedures. Figure 3.1 shows the accession screen recording the acquisition of records from Crewe and Nantwich Borough Council in Cheshire, using proprietary software.

Notes

1. Craig, B. (2004) *Archival appraisal*. München: KG Saur, p. 130.
2. For example, Shepherd, E. and Yeo, G. (2003) *Managing records: a handbook of principles and practice*. London: Facet Publishing, pp. 146–72. This volume has an extensive and useful bibliography.

3. Standards Australia, Australian Standard AS 4390, *Records management.* Homebush, NSW, Part 1, General, p. 6.
4. Reed, B. (1993) 'Appraisal and disposal', In *Keeping archives.* Edited by Ellis, J. Port Melbourne, Australia: Australian Society of Archivists, pp. 157–206.
5. Ham, F. G. (1975) 'The archival edge', *American Archivist* 38: January, 5–13.
6. Menne-Haritz, A. (1994) 'Appraisal or documentation: can we appraise archives by selecting content?', *American Archivist* 57: Summer, 528–43.
7. Jenkinson, H. (1966) *Manual of archive administration,* 2nd edn. London: Lund Humphries, pp. 149–51; Duranti, L. (1994) 'The concept of appraisal and archival theory', *The American Archivist* 57: Spring, 328–44.
8. A useful list of publications on appraisal is provided by Cox, R. (2001) *Managing records as evidence and information.* Westport: Quorum Books, pp. 121–9.
9. Cox, *op. cit.,* p. 108. For more on documentation strategy see Cox, R. J. (1994) 'The documentation strategy and archival appraisal principles: a different perspective', *Archivaria* 38: Fall, 11–36.
10. Mogridge, S. (2003) 'What light can the practice of appraisal in Britain shed on archival theory?' University of Liverpool, unpublished dissertation, p. 59.
11. The National Archives, *http://www.nationalarchives.gov.uk/recordsmanagement/selection/acquisition.htm* [accessed 2 March 2005].
12. The National Archives, *http://www.nationalarchives.gov.uk/recordsmanagement/selection/ospintro.htm* [accessed 2 March 2005].
13. Rothschild Archive, *http://www.rothschildarchive.org/ta/* [accessed 25 August 2005].
14. Wordsworth Trust, *http://www.wordsworth.org.uk/* [accessed 4 March 2005].
15. Labour History Archive and Study Centre, *http://www.nmlhweb.org/archive.htm* [accessed 4 March 2005].
16. Walter J. Rundell, Jr. quoted in Ericson, T. L. (1991–2) 'At the "rim of creative dissatisfaction": archivists and acquisition development', In *American archival studies: readings in theory and practice* (2000) Edited by Jimerson, R. Chicago: Society of American Archivists, pp. 177–92.
17. The National Archives *Standard for Record Repositories,* (2004) 3.2. *http://www.nationalarchives.gov.uk/archives/framework/* [accessed 25 August 2005].
18. Kitching, C. and Hart, I. (1995) 'Collection policy statements', *Journal of the Society of Archivists* 16:1, 7–14.
19. Greene, M. (1998) ' "The surest proof": a utilitarian approach to appraisal', In *American archival studies: readings in theory and practice* (2000). Edited by Jimerson, R. Chicago: Society of American Archivists, pp. 301–44.
20. Willa Samuels, H. (1992) 'Who controls the past', *American Archivist* 55: Winter, 109–24.
21. See Ericson, T. L. (1991–2) 'At the "rim of creative dissatisfaction": archivists and acquisition development', *In American archival studies:*

readings in theory and practice (2000) Edited by Jimerson, R. Chicago: Society of American Archivists, for a critical review of acquisition policies.

22. Honer, E. and Graham, S. (2001) 'Should users have a role in documenting the future archive?' *Liber Quarterly* 11: 382–99. See also Yorke, S. (2000) 'Great expectations or none at all: the role and significance of community expectations in the appraisal function', *Archives and Manuscripts* 28:1, 25–37.

23. Willa Samuels, H., *op. cit.*, p. 115.

24. Cox, R. (1995) 'Archival documentation strategy, a brief intellectual history 1984–1994, and practical description', *Janus* 3, 76–93.

25. Abraham, T. (1995) 'Documentation strategies: a decade (or more) later', paper presented at the annual meeting of the Society of American Archivists.

26. UK National Archives *Appraisal Policy*, 2004, 2.4.3.2. *http://www. nationalarchives.gov.uk/recordsmanagement/selection/pdf/appraisal_policy. pdf* [accessed 7 March 2005].

27. Cook, T. (2004) 'Macro-appraisal and functional analysis', *Journal of the Society of Archivists*, 25:1, 5–18.

28. Greene, M., *op. cit.*

29. Jenkinson, H. *op. cit.*, p. 11.

30. Schellenberg, T. R. (1956) *Modern archives*. Chicago: University of Chicago Press, pp. 139–50.

31. Cook, M. (1999) *The management of information from archives*, 2nd edn. Aldershot: Gower, p. 85.

32. Raspin, G. E. A. (1988) 'The transfer of private papers to repositories', *Society of Archivists Information Leaflet 5*; The National Archives, (2004) *Terms of loan (deposit) for privately owned archives: guidance note for record repositories*, *http://www.nationalarchives.gov.uk/archives/advice/ pdf/loanagreement.pdf* [accessed 4 January 2006].

4

Archival arrangement and description

Introduction

Archival arrangement and description follow on from appraisal and are integral to one of the three core aims of archival management, that of providing access to the materials in our care. They are central professional functions and require the application of some basic theories and principles in order to produce finding aids that will enable the user to access archives easily and effectively.

This chapter will enable you to:

- determine and develop the range of finding aids appropriate to specific working environments;
- arrange archival materials in accordance with accepted principles and practice;
- get to know a range of archival descriptive standards;
- create archival descriptions in conformity with accepted standards;
- develop strategies for retrieving information from archives through indexes and other secondary finding aids.

Finding aids

The information gathered at the point of accessioning an acquisition of archival material provides a basic tool for its internal management. Each collection will have been allocated a unique accession number, a location and brief details of its provenance, content, covering dates and extent (quantity). Staff can now physically identify and locate it in order to undertake the further work necessary to make it accessible for research.

The purpose of intellectual control is to provide access to the content of archival collections for users and staff through a system of finding aids. You cannot browse through boxes of original records in the hope of finding what you want; finding aids are the keys to access. As well as providing intellectual control they:

- represent and interpret the context and content of collections;

- provide evidence and information about an organisation's structure, functions and activities and about the activities of individuals;

- enable archives to be searched from a range of angles and approaches;

- protect records by ensuring only those actually required are produced for the user;

- enable users to help themselves and make choices;

- interpret original records that are in unfamiliar media, language or handwriting.

There are two basic structural models: the horizontally constructed and the vertically constructed finding aid, and repositories are likely to have a finding aid system made up of different kinds of these.[1] Ideally they should be interlinked in a planned manner from the outset. The vertical model describes a single collection at all levels of its arrangement from the collection level down to the item level. This is the catalogue, inventory or list, (depending on your terminology) and is the basic finding aid: for example, the catalogue of the papers of Arthur Wellesley, first Duke of Wellington (1769–1852) held by University of Southampton Library is called MS 61. This basic finding aid is a primary description and describes archives in a way that reflects the system or function that brought them into being: a contextual, provenance-based approach.

The horizontal model brings together a range of collections at the same level: you might have a guide across all your holdings at the collection level (a repository guide) or of a specific kind such as brewing records (a subject guide) or format (catalogue of maps). These secondary finding aids might also include subject, personal and other indexes, thematic guides, information leaflets and other publications that facilitate access to the collection from different user perspectives: these are pertinence- or content-based approaches. Many archives incorporate their own finding aids in on-line systems that are linked into national and international networks and that provide information about (rather than access to digital images of) archival collections in the care of many repositories.

The creation of finding aids is a central archival function. Without them archives are an expensive waste of space and are of use to no one. Many archival repositories hold more collections than they have the immediate resources to catalogue (let alone produce more sophisticated finding aids) and so a planned solution to the problem of backlog is needed. In this situation you should:

- Gauge the overall extent of the backlog and set down some timed aims and objectives for tackling it; and review progress against objectives on a regular basis.

- Prioritise collections for attention. For example, there may be demand for research access, a negotiated agreement with a donor or deadlines imposed by funding bodies that will influence the order in which collections are dealt with. A combined archive service, one that takes in material in-house as well as from external sources, may need to prioritise collections received from the parent body before dealing with external acquisitions.

- Determine what level of descriptive detail is required. Is a description at the top level, the collection level sufficient, or should every item in the collection be listed individually? Details in the accession register or in temporary box lists are adequate in the short term, but they do not permit extensive use of the collections. At the other extreme detailed abstracts or calendars of every record in the collection are luxuries you cannot afford – nor are they the most useful aid for the user.

Records being transferred by a parent body should ideally be accompanied by sufficient information for a seamless transmission to the archives and incorporate finding aids of ongoing value. Most archives will, however, need to construct additional finding aids at this point that cater for the needs of their external researchers. Your job is to make plain to the user both by the way that you arrange the material and in your introduction to the written catalogues both the context and the content of the collection.

Arrangement

The first step on the road to a comprehensive system of finding aids is to create the primary archival description, the catalogue, and this depends on first arranging the material in an ordered way. Arrangement and description are interdependent processes and are central archival functions and core skills.

> Arrangement ... is largely a process of grouping individual documents into meaningful units and of grouping such units in a meaningful relation to one another. An archivist, continually and instinctively, must bring order and relation to unrelated things by sorting and categorizing – to the end of revealing the content and significance of the records with which he works.[2]
>
> Basic to practically all activities of the archivist is his analysis of records. This analysis involves him in studies of the organisational and functional origins of records to obtain information on their provenance – subject, content and interrelations ... Analytical activities are the essence of an archivist's work ...[3]

Arranging and describing archives is quite different from classifying and cataloguing books. Books are single items that do not depend on other items for their meaning. They are catalogued as discrete units, often by subject. However, each archival collection is an aggregate: it comprises a sequence of interrelated documents. It has a collective significance, and significance is lost if documents are treated as single items. Much of the meaning of archives is derived from their context: from an understanding of the origin, functions, administrative or business process that generated the information they contain. Because each collection of archives is unique, a unique arrangement will need to be developed for each. Classification schemes do not apply to archives in the same way as to books: and any standardising systems that are developed (e.g. for the arrangement of business archives or records of non-conformist churches) must remain flexible. Archives should never be arranged by subject unless this coincides with their contextual or functional origins.

At the highest level, all arrangement is based on the principle of provenance. This means that an individual collection should be maintained and described separately from others in order to show its source in a record-creating organisation, individual or function. Archives from one accession should not be mingled with those of another. Even when a donor or depositor makes a subsequent deposit from the same source and creator (often called an 'accrual') it should remain possible to identify each independently, even if catalogue entries are subsequently merged for ease of access. If archives are removed from their proper provenance and arranged with those sourced from elsewhere in a different order, for example by subject or chronology, evidence and authenticity will be lost. In the UK the Public Record Office in a 'flagrant example of misdirected zeal' during the nineteenth century, broke up 15 series of records and re-arranged them by format, such as Ancient Correspondence and Ancient Petitions. In the latter case even the enclosures were separated from the petitions to which they related.[4] Today such an infringement of provenance would be regarded as a serious breach of professional principles.

Arrangement by provenance, original order and ...?

Most textbooks will tell you that the two principles to apply when arranging the content of collections are those of provenance and original order. It is important to be clear about what their application involves and when and how each might be applied. It is equally important to recognise that there will be occasions when the content of a collection has been so disrupted that neither can be discerned, and to have strategies for dealing with this.

Arrangement by provenance

Archives were originally managed by their creators in relation to the activities that generated them. Using this provenance as the framework for arranging and maintaining them will uphold their *evidential* value. Although they *contain* information about different subjects you would not arrange them by subject because this would impose an unnatural order on them and one unintended by their creators. Evidence of context would be lost. You should therefore aim to arrange the archives in order to reflect the administrative machinery that brought them into being. This enables the user to evaluate a document in context and judge its value with reference to the creator, and his or her purposes and actions. Thus, you would seek to establish the structure of the organisation and to define which unit within it produced specific series of records.

However, if using provenance as the basis for arrangement do not be tempted to 'create' administrators or bodies. Just because you have some sales ledgers you cannot assume there was a 'sales department'; or because the organisation has random pieces of correspondence you cannot assume there was such a person as a 'secretary' or 'administrator'. It is much better to take a functional approach (see below) in these instances.

Arrangement by provenance: Crewe Mechanics Institute

Crewe Mechanics Institute was founded in 1845 originally to give technical training to railway apprentices and workmen. Most of the records in the collection are minutes, and the overall covering dates are 1845–1940. In order to establish their provenance it is necessary to find out who the creator or creators of these minutes were, and within which unit they operated. On examination it is clear that the Council of the Institute and various committees such as Finance, Education, Library and Social Club created them. The records will thus be arranged according to Council and Committee.

Also deposited with this collection were the records of the Crewe Scientific Society, the Crewe Engineering Society and the Crewe and District Hospital Society Fund. Why were they in this collection? On the face of it their provenance would not appear to be with the Institute – should they be arranged and listed together because they came in together, or separated? On examination of the records themselves and of histories of Crewe it appears that the Scientific Society was actually part of the Mechanics Institute, so its provenance lies with the collection. The Engineering Society, however, was an independent body that existed from 1879 to 1884, and on closure deposited its minute book with the Institute. Its provenance, too, lies with the Institute, although there might by other Engineering Society records elsewhere with a different provenance. The Secretary of the Hospital Society fund turns out to have been the sometime secretary of the Institute too. Here although its provenance is the same, in that its last location was with the Institute, it formed no part of its activity or records. The best option is to keep it with the Institute's collection, being sure to note its different activity and purpose, to ensure that cross-references are made to and from any other surviving records of the fund and that it is picked up in indexes and search terms. You could alternatively create a separate accession for it, being sure to note its custodial history and provenance.

In cases where organisations undergo change other issues of provenance arise that affect your arrangement decisions:

- in business archives records of subsidiary companies should remain distinguished from those of the parent: they are legal entities;
- in corporate takeovers the records of the acquired company should be listed separately;

- when businesses amalgamate, if the merger is on an equal basis you can treat archives created after the merger as a new collection, otherwise list under the major company (before & after merger) keeping the lesser company separate;

- although organisations and companies may change their name it is not necessary to keep archives under each name separate. You should take the latest, or current, name and list all the records under that, cross refer to earlier names in indexes, and describe changes in administrative histories.

Some organisations may seek to arrange archives that are the subject of constant and ongoing organisational change by series, as described below.

Original order

The principle of original order requires that records should be maintained in the same order as they were in while in active use: a kind of internal provenance. It states that even if the original order appears to be chaotic it should still be retained as evidence of how the individual or organisation operated and is part of its provenance. This is not to do with physical order: records can be stored in all kinds of random locations. It relates to administrative and intellectual order. The records themselves are the best indicator of this, and there may be organisational charts indicating the management structure: file plans, indexes to correspondence, structured electronic databases, directories, folders, etc., to help you reconstruct the administration. Records may have been annotated at the time of creation: file numbers may run in a sequence, or a series of sequences; and volumes and title deeds may have been numbered – these should remain an active part of your arrangement. Beware of later annotations, however: they do not have the same credibility or authenticity as contemporaneous ones. You should certainly not break up any original bundles or dossiers of material without very good reason.

However, more often than not the original order is not detectable. Crewe Mechanics Institute was a well-organised body. Yet the minute books show no overt evidence of 'original order' although it would plainly be nonsense to arrange them in any other way than by Council and Committee – you would certainly lose sense if you arranged all the different committees' minutes chronologically in one sequence, for example. Nor is there any guidance as to which order the committees' records should be arranged. Finance before Education? Social Club before Library? There is no strict rule about this but it is safe to follow administrative hierarchy (Council before Committees) and within series (the minutes) to use an order that reflects most usefully the importance to the organisation of the functions they represent. There is likely to be more than one solution to this. Figure 4.1 shows the arrangement by provenance of the Crewe Mechanics Institute records.

Arrangement by function

When you study the *International Standard for Archival Description* (ISAD(G)) below (see Table 4.1) you will note that it acknowledges that it is not always possible to arrange a collection by provenance in the sense of re-creating, below the level of the group, the actual administrative, structural subdivisions of the originating agency. When that is not possible the Standard allows other methods such as arrangement by functional, geographical, chronological or other groupings. Many practitioners prefer to take a functional approach to the arrangement of the subgroups and series within a collection as being a more consistent way of dealing with multiple collections such as business and higher education records. The functional approach identifies records with the same function or activity regardless of where they were created or their physical medium. This might result in some arbitrary decisions, some functions will overlap (should wages records be placed under the personnel function or the finance function?) and different archivists might discern different functions in the same collection. Arrangement by function is the obvious choice where administrations and corresponding records systems are constructed along functional lines: it is in that context a solution based on provenance.

At a basic level organisational functions can generally be covered by the following categories:

- Administration
- Finance
- Staff
- Production (or other core operation)

However, such loose functional groupings as these might be perceived almost as subjects, leading to placing archives in these categories because that is what the archives are *about* rather than with regard to their origin or context. A more detailed model, the outline of which is given here, can be applied specifically to business records.[5] It suggests the following functions as a basis for arrangement.

- Corporate
- Shareholding
- Internal administration
- Accounting and financial
- Legal (other than property/premises)
- Operational
- Marketing and public relations
- Staff and employment
- Premises and property
- Branch records
- Family papers

Figure 4.2 provides an example of arrangement by function.

Levels of arrangement

Once a general picture of the structure and functions of the organisation or activities of the individual emerges, it is necessary to arrange the records (intellectually) in a structured series of levels or groups. This is done using a top-down approach, with the top level being the overall collection (group or fonds), down through its constituent parts, and moving from the broader, general picture to specific series and items. Such an application is useful and applicable to most archival collections, although there will always be exceptions.

The *International Standard Archival Description (General)*[6] and a number of national guidelines and rules endorse this allocation of levels, and indeed it has long been recognised that archives lend themselves naturally to this treatment.[7] Canadian *Rules for Archival Description*, the UK *Manual of Archival Description* and the American *Describing Archives: a Content Standard* all subscribe to the application of levels to some degree. This is particularly the case for collections of archives that are closed and have been accessioned into repositories. Division into levels is less useful for in-house archives where organisational structures and functions are subject to ongoing change and records continue to be produced, and where records management systems use different solutions. Because this approach to archival arrangement offers a static solution it does not easily align with continuum theories and with electronic systems where records are dynamic. However, it remains a useful methodology for a wide range of collecting and other archives. Different standards use slightly different terminology but the basic structure is constant.

Table 4.1   ISAD(G) levels of arrangement

Level	Description	Examples
Fonds (Group, collection)	The whole of the records, regardless of form or medium, organically created and/or accumulated and used by a particular person, family or corporate body in the course of that creator's activities and functions	Department for Economic Affairs (DfEA) Crewe Mechanics Institute (CMI) George Dutton & Sons, Leather Dressers (GD)
Sub-fonds (Sub-group)	A subdivision of a fonds containing a body of related records corresponding to administrative subdivisions in the originating agency or organisation or, when that is not possible, to geographical, chronological, functional or similar groupings of the material itself	DfEA: Economic Planning Division CMI: Council GD: Corporate Records
Sub-sub fonds (Sub-sub group)	When the creating body has a complex hierarchical structure, each sub-fonds has as many subordinate sub-fonds as are necessary to reflect the levels of the hierarchical structure of the primary subordinate administrative unit	DfEA: Budgetary processing section CMI: Finance Committee; Education Committee, etc.
Series	Documents arranged in accordance with a filing system or maintained as a unit because they result from the same accumulation or filing process, or the same activity; have a particular form; or because of some other relationship arising out of their creation, receipt or use. A series is also known as a records series	DfEA: Registered Files CMI: Finance Committee; minutes; Education Committee; minutes, etc. GD: Partnership agreements

Table 4.1   ISAD(G) levels of arrangement (*cont'd*)

Level	Description	Examples
File	An organised unit of documents grouped together either for current use by the creator or in the process of archival arrangement, because they relate to the same subject, activity, or transaction. A file is usually the basic unit within a record series	DfEA: Minister's Correspondence Jan. – Jun. 1960, File 32/45 CMI: Finance Committee minutes: vol. 1, 1920–1924 GD: Partnership agreements File 1/1
Item	The smallest intellectually indivisible archival unit, e.g. a letter, memorandum, report, photograph, sound recording	DfEA: File 32/45 Letter 2/3/1960 CMI: Finance Committee minutes: vol. 1, page 1. GD: File 1/1 Agreement 22 Mar. 1880

Table 4.1 shows a basic application of levels to some of the records of a fictional Department for Economic Affairs, and the actual Crewe Mechanics Institute and George Dutton & Sons Leather Dressers. Less complex collections will occupy fewer levels but must have a minimum of two: even a single item being all that is left of an organisation's records must have two levels.[8] The top levels, the group (often known by its French title 'fonds') and any lower sub- or sub-subgroups are intellectually constructed: the archivist identifies these for the purpose of hierarchical arrangement. Thus, the records of a government department, school, a business or an individual are located at the group level because they result 'from the work of an administration which was an organic whole, complete in itself, capable of dealing independently ... with every side of any business which could normally be presented to it.'[9] Subgroups represent lower administrative, functional or other divisions that may emerge naturally from the structure of the records, or may, when an arrangement is not obviously apparent, be imposed. At the series level and below we are talking about the actual records. Series are easily recognisable as being sequences of records that result from the performance of a similar function and are kept in the same system, such as case files, minutes, accounts and reports.

Other standards apply additional, higher levels, the repository level and the management group level.[10] The repository level needs to be identified in any description of archives that is to be exchanged or made available more widely than the host repository, for example in on-line networked catalogues. In the UK the National Register of Archives allocates these repository identifiers centrally for national data exchange. For international exchange the appropriate country code as indicated in the ISO 3166 *Codes for the representation of names of countries* should be added. The management group level (repository level in the US) is used to identify the main categories of collections – that is the 'few major divisions on the broadest common denominator'.[11] A UK local authority record office might have such high-level management groups as official, ecclesiastical and private records, each of which is further divided into broad types such as private: estate and family; solicitors; business.

Arrangement by series

There is a common saying that 'records follow functions'. In-house archives are likely to receive on a regular basis continuing series of records that result from a particular function or activity. Over time it is highly likely that the organisation's administrative structures and responsibilities will change but the same functions continue. The same series continue to accrue, regardless of who is in charge at the higher level: this means that the series of records, rather than the administration

Figure 4.1 Examples of arrangement: organisation by provenance

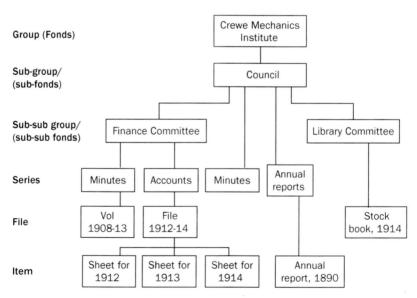

Figure 4.2 Examples of arrangement: organisation by function

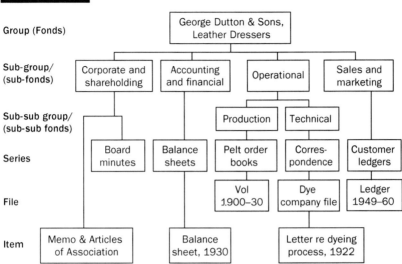

is the more stable element. Systems of arrangement, based on the assumption of static *administrations* are useful for closed archival collections but are less useful here.

Governments and large public bodies undergo frequent administrative change, and the National Archives of Australia was an early advocate of arrangement by series in consequence. In the UK TNA faced the same issue. An example of a continuing series is that of the annual reports of the UK Inspectors of Mines. The function of mines inspection was originally the responsibility of the Home Office, then of the Mines Department, then Ministry of Fuel and Power and finally the Ministry of Power. Once the *series* was accepted as the basis of arrangement regardless of any changes of controlling agency they continued to be placed under 'Ministry of Power' although it had ceased to exist in 1969. In order for this to work, however, it is important that detailed information about the administrative, archival and custodial history of the series in all its incarnations is readily available in order that evidential and contextual evidence is preserved. TNA creates separate administrative histories for this purpose.

In the case of arrangement by series it is thus the *original order* of the files series that becomes more important than the *provenance* of the creating bodies.

Arrangement by format

It is not generally a good idea to arrange archives by format, as we saw in the example of the Public Record Office arranging by format Ancient correspondence, Ancient petitions, and so on. However, where form was clearly the original order it is permissible. For example, in law courts, where records might be arranged by form (writs, affidavits) rather than by case each format is dealt with as a series. The user might be more interested in locating a specific case, however, and so secondary finding aids would be necessary for this.

Arranging personal papers

Records of organisations do not always reveal provenance and/or original order, and if they appear totally disorganised it will be necessary to impose order on them. This is even more likely to be the case in the arrangement of personal papers where their link to the functions and activities of their creator(s) is not always clear and they may arrive in total disarray. It is still worth trying to arrange in terms of provenance and integrity if discernible, but you are likely to have to resort to other types of categorisation too. These might be based around the activities of the individual in relation to different roles in an official or private capacity, and/or by genre or format – type of material, chronologically, alphabetically, for example. It is usual to place official papers before personal ones.

A military man's papers might be arranged chronologically in sections reflecting his service career for example: early career 1891–1908; staff officer, Aldershot Command, England, 1909–11; staff officer, staff college, Quetta, India, 1912–14; staff officer, British Expeditionary Force, 1914–20; diaries, 1900–20; letters received, 1913–18; personal and military photographs, 1900–15.

An author's papers might be arranged by fiction, non-fiction, general correspondence, press cuttings, diaries, printed ephemera, collected publications, personal papers, biographical papers, etc.

Miscellaneous personal papers, where few themes seem apparent, are harder to categorise and sometimes quite arbitrary sections are chosen: these may be chosen in consideration of the needs of users and based around subjects. Whatever solution is chosen it should still be possible to present the final catalogue in compliance with chosen standards – these will allow you to explain why you have chosen a particular scheme of arrangement.

Arrangement of personal papers

William Moore was a wheelwright and coffin maker. His papers include: day books that include details of his clients' orders, interspersed with butter accounts, coffin accounts and lists of when cows were served; two school exercise books; an apprenticeship indenture and some letters that, although interesting, apparently have nothing to do with him. Common sense would tell you to arrange the records of the business in one series and follow this with the personal material – but original order is not relevant here nor is provenance of all the material obvious.

There will be many instances when you can only aim for an approximation of provenance and original order: often you will need to rely on functional, chronological or other arrangements.

Classification

We noted earlier that archives do not lend themselves to classification schemes in the same way as books, because they need unique treatment and present themselves as aggregates rather than as single items. However, archives often fall into predictable families or groups when they are the result of widely implemented functions and common types of administration. Deposits from gas companies, ecclesiastical parishes or schools, for example, are likely to contain similar subgroups and series of material. In these cases classification schemes might be appropriate. The model for the functional arrangement of business archives described above might be regarded as a kind of top-level classification scheme because it is sufficiently general to allow many different kinds of business archives to use it as a framework for analysis, arrangement and description.

The aim of archival classification schemes is to improve consistency and compatibility in the arrangement and description of archives and to avoid the need for repetitive analysis and research. Some schemes are based on divisions by provenance, such as 'personnel department', others on function, such as 'administration', and others on format, for example 'maps' or 'photographs'. They should not be subject-based.[12]

Part of a provenance-based classification scheme for a primary school, arranged hierarchically:

Group/fonds	School
Subgroup	Managers
Series	Minutes
Series	Meeting papers
Subgroup	Headteacher
Series	Log books
Series	Admission registers
Series	Punishment books
Series	Staff files
Series	Pupil files
Series	Correspondence

Classification schemes are useful because:

- they provide a structured approach yet allow latitude for local variations;
- they provide a structure *per se* so that given records can be slotted into the appropriate place;
- they enable you to avoid re-inventing the wheel each time;
- they provide consistency of treatment;
- they are good for managing accruals: you can add to an existing structure;
- they are helpful to the user who likes a consistent approach;
- they help you identify the appropriate place for typical documents with which you might not be familiar.

Classification schemes are less useful:

- if you try to cram things inappropriately into existing classes because the 'right' one does not seem to exist;
- if your scheme is too complicated: over-classification can make decisions difficult;
- if you have only a handful of documents (e.g. for a school) a scheme is unnecessarily complicated;
- when one item falls into more than one category: e.g. when you have one volume containing minutes of four different committees; or does that map go under 'tithe papers' or 'surveys'?

Arranging the content of collections

Having ensured that we respect the provenance of individual collections by treating them separately from those of a different provenance, and having decided on a method of arrangement how do we go about organising and arranging the actual content? Every accession is unique, although some belong to 'families', sometimes known as management groups, such as schools and hospitals. First it is necessary to:

- Gather as much background material about the organisation or individual as possible as you explore the collection.

- Use the notes drawn up by the person who appraised the collection on its accession to help you.

- If you are responsible for the physical transfer of the records the boxing process will give you an initial insight into its original *in situ* arrangement.

- Contact the depositor, or someone else with personal knowledge, if facts do not readily come to hand.

- Survey the *whole* collection (without disturbing its current order) to see whether there appears to be a natural order to it: whether there is any evidence of who created specific records (individuals or bodies with particular functions; councils, boards, committees, departments, for example) and what functions and activities the archives document. Do not approach it piecemeal – you will end up having to re-order and re-number sections you thought complete.

- Once you have a broad idea of the structure analyse in more detail first any subgroups and then series and items.

- Take particular note of any internal finding aids, such as organisational charts, file classification plans and internal telephone directories, to help you in your reconstruction.

- Sketch an initial plan of what the hierarchical arrangement might look like (this might need modifying as the nature of the content becomes clearer).

It is possible to arrange small collections physically into the order in which you will catalogue them: plenty of space for examining and sorting will be needed. How you enter and collate your data will depend on what kind of system you are using. One way is to work through systematically, noting on individual slips of paper or index cards the detail of the item or series of items in front of you, including identification and description of material, covering dates and a temporary number. Add the temporary number (all numbering is done in pencil) to the items too. Alternatively, you might enter data for each item directly into a database and arrange it as you go or subsequently. With larger collections you may not be able to make an initial physical sort: in this case you may need to work through it entering your data in piecemeal fashion before you can get a good overview. You need to arrange your descriptive slips or your database entries into a meaningful structure to obtain a final intellectual arrangement before organising the material itself.

Once you are satisfied with your arrangement you can replace your temporary numbers with permanent ones. Documents can then be stored in acid-free folders and boxes in any convenient space in your storage area. Collections do not need to be stored together: it is much more efficient to store things of a similar shape and size (long maps, large volumes) together, and the intellectual order is preserved in your catalogue. Some media, photographic, magnetic and digital, for example, need different, cooler, storage environments too. You should note the specific location for each box, identified by the catalogue marks of its contents. Thus, the box containing files DDX 1/1–20 may be located in Stack 4, Bay 26, Shelf 1, whereas that with DDX 2/4–13 might be in Stack 3, Bay 5, Shelf 3. Your location index or database should be organised so that you can easily establish:

- where each individual item is stored;
- in which locations an entire collection is stored;
- what each shelf/bay/stack contains;
- how many vacant spaces you have;
- where vacant spaces are located.

The arrangement of collections enables their physical and to some degree their intellectual management to be established. It is now time to consider how to construct the central primary finding aid that will complete the process.

Archival description

By the time a collection has been numbered with temporary or final numbers, boxed and stored in its final location there should exist a reasonably well-structured list of its contents that can be turned into a formal primary finding aid: a catalogue, inventory or list. In offices where the quantity of collections outnumbers resources for listing or cataloguing them, there may only be rough temporary box lists that provide a general idea of what is in each box but where no formal arrangement has taken place. These should be regarded as an interim measure, although all too often they become semi-permanent.

Archival description is the process of capturing and representing the content and context of an archival collection and the catalogue is the prime tool for doing this. It enables both intellectual and administrative control and is the prime source of any subsequent finding aids, whether via paper-based indexes and subject or thematic guides, or electronic access. It is best done in compliance with national and international standards.

Standards

Archival descriptive standards are a recent development when compared with those that developed for the cataloguing of books in the library world. Their acceptance by national and international professional communities and standards organisations mark something of a professional 'coming of age'. It acknowledges that there is a commonly held understanding about the nature and treatment of archives. Standards act as prescribed guides for action, as 'benchmarks' with which practice can be compared and the means by which individuals compare or judge processes and products. It is increasingly the case that overt compliance with standards assists recognition by government and by professional and funding bodies. Finally, it is very difficult to enter the world of retrieval unless finding aids demonstrate the structure and consistency recommended by the recognised standards.

In America, in the search for standards, archives followed the library tradition and adapted bibliographic systems: the Anglo American Cataloguing Rules (AACR) for description and the MARC format enabled machine-readable cataloguing. Subsequently, descriptive rules, which made them easier to apply to an archive, were published by Hensen in *Archives, Personal Papers and Manuscripts* (APPM).[13] Canadian and UK archives were less locked into bibliographic systems than the US and took a different starting point: because of their collective nature, archives were to be dealt with in accordance with archival principles. The Canadian solution was the *Rules for Archival Description* (RAD), first published from 1990 onwards. More recently, a joint project, the CUSTARD project

(Canadian–US Task Force on ARchival Description), tried to reconcile APPM, the Canadian RAD and the *General International Standard Archival Description* (ISAD(G)) to create a set of descriptive rules that could be used with Encoded Archival Description (of which more later) and MARC. The outcome was in fact two standards, an update of RAD and a new *American Standard, Describing Archives: A Content Standard*.[14] In the UK national standards were articulated by the *Manual of Archival Description* (MAD) first published in the 1980s. MAD, now in its third edition, has set the standard of practice for the UK profession and also demonstrates compliance with ISAD(G).[15]

Such standards enable the attributes of archives, particularly their context and the relationships between them, to be properly represented and consistently described. They lay the groundwork for subsequent marking up for on-line display in SGML or XML most usually through the mark-up structural standard Encoded Archival Description (EAD). However, they do not allow archives to be presented in the way that allows users easy to access them: users want specific 'known item' retrieval. For this to be possible specific access points must be identified, such as personal or corporate names, place names and subjects. A further raft of standards provides guidance on how to do this consistently – these are name authority standards for personal, corporate and place names and thesauri for subjects and themes. The main archival (as opposed to library) name authorities are:

- The International Council on Archives' (ICA's) International standard archival authority record for corporate bodies, persons and families (ISAAR (CPF));
- The UK NCA *Rules for the construction of personal, place and corporate names* (NCA Rules).[16]

The three main subject thesauri used are:

- The *Library of Congress Subject Headings* (LCSH);
- *The UNESCO Thesaurus*; and
- The *UK Archival Thesaurus* (UKAT) based on the *UNESCO Thesaurus*.[17]

These authorities define precisely which term should be used in access points in order to provide consistency, coherence and lack of ambiguity. For example, should you refer to the author of *Alice in Wonderland* as Lewis Carroll or as Charles Lutwidge Dodgson? Should the term 'gun' go under 'arms' or 'munitions'? If I search on 'nursery' will I get references to horticulture or children, or both? This is dealt with in more detail later.

General International Standard Archival Description

ISAD(G) was first published by the ICA in 1994: an update with many more examples of how it might be applied came out in 2000.[18] Its purpose is to provide general guidance on how to *structure* archival descriptions – it also gives some advice on what *content* to include. It was developed by a committee drawn from a wide range of countries, and thus is based on common experience and practice. Countries that do not fully subscribe to it (e.g. the US) still recognise many of its general principles. Like many international standards it is a strategic document: although it contains specific guidance it expects practitioners to use it in conjunction with more detailed national standards. Repositories, too, may develop their in-house guidelines – so help is available at a range of levels. ISAD(G) is easily available and so I will only highlight its main recommendations here, together with some examples of how they are applied. I recommend that anyone describing archives use it as a reference point alongside other available standards.

The Standard's objectives are to:

- ensure the creation of consistent, appropriate and self-explanatory descriptions;
- facilitate the retrieval and exchange of information about archival material;
- enable the sharing of authority data (more on this later);
- make possible the integration of descriptions from different locations into a unified information system.[19]

A set of general rules about how to approach description is followed by more detailed recommendations. The first recognises the multi-level nature of archive collections as demonstrated in Table 4.1: the fonds (group collection), subgroup, series, file and item – and any intermediate subgroups or series. This rule explains that a description at the group (fonds) level should be broad and general and cover the whole collection. This is often referred to as 'group-level' or 'collection-level' description, and where information about series, files and items is not given in detail.

When subsequent descriptions of these lower levels are made they may be quite detailed, but will only be meaningful when seen within the context of the whole group or fonds.

Another general rule confirms that description should be from the general to the specific. In order to represent the context and hierarchical structure of the group and its parts, you should supply at each level only the information appropriate to that level. When put together the final result will represent the whole hierarchy of the part-to-whole relationship from the broadest to the most specific. In addition, in order to provide an accurate representation you should only provide information appropriate to the level being described. Thus, a group/fonds/collection-level description of Crewe Mechanics Institute would not give details of how many volumes of minutes there were for the Education Committee series; nor would an item-level description of the monthly cash balances describe top-level information about the constitution of the Institute.

The real meat of the Standard is provided in its description of the rules covering the 26 elements that it considers to be the maximum necessary for any archival description. Some of these elements are obvious – such as title and reference code. Each of these elements is placed within one of seven broader areas: for example, title and reference code fall into the Identity Statement Area. Figure 4.3, taken from the contents page of the Standard, shows this framework, with the areas and elements of description contained within them.

Figure 4.3   ISAD(G) Contents page: seven information areas and 26 elements of description

---

ISAD(G) General International Standard Archival Description, Second Edition.

INTRODUCTION

0. GLOSSARY OF TERMS ASSOCIATED WITH THE GENERAL RULES

1. MULTILEVEL DESCRIPTION
  1.1 INTRODUCTION

2. MULTILEVEL DESCRIPTION RULES
  2.1 DESCRIPTION FROM THE GENERAL TO THE SPECIFIC
  2.2 INFORMATION RELEVANT TO THE LEVEL OF DESCRIPTION
  2.3 LINKING OF DESCRIPTIONS
  2.4 NON-REPETITION OF INFORMATION

Figure 4.3 ISAD(G) Contents page: seven information areas and 26 elements of description (*cont'd*)

3. ELEMENTS OF DESCRIPTION

3.1 IDENTITY STATEMENT AREA

    3.1.1 Reference code(s)

    3.1.2 Title

    3.1.3 Date(s)

    3.1.4 Level of description

    3.1.5 Extent and medium of the unit of description (quantity, bulk, or size)

3.2 CONTEXT AREA

    3.2.1 Name of creator(s)

    3.2.2 Administrative/Biographical history

    3.2.3 Archival history

    3.2.4 Immediate source of acquisition or transfer

3.3 CONTENT AND STRUCTURE AREA

    3.3.1 Scope and content

    3.3.2 Appraisal, destruction and scheduling information

    3.3.3 Accruals

    3.3.4 System of arrangement

3.4 CONDITIONS OF ACCESS AND USE AREA

    3.4.1 Conditions governing access

    3.4.2 Conditions governing reproduction

    3.4.3 Language/scripts of material

    3.4.4 Physical characteristics and technical requirements

    3.4.5 Finding aids

3.5 ALLIED MATERIALS AREA

    3.5.1 Existence and location of originals

    3.5.2 Existence and location of copies

    3.5.3 Related units of description

    3.5.4 Publication note

3.6 NOTES AREA

    3.6.1 Note

3.7 DESCRIPTION CONTROL AREA

    3.7.1 Archivist's Note

    3.7.2 Rules or Conventions

    3.7.3 Date(s) of descriptions

ISAD(G) Contents page: Seven Information Areas and 26 elements of description.

For each element the Standard supplies a rule which:

1. Names the element of description governed by the rule.
2. States the purpose for its inclusion in a description.
3. States what rule(s) apply to the element.
4. Provides examples to illustrate the rule.

If we apply these to the 'title' element as an example, the Standard states:

1. Name of element: title.
2. Purpose: to name the unit of description.
3. Rules: provide either a formal title or a concise supplied title in accordance with the rules of the multi-level description and national conventions.
4. Examples: St. Anthony Turnverein organisational records; Papers of J. Lawton Collins (in our case Crewe Mechanics Institute)

Only six elements are considered mandatory. These are all those within the Identity Statement Area and are

- Reference code
- Title
- Creator
- Dates
- Level of description
- Extent (physical) of the unit of description

Figure 4.3 can be compared with Figures 4.4–4.6 in order to see the different ways in which mandatory, and some non-mandatory elements of ISAD(G) can be applied at group, subgroup, series and item levels. Figures 4.4–4.6 show part of the Crewe Mechanics Institute archive listed at the group, subgroup, series and item level; the records of George Dutton, Leather Dresser, of Northwich, UK, at the group level; and the correspondence of Colonel Hugh Robert Hibbert at series level.

When the archives to be listed are not those of a complete fonds or group, for example when all that remains is a single series and a few items, then series- or file-level description is all that is needed. However, all the elements that are used at group level may also be used at series (or any other) level: the series will still need all the mandatory elements of the Identity Statement Area to be included, and any relevant from the

Figure 4.4 Application of mandatory and some non-mandatory elements of ISAD(G) at group, subgroup, series and item level of part of the archives of Crewe Mechanics Institute

---

CREWE MECHANICS INSTITUTE

Identity statement

Country Code/repository code/reference code: GB 0017 D4807

Title: Crewe Mechanics Institute

Dates of creation: 1845–1946

Level of description: group (fonds), sub-group, series and item level

Extent and medium: .25 cu metres textual material

Context

Name of Creator: Crewe Mechanics Institute

Administrative history: In 1845 the Institution was founded in Crewe, Cheshire, by amalgamating an existing mechanics institute and a technical institute. It was formed to give technical training, in theory and practice to railway apprentices and workmen, and later had a more general educational role and included non-railway members. Its rooms in the assembly hall (later known as the town hall) originally contained a library, newsroom and committee rooms. The library and newsroom had been brought together as one organisation at the end of 1844.

The Institute was controlled by a Council comprising three members elected by the railway, nine elected by members from a list supplied by the railway and nine members from amongst themselves. The 21 members managed three sub-committees; the first dealt with the running of the newsroom and library, the second with the classes and letting of the hall and the third with the public baths; horticultural exhibitions etc. The chairman or president was always the railway locomotive superintendent or in later years the divisional mechanical engineer or works superintendent. In April 1936 the library and reading room were leased to Crewe Corporation for use as the public library; by the 1950s the buildings had deteriorated and they were demolished around 1970.

Archival history: The Scientific Society was part of the Mechanics Institute. The Engineering Society, an independent body formed in 1879,

---

Figure 4.4 Application of mandatory and some non-mandatory elements of ISAD(G) at group, subgroup, series and item level of part of the archives of Crewe Mechanics Institute (*cont'd*)

closed in 1884 and deposited its minutes with the Crewe Mechanics Institute Library. Crewe and District Hospital Sunday Fund was responsible for forwarding church collections and other donations to selected hospitals, mainly those which treated local inhabitants. Its secretary was frequently the secretary of the Crewe Mechanics Institute. The records remained in the custody of Crewe Library after closure of the Institute.

Content and structure

Scope and content: Minutes of Council, 1860–1921 and annual reports 1845–1912; minutes of finance, education, hall, library, games and entertainment, social club committees 1854–1940; correspondence 1903–1922; accounts 1918–1937; leases, inventories and specifications 1901–1934; some records of Crewe Scientific Society 1898–1902, Crewe Engineering Society 1879–1884, Crewe and District Hospital Society Fund 1890–1913.

System of arrangement: The archives arranged according to organisational structure.

Conditions of access and use

Conditions governing access: open access

Council

	Minutes		1860–1921
D 4807/1	Jun 1860 – Jun 1867	1 vol	
D 4807/2	Aug 1867 – May 1872	1 vol	
D 4807/3	May 1872 – Aug 1874	1 vol	
D 4807/4	Sep 1874 – Feb 1883	1 vol	
D 4807/5	Feb 1883 – Feb 1890	1 vol	
D 4807/6	Feb 1890 – Jan 1901	1 vol	
D 4807/7	Jan 1901 – May 1909	1 vol	
D 4807/8	Jun 1909 – Mar 1921	1 vol	

Figure 4.4   Application of mandatory and some non-mandatory elements of ISAD(G) at group, subgroup, series and item level of part of the archives of Crewe Mechanics Institute (*cont'd*)

	Annual reports		1845–1912
D 4807/9	1845–1890	1 vol	
D 4807/10	1891–1899	1 vol	
D 4807/11	1900–1910	1 vol	
D 4807/12	1912	1 doc	

Figure 4.5   Application of mandatory and some non-mandatory elements of ISAD(G) at group/collection level

GEORGE DUTTON AND SONS (NORTHWICH) LTD, LEATHER DRESSERS, NORTHWICH

Identity statement

Country Code/repository code/reference code: GB 0017 DDN

Title: George Dutton and Sons (Northwich) Ltd, Leather Dressers, Northwich

Dates of creation: 1851–1973

Level of description: group (fonds) level

Extent and medium: 2 cu metres textual material

Context

Name of Creator: George Dutton and Sons

Administrative history:
The firm was founded in the mid 19th century as Dutton and Lamb but in March 1870 this partnership was dissolved and the company came into the sole possession of George Dutton. In January 1920 it became a limited company known as George Dutton and Sons (Northwich) Ltd, making roller leather for cotton spinning, hat leathers, skivers and shoe linings and clothing and fancy leathers.

Content and structure

Scope and content: Corporate records 1870–1969; share records 1925–1959; internal administration 1873–1880; accounting and financial

Figure 4.5 Application of mandatory and some non-mandatory elements of ISAD(G) at group/collection level (*cont'd*)

records 1851–1970; operation: production records 1895–1970; operation: technical records 1888–1963; sales and marketing records 1905–1955; personnel records 1855–1963; premises and property papers 1910–1973.

System of arrangement: Owing to a lack of information on the administrative background of the company, the records have been arranged to reflect the functions of the company rather than its structure.

Figure 4.6 Application of mandatory and some non-mandatory elements of ISAD(G) at series level

COLONEL HUGH ROBERT HIBBERT: LETTERS AND PAPERS

Identity statement

Country Code/repository code/reference code: GB 0017 DHB

Title: Colonel Hugh Robert Hibbert: letters and papers

Dates of creation: 1845–1865

Level of description: series level

Extent and medium: 3 files of correspondence

Context

Name of Creator: Hibbert, Hugh Robert, Colonel, 1825–1865

Biographical history: Colonel Hugh Robert Hibbert DL, JP, of Birtles Hall, Macclesfield, served with the 7th Royal Fusiliers in the Crimean Expeditionary Force from embarkation in April 1854 until the Second Assault on the Redan at Sebastopol in September 1855, when he was severely wounded and sent home. Having first entered the Army in 1847 as an Ensign in the 39th Foot, he was commissioned Lieutenant in the 7th Royal Fusiliers in 1850 and served continuously with that Regiment until his retirement in 1871 as Colonel commanding the First Battalion, 1864–71. During the Crimean War he was actively engaged in the Battles of the Alma

Figure 4.6   Application of mandatory and some non-mandatory
elements of ISAD(G) at series level (*cont'd*)

---

and Inkerman and at the Siege of Sebastopol, being twice wounded. In
1858 he took part in military operations in suppression of the Indian Mutiny
and subsequently served for several years in India.

Allied material area

Existence and location of copies: Letters copied and edited by
Mrs. Hibbert at the time of receipt have been attached to the originals.

Publication note: The Crimean War historian, A. W. Kinglake quoted from
Colonel Hibbert's reminiscences in *The Invasion of the Crimea* (1877); Major
General W. R. Baring Pemberton used some letters in *Battles of the Crimean
War* (Batsford 1962).

Content and structure

Scope and content:

Hibbert's Crimean letters, most of which were addressed to his mother, give
graphic descriptions of active service conditions in the Crimea.

Correspondence 1845–1865

DHB 1–39	Letters from Hugh Robert Hibbert to his mother, Mary Caroline Henrietta Hibbert of Birtles Hall, Macclesfield (39 items)	1845–1865
DHB 40–52	Letters from Hugh Robert Hibbert to his father, Thomas Hibbert of Birtles Hall, Macclesfield (13 items)	1845–1864
DHB 53–57	Letters from Hugh Robert Hibbert to various family and friends: including his sister, Georgiana Charlotte Hibbert. (5 items)	1854–1855

---

other areas too. The most useful of these will be details of the creator, an
administrative history, and the scope and content.

Different repositories will present information in different ways and
are likely to use less formal terminology than that of ISAD(G) if it suits
them. Many repositories confine their descriptions to collection/group
level. Group-level descriptions provide basic intellectual control and take
less time than more detailed item descriptions. However, it may be

difficult to provide physical access to the contents of collections that only have a group-level description, unless the items are separately identifiable.

Practical issues

International standards such as ISAD(G) provide a useful framework of principles and practice. National standards, such as the *Manual of Archival Description*, and a repository's in-house guidelines will offer more detailed advice on local conventions and procedure. Sometimes, however, it seems that none of the guidance seems to fit *this* particular collection. In general catalogues and finding aids should:

- be concise and laid out as clearly as possible: they should lead users to what they want to know by the shortest possible route;
- include sufficient management information for documents to be identified and retrieved by staff;
- be presented objectively in layperson's language, without using obscure archival terminology ('fonds' is meaningless to non-archivists) or unnecessarily showcasing the archivist's knowledge;
- supply users with only sufficient descriptive information to indicate an item's possible relevance to their enquiry;
- cater for a broad range of research: the archivist needs to be aware of areas of potential interest;
- not attempt to take the place of the original: detailed abstracts of documents are not cost-effective;
- indicate which access points are to be extracted for indexing, using specified authorities, to allow searching from such user angles as personal, corporate, place names and subjects.

Depth of description

Accurately and concisely describing archives is an underrated skill. The *depth* of description, i.e. the amount of detail that is included, is usually a matter of office policy. Some offices, for example, require each title deed to be listed in detail; others seek no more than a file-level (deed bundle) description. This is a matter of judgement, based on available resources, likely level of research use and perceived 'value' (including commercial) of items.

When describing at the series or file level it is important to provide succinct and consistent descriptions that give a 'flavour' of the contents with as little bias as possible. The decision not to catalogue these at the item level may be soundly based: indeed, these file-level descriptions can be more useful than endless item-level ones, where the informational value is low. If you are unsure about the informational value of what you are cataloguing, consider whether it is 'worth' indexing, or providing access points for, because your description will provide the basis for subsequent searches.

Thus, you might create a file-level description for bundles of correspondence between a husband and wife that highlights the unusual while noting the main components (Table 4.2).

Note that 'correspondence' refers to letters *between* people; if you only have one side of it then you should describe it as 'letters to/from'.

Property deeds may also be described either at item or file level: usually those earlier than 1600 are listed at item level, with later ones being dealt with more summarily. It is conventional to retain the spelling of surnames in early deeds while modernising place names and forenames. When described at file level care should be taken to be consistent, always highlighting the same things, such as those that provide additional evidence of title (probate copies of wills) summaries of contents (abstracts of title) or other useful information (sale particulars, plans, etc.) (Tables 4.3 and 4.4).

Table 4.2   Correspondence: file-level description

Correspondence [Series level] Letters to Mrs Elizabeth Dobson, Birches Hall, Great Budworth [File level]		
DSS 1/4/57	Letters from Edward Dobson at Grays Inn, London, Esq., to his wife, relating to legal, business, domestic and personal matters. Includes references to Parliament and preparations for war with France, 1678 [no. 6]; the 'great comet' of 1680 [no. 9]; the conveyance of cheese from Cheshire to London [no 4]. (13 items)	1676–1682

Table 4.3 Deeds: item-level description

	Agden, Cheshire	1401/2
DVA 1/1	1. William le Spencer and John de Norton, chaplains 2. Ellen, formerly wife of Thomas Warburton of Agden Feoffment from 1. to 2. of all lands, tenements, rents and services in Agden, with reversion of lands etc. of William le Walker in Agden for her life; and after her death to Ellen, wife of William le Venables and their heirs. Witnesses: John le Massy esq., Roger de Merynton, Robert de Werberton 31 Jan 1401/2	

Table 4.4 Deeds and papers: file-level description

	Chester	
DDC 2877/1	Deeds and papers relating to property at 26 and 27 Middle Crane Street, Chester, of the Peers family of Anglesey and Chester, including abstract of title, 1897, reciting from 1790 [no.22]; sale particulars with plan, 1850 [no.20]. 22 items	1825–1897

Volumes

Volumes should normally be listed individually, at item level. Check the contents carefully – it is often the case that entries are made at the back as well as the front, for example by different committees. For volumes in the same series a scope and content note at the series level can supply the general contents, for example 'the committee's function was to allocate funding to applicants and to receive reports on the activities of those who were successful'. Where there is unusual content, this should be noted at the individual file (volume) level. Loose papers in volumes, if worth keeping, should be removed and catalogued separately, making sure that their original location is noted.

Composite files and series

In an ideal archival world, series and files would make themselves immediately identifiable as in the case of the Crewe Mechanics Institute (Figure 4.1), and often in their original order. All too often, however, you will find that you have to impose some kind of order on a random collection of material, and that this involves 'creating' miscellaneous or composite series and items – I referred to this when discussing the arrangement of personal papers. This is done by bringing together an assortment of items with different physical and/or informational characteristics, on a functional, chronological or – failing all else – subject basis. Examples of these would be 'papers relating to the construction of the church hall', 'legal papers relating to the case Disraeli v. Gladstone', 'newscuttings and other printed ephemera relating to local elections' and 'photographs of Gotham City summer festival'. The series title 'miscellanea' should be a last resort, only used where there are items whose reason for being in the collection is entirely unclear – yet of sufficient interest to be kept. You can often judge the quality of a catalogue by the length of its 'miscellanea'.

Reference codes

Again conventions vary from repository to repository. Those closely associated with libraries sometimes have variations of a Dewey system, although this is not usually satisfactory because Dewey is subject-based. It is quite usual for an office to use alpha-numerical systems for referencing documents. At the higher levels, management and group, letters may be used: FO for Foreign Office, E for Ecclesiastical records, D for Deposited records, and so on. Numbers are used at the lower levels. These may reflect the structure and arrangement of the archive, or be used as a sequence of running numbers.

For example, the reference of the first minute book of the Council of the Crewe Mechanics Institute might either be

> D 4807/1 – D (deposited)/4807 (accession number)/1 (first item in collection),

or reflect the hierarchical arrangement of the archive and be allocated

> D 4807/1/1/1 – D (deposited)/4807 (collection reference)/1 (1st subgroup Council)/1 (1st series Minutes)/1 (1st item of 1st series of 1st subgroup).

Office practices vary considerably. While ISAD(G) anticipates a hierarchical use of references, the prime function of the reference code is to be able to locate the item concerned physically – it does not have to reflect an intellectual structure.

Presentation formats for archival description

Although many archives continue to produce paper-based catalogues and other finding aids, most aim to generate them for digital viewing too. This may be done for internal purposes by entry into a relational database, often that used for other management functions such as accessioning, location and conservation. However, for wider distribution networking facilities are necessary. An early US solution was to include descriptions of archives in the library bibliographic systems based around AACR and MARC.

More recently, the development of EAD, a data structure standard that supports the hierarchical nature of archival finding aids and their content, has enabled the archival community to disseminate catalogues, as well as a range of other finding aids, on the Internet. It is mapped to ISAD(G) and comprises a set of rules for 'designating the intellectual and physical parts of archival finding aids so that the information contained therein may be searched, retrieved, displayed, and exchanged in a predictable platform-independent manner.'[20] Specific pieces of information are encoded (tagged or marked-up) in such a way that the computer will recognise which section is 'title', which is 'dates' which is the 'name of creator', and so on.

EAD comprises a Document Type Definition (DTD) for encoding archival finding aids [others exist for different materials, such as the Text Encoding Initiative (TEI) DTD for literary texts]. It is written following the syntactic rules of Standard Generalized Markup Language (SGML) and Extensible Markup Language (XML).[21] Marked-up sections can be 'nested' inside each other in order to present archival description hierarchically. Table 4.5 shows how EAD tags represent the data elements in the Identity Statement Area of ISAD(G).

EAD elements can be further refined through the use of 'attributes'. In Figure 4.9 below, the Country code and Repository code attributes enable the required ISAD(G) reference code element to be encoded in more detail.

Figures 4.7–4.9 show how the catalogue entry for the Preston Brook Methodist Chapel records can be displayed in three different ways. The first is for internal management use, and has been largely derived from

Table 4.5 Mapping ISAD(G) elements with EAD tags[22]

ISAD(G): Identity Statement Area	EAD
3.1.1 Reference code(s)	\<unitid\> COUNTRYCODE and REPOSITORY CODE attributes
3.1.2 Title	\<unittitle\>
3.1.3 Dates of creation	\<unitdate\>
3.1.4 Level of description	\<archdesc\> and \<c\> LEVEL attribute
3.1.5 Extent of the unit	\<physdesc\>, \<extent\>

the data entered in the accession database. The second shows the same data displayed in the public access catalogue, and the third shows part of the catalogue tagged in EAD mark up.

The development of EAD began in 1993 at the University of California and its application is spreading rapidly. The most recent version of the standard is EAD Version 2002 and this and much other guidance can be found on the official EAD website hosted by the Library of Congress.[23] Two issues of the *American Archivist* have discussed its development, and practical step-by-step guidance in its use is given in the *EAD Cookbook*,

Figure 4.7 Catalogue entry displayed in DS Calm

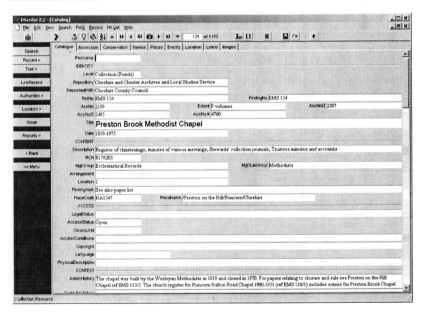

Figure 4.8 Catalogue entry displayed in DServe public access catalogue

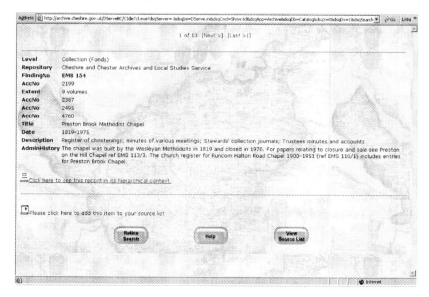

Figure 4.9 Part of fonds-level description displayed in EAD

```
<CORPNAME SOURCE="ncarules">Preston Brook Chapel, Cheshire</CORPNAME>
</ORIGINATION>
<PHYSDESC LABEL="Extent" ENCODINGANALOG="315">
<EXTENT>9</EXTENT> <GENREFORM>files</GENREFORM>
</PHYSDESC>
<REPOSITORY ENCODINGANALOG="311" LABEL="Held at:">
<CORPNAME SOURCE="ncarules">Cheshire and Chester Archives and Local
Studies Service</CORPNAME></REPOSITORY></DID>
<ADMININFO>
<ACQINFO ENCODINGANALOG="324"><HEAD>Immediate Source of
Acquisition</HEAD>
<P>Acc 2199(pt), 2387(pt), 2495(pt), 4760(pt)</P>
</ACQINFO>
</ADMININFO>
<SCOPECONTENT ENCODINGANALOG="331"><HEAD>Scope and Content</HEAD>
<P>Minutes, register of christenings, collection journals</P>
</SCOPECONTENT>
<BIOGHIST ENCODINGANALOG="322"><HEAD>Administrative History</HEAD>
<P>The chapel was built by the Wesleyan Methodists in 1819 and closed
in 1970. For papers relating to closure and sale see Preston on the
Hill Chapel ref EMS 113/3. The church register for Runcorn Halton
Road Chapel 1900-1951 (ref EMS 110/1 includes entries for Preston
Brook Chapel.</P>
</BIOGHIST>
```

developed by the University of Virginia.[24] In the UK EAD has been exploited widely, particularly in the university sector. A number of catalogue networking initiatives have developed that are dependent on EAD; the largest of these are Access to Archives (A2A) and the Archives Hub.

Archival description of electronic formats

Increasingly, new archival material will only exist in digital form. Records managers should be actively involved in the management of electronic records within their organisations with a view to capturing and preserving them for as long as they are required for business purposes. Some will be identified as archival from their point of creation, others at some point during their active life. Selection of enduring non-proprietary formats and the application of appropriate metadata are of central importance in ensuring longevity. In-house archives will be facing these issues now, and national archives are providing good models to follow. Collecting archives may not yet have been approached with a view to taking in digital archives: when they do they are likely to have a more difficult time providing the necessary support. Electronic records can exist in an enormous variety of formats, such as office-suite documents, applications, databases, virtual-reality models and audio-visual material. Unless their ongoing maintenance is factored in early in their active lives archives are unlikely to be able to manage them.

In terms of the description of archives created and maintained electronically there are one or two models to follow. Examples that have reached the UK National Archives include records of public enquiries, parliamentary committees, royal commissions and government department websites.

The UK Committee on Standards of Conduct in Public Life was announced by the Prime Minister in the House of Commons on 25 October 1994. This is a standing committee and its records are routinely transferred to the National Archives. Some of its records are paper-based, whereas others were transferred on CD-ROM. Both are described in line with TNA and ISAD(G) standards in the on-line catalogue, with details of media and format for the digital records supplied as follows:

Describing digital archives

'The records were originally created in Word Perfect 5.1. The files were transferred to the Public Record Office on floppy disks and were then copied into Word 6 format and verified to confirm the integrity of the data. The Word Perfect files were later copied into Word 7 format and printed to Postscript files for permanent preservation.'[25]

Figure 4.10	Cataloguing data sets

Department	Series	NDAD ref	PRO ref
Agricultural Departments	Agricultural and Horticultural Census	CRDA/4	MAF 408 MAF 410
	Coast Protection Survey of England	CRDA/10	MAF 406
	Internal Drainage Board Database	CRDA/9	MAF 407
British Railways Board	British Rail Electronically Archived Documents	CRDA/37	AN 186
Countryside Agencies	Survey of Rural Services	CRDA/30	D 16 D 10
Department of Culture, Media and Sport	National Lottery Awards Database	CRDA/39	PF 1
Department of Trade and Industry	Oil and Gas Directorate, North Sea Geographical Information System	CRDA/26	EG 17
Education Departments	Grant Maintained Schools Database	CRDA/36	ED 278
	Learning Partnerships	CRDA/53	NV 4
	Learning and Training at Work	CRDA/52	NV 3
	Register of Educational Establishments	CRDA/47	NV 2

Describing data sets

Computer data sets produced by UK government departments and agencies are managed and made available by the National Digital Archive of Datasets (NDAD) on behalf of the National Archives.[26] This body is experienced in the management and preservation of large quantities of often statistical digital data, particularly in hierarchical storage management systems. Despite the differences in format and content these datasets can still be described using the elements of description in ISAD(G) (Figure 4.10).

Retrieving information from archives

The value of applying standards becomes clear when you start searching for data in response to enquiries. The phrase 'garbage in, garbage out' means that if you do not create consistent and accurate content what comes out will be unreliable and partial. Your finding aids need to be able to answer a range of different types of research question: and although a few people might be interested in the archives as created by the organisation, most will be seeking information about a specific person, place or subject, irrespective of who created it.

We can perceive this activity as a two-way process. At one end the 'indexer' or whoever is creating the finding aid acquires records and describes, classifies and indexes them, produces an index or finding aid and then stores the records. At the other end the user initiates a query, adopts a search strategy, searches the finding aid or index for references, and ultimately accesses the stored record. He or she goes through a similar process to the indexer but from a different starting point. The challenge is to match 'input' with 'output': in other words the terms input by the indexer to represent its content should match as far as possible those used by the searcher looking for information. Of course, manual, paper-based indexes as separate entities are much more visible than those created through a computer. Finding specific terms in computerised data is done through searching for entries containing specific words, perhaps in particular fields, such as in the collection title or dates field. This may be done through free text searching and by controlling terms used by applying authority standards.

There are two main types of information requests presented by researchers. These demonstrate either a 'known-item need' or a 'subject need'. In the first, the request is for access to or information about a document that is known to exist. For example, 'I need a copy of the contract we made with Sue, Grabbit and Run in 1987 or 1988' or 'Can I see my great grandfather's apprenticeship indenture? I know you have it here'.

A subject need is expressed in more general terms. For example, 'I am sure the bank has information about business relations with China over the last ten years. What can you find?' or 'What do you have on poverty in twentieth century Bolton?'

How do you respond? Firstly check that the searcher is asking the 'right' question. It is quite easy to undertake extensive research on, say, poverty in Bolton only to discover that the 'real' question was 'Where was the workhouse located in Bolton?' Thus, what is presented as a subject need might actually be a known-item need, and vice versa. A basic reference skill is getting to the bottom of the question.

If you do not have extensive secondary finding aids – indexes or computerised search capabilities – that will locate the information easily you will need to have a very detailed knowledge of the content of your collections. You will also need to be able to translate the question from 'what records do you have *about*' to 'which organisation or individual will have *created* records' to satisfy the request. You will need to know, for example, that organisations dealing with poverty in the twentieth century included the parish and township, quarter sessions, boards of guardians, poor-law unions and workhouses and that the records they produced are core resources here. This is the kind of information you would expect an archivist to know. What is harder to determine is where there is useful but incidental information *about* poverty in unexpected sources: in personal papers, diaries, correspondence, for example. Unless you capture this in some kind of finding aid it may remain unused.

'Poverty in Bolton' is relatively easy. But what will you say to the researcher whose topic is 'representations of motherhood in the urban environment' or 'qualitative responses to diet in the working classes'? Advanced research topics are harder to unpick, and although the archivist should be aware of likely research areas responsibility also rests with the researcher to interpret advanced topics on our behalf.

Indexing and authority standards

Using authority standards in the creation of finding aids will make life easier. These standards control the language used in the creation and use of access points (in indexes or as keywords) so that it is consistent and unambiguous. Access points are those names or keyword index terms by which a description may be searched, identified or retrieved. Indexing provides *multiple* access points to enable records/archives to be searched and retrieved: it is the process of labelling for retrieval and involves analysis of the concepts within the documents and translation of them into the language of the system. Authority standards exist for personal, corporate, family and place names as well as for subjects.

It is possible to index using 'natural language', i.e. using terms taken directly from the text of the original, or using your own terminology. This means there is no control over the choice of terms used. As free text searching is quite common, and will yield results even if they are not comprehensive, this might seem tempting. 'Controlled language' imposes an artificial or controlled vocabulary so that there is only one term in the vocabulary to represent any one concept. It requires the indexer to establish from the appropriate authority standard which is the designated word to use. This may seem labour intensive at the input stage but will yield much more comprehensive output.

The examples below demonstrate four problems that arise if controlled vocabularies are not used to define specific subject terms.

- Volume of first-day postal covers collected by James Brown, Sheffield, 1950s.

- Photographs of Mamma Mia's children's nursery, Rome, 1982.
- School exercise book of Richard Walter Jenkins, 1932.
- Catalogues of shrubs and perennials, of Bees Nurseries, Birmingham, 1970–1975.
- Records of the Center for Alternative Technology, 1980–1991.
- Draft copy of *Stamp collecting for beginners*, by James Brown *c.* 1958.
- Invitation to tea dance at the Elderly Person's Day Centre, Bournemouth, 20 December 1920.
- Records of Black and Sons, Philatelist, Toronto, 1902–1937.

The problems are:

- Different words with similar meanings (synonyms): philately, first-day covers, stamp collecting – all related to collecting of stamps.
- Similar words with different meanings (homonym): nursery (horticulture) and nursery (child care).
- Different legitimate spellings of the same word: Centre and Center.

Unless guidance is supplied on which word to use to represent the natural terms in each of these cases, searching will result in only part of the information available being retrieved.

The same problem occurs in personal, corporate and place names.

- Should the actress Diana Dors be indexed under this stage name or her birth name Diana Mary Fluck?
- Should the Duke of Wellington be indexed under the title Wellington or under the family name of Wellesley?
- Which is 'right' – Worshipful company of Clothworkers or Clothworkers' Company?
- Should the Irish town of Dun Laoghaire be placed under this or its previous name of Kingstown? Wiche Malbanke or Nantwich?

Standards are indispensable here. ISAAR(CPF) and the UK NCA Rules enable us to define which term to use for the corporate, personal and family creators of records while the thesauri (UNESCO, LCSH and UKAT) offer unique terms to represent subjects. Each provides a term which is the one that is *used* or *preferred*, providing alongside it references from *unused* or *non-preferred* terms that are similar. Below are just a few examples of some of the rules.

Personal names

The NCA Rules explain that the entry for Diana Dors should be under her stage name because she used it in all aspects of her life, not just when acting. It should be shown as:

Dors/Diana/1931–1984/actress with a cross reference to *x* Fluck | Diana Mary

Like the NCA Rules, ISAAR(CPF) states that titled people are indexed under the family name rather than a title, which may be transient

5.1 IDENTITY AREA
    5.1.1 Type of entity: Family
    5.1.2 Authorized form of name: Noel family, Earls of Gainsborough
    5.1.5 Other forms of name: Noel family, Barons Noel

        Noel family, Barons Barham

        Noel family, Viscounts Campden

        Noel family, baronets, of Barham Court

So the Duke of Wellington should be indexed under his family name:

Wellesley / Arthur / 1769–1852 / 1st Duke of Wellington

Place names

The NCA Rules explain that you should use the form of the name that is contemporary with the primary source being described and that where there has been a change of name there should be reciprocal cross-references. Thus,

Dun Laoghaire
xx Kingstown
Kingstown
xx Dun Laoghaire

Corporate bodies and subjects

ISAAR(CPF), which is based around areas and elements similar to those in ISAD(G), also states the rules and provides examples. It includes additional detail to the authority entry in its description of corporate bodies that provides contextual information:

5.1 IDENTITY AREA

    5.1.1 Type of entity: Corporate body

    5.1.2 Authorized form(s) of name: Department of State. Peace Corps. (03/03/1961–07/01/1971)

    5.1.2 Authorized form(s) of name: ACTION. Peace Corps. (07/01/1971–1982)

    5.1.2 Authorized form(s) of name: Peace Corps. (1982–)

    5.1.4 Standardized forms of name according to other rules: AACR2R Peace Corps (US)

5.2 DESCRIPTION AREA

    5.2.1 Dates of existence 1961–

    5.2.2 History: The Peace Corps was established as an operating agency in the Department of State by Department of State Delegation of Authority 85–11, effective March 3, 1961, pursuant to Executive Order (E.O.) 10924, March 1, 1961. It was recognized legislatively by the Peace Corps Act (75 Stat. 612), approved September 22, 1961. The Peace Corps was reassigned to the newly established ACTION by Reorganization Plan No. 1 of 1971, effective July 1, 1971. It was made autonomous within ACTION by E.O. 12137, May 16, 1979, and was made an independent agency by Title VI of the International Security and Development Corporation Act of 1981 (95 Stat. 1540), February 21, 1982. The Peace Corps administered and coordinated Federal international volunteer and related domestic volunteer programs including the areas of agricultural assistance, community development, education, environmental protection, and nation assistance.

5.2.5 Functions, occupations and activities: Agricultural assistance, Community development, Education, Environmental protection, Nation assistance.

This last example shows how detailed some of these authority records are. You may well find that you do not need to go to these lengths, but understanding the rules behind their construction is important.

However, anyone with archives created by, say, the Duke of Wellington or the Peace Corps should be able to use existing authority records like these for their own purposes, and indeed create their own for other people to use. The ways in which access to this information can be carried out have not yet been fully worked out. Some archives have imported the NCA Rules and one of the various thesauri into their cataloguing databases and on-line catalogues so that they can use the approved terms both for input and retrieval.

Subject thesauri adopt similar rules for narrowing down terms. The UNESCO thesaurus provides structured lists of descriptors (preferred terms) for indexing and retrieval in the seven major fields of interest to UNESCO: education, science, social and human science, culture, communication and information. These are presented in two ways: hierarchically and alphabetically. The hierarchical list is broken down into microthesauri (smaller subject areas), which allow you to gain a quick overview of the subjects. The alphabetical list displays descriptors and non-descriptors (non-preferred terms) alphabetically, showing which are the preferred and which the non-preferred subject terms. A number of archives, especially in the US and in archives based in libraries, use Library of Congress Subject Headings (LCSH) and find it caters better at a detailed level. For example, a search for the term 'nurses' in UNESCO requires you to use 'paramedical personnel' as the preferred term, whereas LCSH allows 'nurses' to be used. Archives often find that the 'right' terms are not offered, and that local records need local terms. If your archive holds large holdings relating to coal mining, for example, general thesauri cannot provide sufficiently detailed access points. There are other difficulties for archivists, particularly when use of language changes. For example, records relating to unmarried mothers were created by the Moral Welfare Association, House of Mercy, House of Refuge, among others, terms which would be unlikely to be found in current thesauri.

UKAT, which is becoming the most useful thesaurus for UK archivists, has been created for the archive sector in the United Kingdom (Figure 4.11). Its key aims are: 'to improve access to archives by subject; to ensure that users of archives can carry out effective subject searches of

Figure 4.11   UKAT Thesaurus

the national archives network; and to promote the involvement in archives by groups which are under-represented among archive users, by providing subject terms which reflect their histories and experiences.'[27] It is based on the UNESCO thesaurus and enhances it to include terms of relevance to the archive community and its users. It is being constructed from terms contributed by archive services, archive projects and users of archives who submit them for approval by the central team.

Notes

1. Cook, M. (1999) *The management of information from archives*, 2nd edn. Aldershot: Gower, pp. 132–4.
2. Schellenberg, T. R. (1965) *The management of archives*. New York: Columbia University Press, p. 81.
3. Schellenberg, T. R. (1999) in Cook, *op. cit.*, p. 102.
4. Roper, M., (1992) 'Provenance', In *The archival imagination: essays in honour of Hugh A. Taylor*. Edited by Craig, B. L. Ottawa: Association of Canadian Archivists, pp. 134–53.
5. Freeth, S. (1991) 'Finding aids', In *Managing business archives*. Edited by Turton, A. Oxford: Butterworth-Heinemann, pp. 282–4.
6. International Council on Archives (2000) *General International Standard Archival Description (ISAD(G))*, 2nd edn. Ottawa: International Council on Archives.
7. Holmes, O. W. (1964) 'Archival arrangement – five different operations at five different levels', In *A modern archives reader: basic readings on archival*

theory and practice. Edited by Daniels, M. F. and Walch, T. Washington: National Archives Trust Board, pp. 162–80. First published in *The American Archivist* 27: January, 21–41.

8. Procter, M. and Cook, M. (2000) *Manual of archival description,* 3rd edn. Aldershot: Gower, p. 19.

9. Jenkinson, H. (1966) *Manual of archive administration,* 2nd edn. London: Lund Humphries, p. 101.

10. Procter, M. and Cook, M. (2000) *op. cit.,* pp. 13–14.

11. Holmes, *op. cit.,* pp. 164-5.

12. Procter, M. and Cook, M. (2000) *op. cit.* pp. 40–1.

13. Hensen, S. L. (1989) *Archives, personal papers and manuscripts: a cataloging manual for archival repositories, historical societies and manuscript libraries,* 2nd edn. Chicago: Society of American Archivists.

14. Society of American Archivists (2004) *Describing archives: a content standard.* Chicago: Society of American Archivists.

15. Bureau of Canadian Archivists (1990) *Rules for archival description.* Ottawa: Bureau of Canadian Archivists; Procter, M. and Cook, M. (2000) *op. cit.*

16. International Council on Archives (1996) *International standard archival authority record for corporate bodies, persons and families* (ISAAR (CPF)). Ottawa: International Council on Archives, *http://www.ica.org;* National Council on Archives (1997) *Rules for the construction of personal, place and corporate names* (NCA Rules). London: National Council on Archives, *http://www.ncaonline.org.uk/* [accessed 25 August 2005].

17. *Library of Congress Subject Headings,* 28th edn. 2005, *http://www.loc.gov/ cds/lcsh.html;* UNESCO *Thesaurus, http://databases.unesco.org/thesaurus/;* *UK Archival Thesaurus, http://www.ukat.org.uk/* [accessed 25 August 2005].

18. International Council on Archives (2000) *General International Standard Archival Description,* 2nd edn. (ISAD(G)). Ottawa: International Council on Archives, and available at: *http://www.ica.org* [accessed 25 August 2005].

19. (ISAD(G)), p. 16.

20. Society of American Archivists *Tag Library,* Version 1.1 quoted by Hill, A. in 'Introduction to EAD', *http://www.archiveshub.ac.uk/arch/training0201 .shtml* [accessed 25 August 2005].

21. EAD Application Guidelines, *http://www.loc.gov/ead/ag/agcontxt.html* [accessed 25 August 2005].

22. EAD Application Guidelines for Version 1.0 Appendix B: EAD Crosswalks, *http://www.loc.gov/ead/ag/agappb.html* [accessed 25 August 2005].

23. Encoded Archival Description official website, *http://www.loc.gov/ead/* [accessed 25 August 2005].

24. Society of American Archivists (1997) *American Archivist* 60: 3–4; *EAD Cookbook,* University of Virginia.

25. The National Archives, *Committee on Standards of Conduct in Public Life,* ref. JN1–3.

26. National Digital Archive of Data sets (NDAD), *http://ndad.ulcc.ac.uk/* [accessed 25 August 2005].

27. UK Archival Thesaurus, *http://www.ukat.org.uk/* [25 August 2005].

5

Access, reference and advocacy

Acquisition and selection, arrangement, description and preservation are all preparation for the ultimate archival function, that of making archives available to an ever-widening audience and in increasingly diverse ways. This chapter will explore issues of access from the international to the local and from legal, ethical, intellectual and practical perspectives and consider ways of reaching out to the uninitiated. This chapter also introduces:

- Access: international and ethical issues – making the case for access;
- The UK access agenda;
- Access, privacy and copyright legislation;
- Legislation and access in the private sector;
- Access standards and policies;
- Access and reference services: the user base;
- Providing a reference service;
- Advocacy and outreach;
- Outreach activities and audience development;
- Assessing the impact of services.

Access: international and ethical issues

Access encompasses the political, legislative, cultural and social climate in which records and archives are (or are not) made available to people across the world as well as the practical and intellectual means by which access may be delivered. We might perhaps reflect that whereas openness, transparency, accountability and freedom of information are ideals to which we might aspire in the western world, this is not universal. It is important to consider our local approaches to access in a wider international context and to note that issues of access are central to international and national codes of ethics.

> Archives are not simply a leisure interest for a tiny minority, they are a vital element of our cultural heritage and part of the infrastructure of a modern democratic society in which information, and access to it, is properly valued.[1]

This view reflects an altogether broader vision and a wider challenge than simply the provision of access to a local constituency. Concern for equality of access to archives across countries and communities has led to the introduction of national and international standards and ethical codes. In 2000 the Council of Europe Committee of Ministers formally adopted a policy on access. Among other preliminary remarks it stated that:

> ... a country does not become fully democratic until each one of its inhabitants has the possibility of knowing in an objective manner the elements of their history ...[2]

It notes that the complexity of problems concerning access is due to differences in constitutions, legal frameworks, the conflicting requirements of transparency and secrecy, and privacy and access in different countries. This is a high-level and political statement about access and human rights. It highlights problems that result from the different perceptions of access held by different countries. It acknowledges that different cultural attitudes affect the level of a country's attitude to openness and secrecy, and so makes recommendations rather than proposing a set of uniform rules.

These are:

- Access to public archives is a right ... [and] should apply to all users regardless of their nationality, status or function.
- Access to archives is part of the function of public archives services and should be free.
- Each country should set out principles governing access to its archives through legislation.
- Attempts should be made to bring arrangements for access to private archives in line with those for public archives.

- Each country should spread the information in this standard as widely as possible.

- Finding aids should be provided, and should cover all archives, including closed archives.

- Guidance for application for permission to access closed documents should be available.

The issue of access forms an important part of ethical codes. Codes of ethics and conduct are often considered a hallmark of professional identity and the archives and records management profession is no exception. The ICA formally adopted its *Code of Ethics* in 1996. Although it uses the term 'archivists' throughout it makes it clear that it is intended to 'encompass all those concerned with the control, care, custody, preservation and administration of archives'. Less of a political statement than that of the Council of Europe, the *Code of Ethics* concentrates more on the actual policies and practices which organisations should subscribe to if they are to provide an ethical and fair service to all. Both, however, articulate a clear commitment to provide access to archival material, and provide useful benchmarks for countries and organisations to measure up to.

Code of Ethics Principle 6[3]

'Archivists should promote the widest possible access to archival material and provide an impartial service to all users.

Archivists should produce both general and particular finding aids as appropriate, for all of the records in their custody. They should offer impartial advice to all, and employ available resources to provide a balanced range of services. Archivists should answer courteously and with a spirit of helpfulness all reasonable inquiries about their holdings, and encourage the use of them to the greatest extent possible, consistent with institutional policies, the preservation of holdings, legal considerations, individual rights and donor agreements. They should explain pertinent restrictions to potential users, and apply them equitably. Archivists should discourage unreasonable restrictions on access and use but may suggest or accept as a condition for acquisition clearly stated restrictions of limited duration. They should observe faithfully and apply impartially all agreements made at the time of acquisition, but, in the interest of liberalisation of access, should renegotiate conditions in accordance with changes of circumstance.'

National archival and records management societies maintain their own ethical codes too; these are invariably available on their websites.[4] Such policies and codes underpin the notion that democracy can only exist in countries where people have the opportunity to 'know their history' through access to archives. By referring to such statements as these you should be able to argue the case for access in almost any situation.

The UK access agenda

While international codes and standards provide a framework against which we can set local policies, our own national government policies must also be taken into account, and may have a direct bearing on what we do in our own environment. In the UK there is a clear relationship between government policy and record-keeping practice.

In its 'Modernising Government' white paper, first published in March 1999, the UK Government set out its programme for change in the public services over the following ten years. It focused on the

> delivery of responsive, high quality public services which meet what customers need and want regardless of organisational boundaries, using new (information age) technologies to improve accessibility and effectiveness.

The effect of this mission in the archival domain in the UK has been profound. It has influenced in equal measure the two main strands of professional activity: the management of records as evidence and the promotion of records, as archives, for cultural purposes. It is useful to focus on these through the lens of the first ever *Government Policy on Archives*, also published in 1999, which was a direct outcome of the Modernising Government white paper. The *Government Policy on Archives* was produced by the Inter-Departmental Archives Committee (IDAC), which is the co-ordinating mechanism within government for the handling of archive policy.[5] It defined how archives could contribute to seven of the government's most important policy areas. These were public access, modernisation of public services, open and accountable government, education, social inclusion, economic regeneration and regionalism.

The 'public access' and 'open and accountable government' objectives affect both the evidential and the cultural aspects of our work in terms of access, and in both current record-keeping and archival policies and practices.

The stated objective for 'public access' was 'to ensure that ready access to archives, in the most useful and convenient way, is offered to all the nation's citizens and to other users'. Alongside this are objectives focusing on access to archives for education in schools and for life-long learning and as an aid to social inclusion, using archives to help bridge the gap between those who could afford access to information and those who otherwise could not.

The aim for 'open and accountable government' is expressed thus:

> The Government wishes to do away with the climate of excessive secrecy by establishing a general citizen's right of access. The right of access to official records, whether through Freedom of Information, Data Protection or more open government generally, will increasingly depend upon effective records management. This encompasses the creation of reliable records and arrangements for their speedy retrieval when requested.

TNA has also been heavily involved in promoting the cultural access mission, alongside other UK Government bodies. The Museums Libraries and Archives Council (MLA) is the body set up by the Department for Culture Media and Sport (DCMS) as the strategic organisation to advise on the ways in which museums, libraries and archives could work together to pursue the government's cultural agenda.

MLA like the National Archives, implements government policies, and its *Developing the 21st Century Archive*[6] identified three key priority areas:

- identifying strategic needs and priorities based on user needs and perception;
- exploiting the potential for archives to contribute to the learning and access agenda;
- promoting training, career development and skills.

The first two of these priorities pick up elements specifically mentioned in the *Government Policy on Archives* and clearly have the greatest implications for access.

More recently, MLA was invited by the DCMS to implement a 'root and branch review of archives in Great Britain ... with the highest possible level of support' by means of an Archives Task Force. This body published its report, *Listening to the Past, Speaking to the Future*, in April 2004.[7] The Task Force's view on access is that 'delivering effective, universal access calls for new strategies and techniques that will engage those who currently benefit least from this archival heritage: the non-specialist individual, community groups and the student in school.' Again this is very much about making access more inclusive, under the banner of 'social inclusion'.

A good way to explore ideas on how to increase your audience is to have a look at the National Council on Archives' report about widening access. It provides a snapshot of the policies and practice current in the sector, demonstrating how different archives are tackling the social inclusion issue.[8] It is worth looking at firstly for ideas on how you might improve *your* service, and secondly because it does describe some of the difficulties – e.g. the limitations of project funding in delivering sustainability – that it raises in practical terms.

It is obvious that the issue of access is driving a number of initiatives at the highest level. Each archival organisation will have its own policy about the level of access it provides and this will depend on its overall business objectives: what level of priority does it have in your organisation? Those in public sector records and archives will be the most directly affected by government policy objectives. Archives in the private, business and commercial sectors cannot offer the open access that publicly funded repositories aim to. However, government 'wishes to do all it can to encourage private organisations and individuals holding historically significant archives to make their own contributions to these objectives', so there are expectations here for all of us.[9]

Access: legislation, standards and policies

Legislation can define who has access to records and to which records in particular. As Principle 7 of the ICA's *Code of Ethics* states:

Principle 7 ICA Code of Ethics

'Archivists should respect both access and privacy, and act within the boundaries of relevant legislation.

Archivists should take care that corporate and personal privacy as well as national security are protected without destroying information, especially in the case of electronic records where updating and erasure are common practice. They must respect the privacy of individuals who created or are the subjects of records, especially those who had no voice in the use or disposition of the materials.'

Access and privacy legislation

Balancing the requirements for access with those for maintaining the privacy of individuals is a significant responsibility for archivists and records managers. Many countries have freedom of information laws that give enforceable rights of access to government and other public records. These include the USA, Canada, Australia, New Zealand, France, Denmark, Germany, Holland, Norway, Greece, Hungary, Japan and Sweden (Sweden since 1766). The UK joined the group with the passage of the Freedom of Information Act (FoIA) in 2000 and the Freedom of Information (Scotland) Act 2002: Ireland passed its own act in 1998. In these countries for the main part responsibility for both access and privacy legislation come under one official body: in the UK this is the Information Commissioner.[10] Balancing this is legislation that protects personal information about individuals – in the UK under the label of 'data protection'.

This access and privacy legislation changes the whole climate of access in the UK: the presumption is that the records are open (with certain exemptions) rather than closed (with certain exemptions). Attitudes of those generating and maintaining information have had to change accordingly: no longer can you send an e-mail saying 'this person needs locking up' or 'don't use this business – it's run by a load of crooks' unless you are prepared for it to become public and you can defend your opinion with very sound evidence. In addition, archives that have been routinely closed for a set number of years (e.g. hospital patient records) are quite likely to be accessible in certain situations: it is no longer possible to apply a blanket closure to a class of records, because the circumstances of each application have to be considered before a decision about access can be made.

In England and Wales a suite of legislation governs access:

- The *Freedom of Information Act 2000* enables access to all information held by public authorities other than that covered by

- *Environmental Information Regulations 2004*, which enables access to environmental information in public authorities, and the

- *Data Protection Act 1998*, which enables access to personal information in public authorities and private organisations of which the applicant is the subject.

These acts directly impact on our working practices, particularly those of records managers dealing with current records and information.

Archivists need to be aware of the general provisions of these acts too, and how to respond when situations arise in their own workplace. FoIA creates rights of access to information held by public authorities. Public authorities include government departments, the houses of parliament, the armed forces, local government bodies including local authorities, the National Health Service, state schools, police forces and a variety of others ranging from the British Potato Council to the Place Names Advisory Committee. The Act came into effect in January 2005 and has superseded the access provisions of the Public Records Acts 1958 and 1967.[11]

Briefly, the FoIA

- creates a general right of access to recorded information irrespective of its age (there are some exemptions such as that relating to security, defence);
- requires public authorities to issue a 'publication scheme' that describes all classes of information that are routinely made available;
- requires them to respond to requests for information (i.e. that is not included in the publication scheme) within 20 days;
- states that many exemptions cease at 30 years when records become 'historical records';
- requires the Secretary of State and the Lord Chancellor to put forward codes of practice for guidance on specific issues.

As far as the last point is concerned, records managers and others are provided with specific guidance in the Lord Chancellor's Code of Practice on good practice in records management. If you are looking for support in making the case for sound records management this is particularly useful. Part iii of the foreword states:

> Any freedom of information legislation is only as good as the quality of the records to which it provides access. Such rights are of little use if reliable records are not created in the first place, if they cannot be found when needed or if the arrangements for their eventual archiving or destruction are inadequate.[12]

The Act has been in full operation since January 2005 and public authorities are now able to get an idea of what information that is not provided in publication schemes is most frequently sought. A typical local authority in England finds that many information requests relate to money: the pay of senior officers; the cost of overseas trips of elected members; the management of the pension fund and its investments; details of commercial contracts. Environmental information is often sought [under the Environmental Information Regulations (EIR)] about waste management, landfill sites and illegal tipping. People involved in local disputes seek to find the source of a complaint – although they are unlikely to be supplied with the *name* of a complainant. Some might seem trivial: must you take seriously a request for information on how much the authority spent on biscuits in the current financial year; how many biscuits were purchased; what was the policy on allocation of biscuits per person per meeting; whether different quality biscuits were available at different levels of meeting? Those requesting information are not obliged to say *why* they want the information, but in this case if such an enquiry is made of all local authorities quite a good picture of each authority's approach to its hospitality budget (and whether extravagant or parsimonious) might reasonably be drawn.

Requests for information can of course be refused on a variety of grounds, but where this is the case the enquirer must be told the reason. It might be that it comes under an exemption such as national security, defence, or law and order. However, because the assumption is that records should be open, just because a request relates to an exempt category it does not automatically mean that the records are closed. The 'harm test' or 'public interest' test may be applied: even though the records may fall into an exempt category does the public interest in maintaining the exemption outweigh the public interest in disclosing it?

Archivists are accustomed to responding to requests for information from archives (rather than current records) on a daily basis (in private as well as public and authorities). In a sense, provided public archives respond within 20 days, little has changed. However, what about requests to access archives that have not been catalogued? Before FoIA the enquirer might have been simply told that these were therefore inaccessible. Now the public authority archives service can argue for exemption from providing access under Section 22 of the Act on the grounds that the 'information is intended for future publication'. This is not very helpful for the user, however, and archives are unlikely to offer such a response. They are more likely to put such archives at the head of the cataloguing queue and negotiate a time when they will become available to the user.

One other issue that has yet to be fully clarified is whether private archives that are held on deposit by repositories (but remain in the ownership of the depositor rather than the public authority) are subject to the act or not. The Information Commissioner's view on this issue is that it depends whether such archives are held for the benefit of the repository (and its users) or the owner. Because they are more likely to be held for the benefit of the former (otherwise why would they have been accepted by the archive?), it follows that they should be available under the same terms as other recorded information held by the public authority.

Although FoI enables individuals to access information about the activities of public authorities, *Data Protection* enables access to personal information of which the applicant is the subject. The 1998 Act (DPA) seeks to prevent the inappropriate disclosure of information about living individuals so that individuals' right to privacy is protected and any decisions made about or affecting them are made on the basis of being error-free information.[13] We are all familiar with stories of people being refused credit, for example, because the information held by credit reference agencies refers to debtors who previously lived at the same address.

An individual, or 'data subject', seeking access under DPA has various rights, including to request a copy of the relevant data and where appropriate demand correction, know why it is held and to know where information came from and where it might be sent to. The knowledge that such data are available to the data subject should encourage those processing data to be careful about what they record, as the James Cameron case outlined below shows. As a result of Cameron's demands for information about him the Foreign Office was obliged to admit it had been seeking to silence him.

'Foreign Office doubts on a visa witch hunt'

In 2004 James Cameron, the former British Consul to Bucharest, applied under the Data Protection Act for access to data held on him by the Foreign Office relating to an ongoing case. He was at that time under a Scotland Yard inquiry accused of taking backhanders or obtaining sexual favours in exchange for granting visas. This action against him followed his disclosures to David Davis, the Shadow Home Secretary, that he and other embassy staff were being instructed by the Home Office to turn a blind eye to fraudulent visa applications. These included work permits being issued to a one-legged roofer and an electrician without any fingers. Cameron's friends said the allegations were smears to discredit him and punish him for speaking out. The Foreign Office dossier showed that Cameron's superiors regarded him as an awkward employee even before he exposed the visa scams. 'He has a history of odd and erratic behaviour,' said one. 'There are also other strange happenings ... He has an uncanny knack of being in the spot where lightning strikes (numerous break-ins, a mugging and other strange goings-on). This latest episode shows poor judgment and a degree of bloody-mindedness.'[14]

Archivists are not generally at the sharp end of data protection issues. However, they do need to be aware of at least two of the eight data protection principles because they apply to the availability of personal data for research. These require that personal data must be:
Principle 2

- obtained only for (a) specified and lawful purpose(s) and not be further processed in any manner incompatible with the purposes stated

Principle 5

- kept for no longer than is necessary for the purposes notified

These principles appear to disallow keeping records for research purposes – a prime archival function. Principle 2 implies that personal data should only be used for the purpose for which it was created – and research for other (e.g. historical or statistical) purposes would be in breach as it would be further processing in a manner incompatible with the original purpose for which it was obtained. Thus, a school admissions register, compiled for the purpose of informing educational authorities on school populations, ought not to be used for organising a school reunion. Principle 5 states that you should not keep any personal data for longer than is necessary to fulfil its original purpose. This would enormously inhibit research, because, if implemented, the records would simply be destroyed once a person had died.

However, section 33 of the Act does allow 'research exemptions', which enable personal data to be stored indefinitely and for research purposes provided that two 'relevant conditions' are observed. These are that the data are not processed to support measures or decisions with respect to particular individuals; and are not processed in such a way that substantial damage or substantial distress is, or is likely to be, caused to any data subject. Thus, in certain cases third parties are able to have access to personal data in archives. However, authorities must still notify the Information Commissioner that they intend to process data for research purposes.

Of course this is all about data relating to *living* individuals. Once a person has died the provisions cease to apply in this form, and access to people other than the data subject may be permitted. However, all sorts of complications can still arise. A school or hospital admissions register of fairly recent date that prior to the 1998 Act may have been readily accessible may be no longer because it contains information about people who are still alive.

Prior to the FoIA and DPA access to sensitive *archival* records was managed under a system of blanket closures. Thus, sensitive personal records such as hospital case registers and files would be closed for 100 years, some coroners records for 75 years and certain magistrate courts records for 30 years. Now applications, whether to current or to archival records, have to be dealt with on a case-by-case basis – and it may be that while someone might apply under FoIA the response might have to be delivered under the Environmental Information Regulations or Data Protection. Thus, an application under FoIA about archaeological excavation of old waste sites would be dealt with under EIR, while another about child abuse might be a Data Protection issue.

Useful guidance includes the *Code of Practice for Archivists and Records Managers under Section 51(3) of the Data Protection Act 1998* (Version 2 April 2002), produced by the Society of Archivists and Records Management Society, and the Public Record Office's *Data Protection Act: A Guide for Archivists and Records Managers, 2000.*[15]

Copyright

Although arguably only tangentially related to access, it is worth mentioning copyright here, alongside other issues relating to legislation. If you are involved in providing copies of records and archives to users you will already be aware that access to records and archives in this way must take into account the issue of copyright. Copyright is a property right and of course different countries have different legislative provision. In the UK it is protected by the Copyright, Designs and Patents Act, 1988, as amended by the Duration of Copyright and Rights in Performances Regulations 1995 (Statutory Instrument 1995/3297).

Copyright restricts the extent to which anyone other than the copyright owner may reproduce, publish or adapt in whole or in part any original literary, dramatic, musical or artistic work, or any sound recording or film. Copyright resides with the author of a work and descends on the death of the author to his or her legal heirs. Like other property it can be sold or given away (for example, J. M. Barrie gave the copyright of the play *Peter Pan* to the Great Ormond Street Hospital). The ownership, duration and publication rights of works all need to be taken into account when considering publication or the provision of copies. Fortunately, a useful guide for archivists to this complex subject is available.[16]

Legislation and access in the private sector

Freedom of information legislation affects all public authorities; but *all* organisations, both public and private, must comply with the Data Protection Act. Sector-specific access legislation in the UK covers the records of the Churches of England and Wales and some specific types of private records.

The Parochial Registers and Records Measure 1978, passed by the General Synod of the Church of England, amended 1992, provides for statutory access to registers of baptisms, marriages and burials in diocesan record offices (normally the local authority record office) and in parishes where such records remain, 'at all reasonable hours' and for the provision of certified copies. In Wales an agreement between the Representative Body of the Church in Wales and the Welsh County Councils in 1976 enabled ecclesiastical parish records to be deposited and accessible in county record offices in addition to the National Library of Wales.

There is no legislation that makes access to business records compulsory for purposes of research. Such access requirements as are in place through the various Companies Acts are to do with audit and accountability for current purposes. Companies have to make their minutes and accounts, known as the 'statutory books', available for inspection, but are not obliged to keep anything indefinitely. However, a number of business archives are keen to permit research, particularly of an academic nature.

There is no requirement on private individuals owning archives to make them accessible, although, of course, many have deposited their records on loan in local and specialist repositories. However, a statutory right of access does exist to manorial documents, for example manorial court rolls and surveys, under the Manorial Documents Rules, 1959 (SI 1959/1399) to those 'persons having an interest in their contents for legal purposes' – although they will normally be on open access if deposited in a local repository. Similarly, tithe maps and apportionments, created after 1836 and which cover many parishes in England and Wales, are accessible under the Tithe Rules 1960 (SI 1960/2440) 'for inspection and copying by persons appearing to be entitled to do so or requiring them for historical research'. The Historical Manuscripts Commission, now part of the National Archives, exercises the statutory responsibilities both for manorial and for tithe records.

Access standards and policies

Any organisation that is involved in the provision of access to records and archives, whether to internal or to external clients, needs to operate within a framework of standards. At a strategic level The Council of Europe Committee of Ministers' recommendation on access to archives noted above is a political document and sets a benchmark against which to measure the provision of access to archives in European countries at a national level. Countries that do not comply with these recommendations may find it difficult to offer services at an operational level.

National archives and professional associations also contribute to the development of national standards for access: whether or not supported by legislation they will offer useful guidance to professionals. For example, Archives New Zealand has provided a national standard, and the American Library Association jointly with the Society of American Archivists a professional standard on access.[17]

In the UK the Public Services Quality Group (PSQG), a group of professional archivists, has drawn up the *Standard for Access to Archives*. It

> ... defines quality in archive access services. Access services are the means by which records are offered for use either directly or indirectly through mediation.

Any archive that provides public access to its collections can measure itself against this standard. It is offered as a framework on which to build systems for access, and it suggests that individual archive services might use it to build specific good practice guides.[18] Although it concentrates on access to archives, it can also apply in a records management operation for internal users because so many of its recommendations are concerned with delivering best practice for the 'stakeholders' of any service where access is at issue.

If you look at the standard's two access objectives you will see that it is not size or resources that count, but a service's *approach* to its users. The objectives are to ensure that:

- it is clear who the archive service is intended to serve, and

- it is clear what the archive service is intending to achieve in providing access to its collections.

It emphasises that it does not seek to define *what* the purpose of an archives or reference service should be in providing access or *how* that purpose is fulfilled. Instead it recognises that services are all very different and must therefore be assessed in relation to their success in fulfilling their particular stated purposes rather than to some absolute form or standard of service.

It suggests that in providing access you apply four key principles. These relate to:

- *Equity*: to serve all users in a community, without discrimination.

- *Communication and openness*: to offer open, two-way communication with your community and policies which are available for scrutiny and comment.

- *Responsiveness*: to respond effectively to comments and complaints; review performance and make improvements; reflect views and interests of stakeholders.

- *Effectiveness and efficiency*: provide best value for money; seek innovation; actively managing risk.

If you are considering writing an access policy or reviewing an existing one you should use the *Standard for Access to Archives* as a benchmark. For more specific guidance on the *actual* minimum standards to which archives open for public access should comply, see the National Archives *Standard for Record Repositories*. This includes sections on constitution and finance, staff, acquisition, as well as access.[19]

Access policies

In order to make your access principles and practices clear to everyone, your repository needs to develop an individual access policy for reference by staff and users – indeed by any of those with an interest, as stakeholders, in what you do. The access policy should reflect the specific mission and objectives of your organisation and might include:

- a description of your user base;
- details of any legislation that impacts on access to collections;
- statements about freedom of information and data protection;
- guidance in the use of sensitive or confidential records;
- statements about equality of access;
- information about copyright and publication rules;
- details of how records are made available (digitally, physical access only, stored elsewhere, collections with restrictions on access?);
- conditions of access to fragile records;
- rules about using surrogates (e.g. microfilm) of heavily used records rather than originals;
- an explanation of security procedures;
- an explanation of access procedures;
- any charges which operate for specific services.

It is important that your access policy provides a clear statement of available services and how to use them. It should be couched in terms that make it clear that in providing this public service your archive, museum or other reference service realises that it has entered the world of service industries. Although you, as archivist, might have expectations of how users should behave, do not forget that users ought also to have a view of how you should treat them – and indeed what constitutes an acceptable level of service. However, the first-time user – more familiar perhaps with practices in libraries – may have no idea what to expect, and you need to develop tactful ways of advising people of what they, and you, might expect of each other. I will now look more closely at some of the elements of an access policy.

Access and reference services: the user base

Who are our users? Recent studies have shown that archives services, far more than libraries and museums, have concentrated more heavily on the materials – particularly the records – in their care than on the people who use them. Indeed, Sir Hilary Jenkinson said that the archivist was the servant first of the archives and secondly of the public but that 'it may be maintained with some force that his first duty, adequately carried out, would leave him no leisure for the second.'[20] He would not get away with that today. Knowledge of patterns of use of archives, in terms of both the profile of users themselves and the nature and methods of enquiry undertaken by them is patchy but improving.

In the past we might have defined users as readers, researchers or searchers who consult records in a search room or reading room. Clearly this definition is no longer sufficient: it appears exclusive, and assumes on-site access to original records by people who know what they are looking for. The PSQG *Standard for Access* suggests that users are actual or potential customers of any of our services, part of a wider body of stakeholders. Users may be internal or external, and access services on site or on line, and potential users – and those not yet born – need to be considered too. Service providers need to analyse their user base in relation to the resources they offer and to consider whether it can be broadened. Museums and archives are likely to concentrate on providing access for the external user and develop their finding aids accordingly, but will also receive internal enquiries. Business archives generally cater for internal clients and although providing limited access to external users archivists are more likely to undertake research on their behalf than to provide physical access. Internal clients are likely to be using resources for corporate purposes, external clients for research. Both are increasingly likely to access these services from a distance when possible, via e-mail, websites, digitised finding aids – file plans and catalogues, and, increasingly born-digital and digitised original documents.

What do our users want? Government drivers for access, increased funding for access-based projects and the closer integration of archives with other heritage 'providers' such as libraries and museums (where interest in and analysis of user needs is more advanced) have forced the archival community to focus more clearly on identifying user needs. It is generally admitted that the 'archival community does not have a good understanding of its current or potential user community, their interests ... or their needs.'[21] A UK report notes that

> the connection between these [archival description] standards and actual user satisfaction is not fully understood. More generally, the needs of archive users and what they find useful is largely only understood indirectly or anecdotally. While archivists have a profound knowledge of user needs established through close interaction with users in archives, less is known about user behaviour outside the archive and thus on the determinants of ultimate user satisfaction.[22]

The PSQG has generated basic profiling data about on-site visitors to archives in Britain and Northern Ireland through regular surveys of visitors, most recently in 2002. That for 2001 surveyed 126 archives from which 13,200 questionnaires completed by users were returned. Questions were based on three areas: about your visit; about yourself; and about the wider cultural and economic role archives play in the community.

It showed that:

- 79% of users were over 44 years old, 43% over 60 and only 3% under 24, with about 2% from ethnic minority groups;

- 30% had a first degree, while 13% did not claim any qualification;

- 50% of visitors lived within 20 km of the repository and 2.6% of users came from overseas;

- 83% of visitors to archives come because of personal interest or a hobby.[23]

These statistics clearly show the parts of the nation that archives are failing to reach – and what areas lifelong learning and social inclusion policies might target.

The PSQG's survey is large-scale and strategic. But at local level information about your users can be gained through simple questionnaires and exit interviews. Increasingly, we need also to discover the profile of remote users: a much harder job, but all the more necessary as online access is increasing, and causing a reduction in the number of users physically visiting archives. How do users approach online finding aids? The LEADERS project recruited volunteer archivists, and academic, educational and leisure interest users to test online finding aids based on the George Orwell Archive and the University College London

Archive in order to assess user needs and behaviour when accessing online finding aids.[24] The aim of the project was to investigate methods of integrating digital archive documents with contextual information and of presenting such integrated resources in online environments. The group explored how easy or difficult it was to use digitised images of documents, together with transcripts, and authority records to enable searching for personal, corporate and place names, and topics (see example in Figure 5.1.

The project found that different types of user needed different levels of interpretation of documents and the provision of more or less contextual information.

For example:

- Leisure users and those less familiar with online searching were happy to have index terms provided.

- Professionals and academics thought provision of index terms limiting: they argued that such pre-selection was a hindrance, preferring free text searching.

- Users with academic backgrounds preferred to browse the finding aids prior to looking at originals or transcripts rather than use indexes.

Figure 5.1 LEADERS project: digitised image with transcript

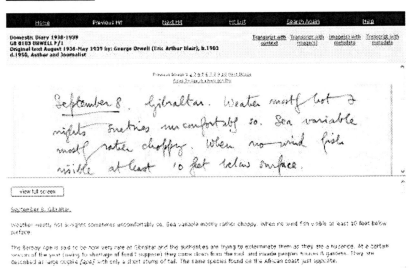

- Leisure users were more likely to use the indexes, describing the finding aids as daunting and unfamiliar.

- Professional and academic users wanted transcripts to follow the originals as closely as possible.

- Educational and leisure users wanted added extras such as a glossary or dictionary of terms: some academic users felt this to be intrusive.[25]

Projects such as these are important in building up a picture of the needs and abilities of the different user groups. They can help us to plan more effectively our own online resources. What it seems to show is that the 'known-item' approach discussed elsewhere will be more readily satisfied via indexes and controlled language and the 'subject-based approach' through finding aids that offer the capacity to browse and free-text search.

Providing a reference service

Reference services provide the environment for a range of access activities. These will differ depending on whether you are working in a national archive, a combined library and archive service, a university or a business archive, for example. There is, however, a range of common factors that will influence the nature and extent of the service provided. In order to plan your service effectively you will need to establish details of each of these:

- Mission and purpose of the organisation;
- Resource base of the archive (or other reference) service;
- Nature of client base;
- Priority given to reference services in relation to other records/archives functions;
- Nature of holdings: primary and secondary sources;
- Nature and quality of finding aids;
- Degree of staffing and supervision required;
- Level of demand.

Let us take a business archive as an example. In this case organisational resources might be plentiful, but the principal corporate mission will not depend on the archive service nor is access to it a business objective. The reference service priorities are likely to focus on promotional activities such as publications and exhibitions, for business purposes. The client base will primarily be the internal user; the holdings will be primary sources that relate solely to the organisation; secondary sources such as a reference library may be small and again relate only to the business. Basic finding aids will probably be sufficient. Relatively few resources will be required for the purposes of supervision as the user base will be small.

Once you have completed this analysis you will be able to prioritise activities and plan where to place your resources. A task you will need to do fairly early on is to provide information:

- about the range of services you provide,
- about the holdings in your care,
- to assist on-site research visits, and
- in response to enquiries, from the content of the holdings.

Information about the range of services provided

The best way to disseminate useful information about your services as widely as possible is via a website and in the form of an introductory leaflet. This will help people to judge whether a personal visit will be necessary. In addition to on-site research facilities, services provided may include reprographic services, research consultancy services, exhibitions, school visits, talks and training days, and sales of publications and other items. All archives providing a public service should by now have a website and e-mail services. In addition, many are moving into e-commerce whereby charges for the various services can be managed on line.

Here is a checklist of possible contents of an introductory section on a website or in leaflet form: does it include?

- introduction to the service;
- contact details and opening hours;
- location, including a map, transport and parking facilities;
- outline of archival and secondary materials available;
- searchroom facilities: accommodation, film, fiche, Internet access, laptop use;

- planning a visit: readers' tickets; whether an appointment is necessary; items to bring (pencils, identification); refreshment facilities;
- brief version of collections and access policies and searchroom rules;
- services for those unable to visit;
- services for schools, colleges and other groups;
- reprographic and research services;
- how to get more information on the holdings and other services;

Information about the holdings

A reference service can be judged by the range and quality of its finding aids. They not only demonstrate how far you have intellectual control of your holdings, they also enable your users to make an informed decision as to whether what they are seeking is available and whether they need to make a personal visit to view it. Only a minority of archives will ever be digitised, and so personal visits will continue to be core to service provision. But with the ability to view catalogues online many wasted journeys will be prevented.

Your finding aids system should provide, at different levels of detail, information about your service's holdings. As discussed in Chapter 4, collection-level guides to an entire repository's holdings will provide a broad view of what is available; subject and thematic guides will concentrate on dedicated areas, and the catalogue or inventory will provide more detailed information about individual collections. Indexes provide access points into collections, as can authority-controlled and free text searching. If you can add any or all of these to a website so much the better. Supporting information about the collections can be provided in different ways. As we saw, the LEADERS project aimed to integrate contextual information alongside transcripts and images of original documents with the option of adding additional guidance, glossaries, and so on. This works well for fairly small, clearly defined projects. By contrast, large national collections can provide a range of linked finding aids that incorporate generic 'how-to' guidance alongside other information and subject leaflets which ultimately take you to the catalogue entry itself (and in rarer cases to a digitised image of the original).

This can work in practice as follows. A search for an ancestor who had served in the Royal Flying Corps during World War I starts from the homepage of the National Archives website (Figure 5.2) and invites me to select 'military history'.

This takes me to a guide to resources for military history, and to what sources are available online and which must be accessed on site. It gives me the option of viewing an online exhibition on World War I or selecting a 'topic to research', in my case the Royal Air Force and its predecessors. The next screen allows me to select 'Royal Flying Corps', from where are links to three other research guides and to the catalogue reference itself – in my case WO 363 (Figure 5.3).

Here I learn that the original documents are available only on microfilm because the originals had been burnt during bombing in London during World War II. I need to have full details of my serviceman's name as I will have to search the film (some of the contents of which are not in alphabetical order) to find any reference to him.

This is an example from a single archive. There are also initiatives that support the networking of catalogue information across a range of repositories so that the user has the opportunity for the first time to access information about specific topics from more than one repository simultaneously. An example of this kind of 'supra-repository' provision is the A2A project. The A2A database contains catalogues contributed by over 340 record offices and libraries, museums, and nationalist and specialist institutions. A search for William Wordsworth finds 49 references, the first seven of which are all located in different archives,

Figure 5.2   The National Archives Home Page, 11 August 2005

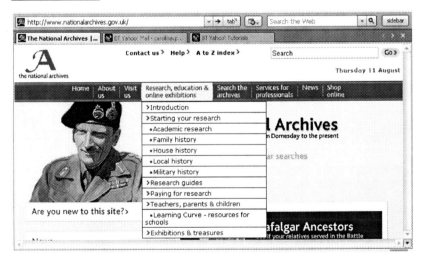

Figure 5.3 The National Archives catalogue entry for 'other ranks' of the Royal Flying Corps

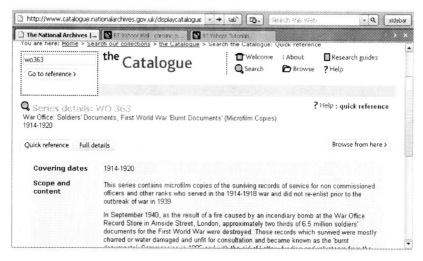

arranged in order of number of hits in each archive (Figure 5.4).[26] Most related to the poet, but I could have narrowed my search by defining the dates more exactly, the region of the country or even the particular archive whose holdings I wanted to trawl.

Figure 5.4 Search for William Wordsworth on A2A

49 catalogues were found to match **William Wordsworth**
Shown below are catalogues 1 to 25 (of 49)

		next
Sheffield Archives: Crewe Muniments	1311-1939	21 hit(s)
Cumbria Record Office, Kendal: National Trust, Westmorland	1602-1968	10 hit(s)
Cumbria Record Office, Carlisle Headquarters: Lowther Family of Lowther, Earls of Lonsdale [D LONS/L1 - D LONS/L2]	1530-1975	9 hit(s)
Birmingham University Information Services, Special Collections Department: Hannah Maria Phillip's Autograph Album	1734-1883	3 hit(s)
Sheffield Archives: Spencer Stanhope Muniments [SpSt/1 - SpSt/172]	1387-1846	3 hit(s)
Lancashire Record Office: The Stephen Marshall Documents	1675-1903	3 hit(s)
Liverpool Record Office and Local History Service: Diary and letter of Thomas De Quincy (1785-1859)	1803-1803	3 hit(s)

Information from the content of the holdings

Depending on the number of telephone, e-mail and written requests you receive, your archive service will need to have a policy about what level of response you can realistically provide. What degree of research can you undertake into the content of your holdings in response to enquiries? If your main clients are internal you may need to respond quite fully, as may business archives in response to external enquiries when personal access is not provided as an option. It is best to have a stated policy about the length of time it takes to respond to enquiries – say five days – and ensure that this is complied with. As far as research into *content* is concerned, because equality of access is one of the ethical standards to which most services aspire, arguably we should not disadvantage those unable to visit, and a consistent approach to these requests must be apparent.

Services in this situation will usually offer without limit information *about* their holdings, but will set a time limit (say 30 minutes) on how long they will spend researching a particular request for free. If longer is required than the permitted time, you might either refer the applicant to a list of professional researchers (in which case the archive takes no responsibility for the quality of the work undertaken) or employ an in-house research consultant. This consultant will become an expert on the contents of the archive and will also generate useful income.

On-site research visits

It is important that you supply the researcher who plans to visit in person with plenty of information in advance of a visit, and ensure that this is easily accessible. Increasingly, national online portals provide contact details of local archives, and links to their websites. In Australia the site 'Archives around Australia' provides state-by-state details of some government and institutional archives, research collections and personal archives, with a link to the more detailed Directory of Archives in Australia.[27] In Canada the Archives Canada site provides contact details for repositories, enables a search of archival holdings, and permits access to provincial and territorial archival networks.[28] In Britain the ARCHON site includes contact details for all record repositories and links to their websites.[29] The information you place on your website should include enough (such as that suggested for an introductory leaflet above) to reassure the first-time user. You will find that first-time users fall into two categories: those who have used archives elsewhere and those who have never been to an archives before and are unfamiliar with how they operate.

Archives can be fairly daunting places for the uninitiated, given the security measures, complicated finding aids, high levels of supervision and apparently strict rules of behaviour. Your role is to make the experience of researchers comfortable and rewarding (even if the information sought is not found) and leave them confident to visit again. You will need to explain the most efficient way of using the service while introducing the notion of what is acceptable behaviour. Some archives services use entrance interviews in order to find out what the researcher is trying to find out and to provide him or her with necessary information, and then use exit interviews to evaluate the user's experience of the visit. In busy offices this is often not possible, and although nothing can replace the personal conversation, well-written guidance should also be available. Larger offices may require new users to view an introductory video or be given a tour before starting their research.

In general the process of a visit involves the following stages:

1. *Registration of researcher.* This involves the confirmation of identity, address details (with confirmation of both) and topic of research. Some archives issue reader tickets that can be produced on subsequent visits. Registration is necessary:

   – for security purposes: it conveys the idea that archives are unique and therefore need special care;

   – because if we know who our users are and where they are from we can contact them in case of need;

   – so that we understand our users, can tailor service to their needs and use the information for statistical purposes.

   Registration can seem very bureaucratic to the anxious researcher and is best kept short. All personal belongings other than those needed for research (laptop, notebooks, pencils, own reference works) should be left in a secure area at this point.

2. *Determination of researcher's needs.* Identifying the user's research question is a skilled process, particularly with inexperienced users, so be patient. If we are to succeed in making sure each user gets the best experience possible, we need (without compromising security and preservation) to be able to empathise with them. Good customer care is central: we may deal daily with dozens of enquiries; each enquirer will judge the service on the basis of the response he or she received,

and reputations can be made and lost. Customer care equips us with the skills to deal with stressful and demanding situations, to explain sensitively rules and procedures, and to find out what the user really wants (which may not be what they first ask). We want them to go away with confidence in our service.

3. *Introduction of repository rules.* With the act of registering and signing-in the user undertakes to abide by the repository's rules, and you can make them available at this point. These rules need to make clear what users can expect from your service and what you expect from them. No one likes rules, but they do make sure users are dealt with in a consistent manner and to an objective standard. They do not have to sound bossy, however, and are best phrased in a way that explains the reason behind them. 'Do not use pens' is less helpful than 'Pencils only should be used to take notes from original documents'. Other rules relate the ordering, use and copying of documents; restrictions on eating, drinking and smoking; and consideration for other users. You might use the National Archives *Standard* for reference when developing your own rules.

The National Archives Standard for Record Repositories section on access[30]

4.1 The governing body should provide a designated study area sufficient to satisfy normal demand for public access to the records and suitable for their inspection under constant invigilation.

4.2 The health and safety of the public must be provided for.

4.3 Reasonable measures must be taken to meet the special needs of disabled readers and it is desirable to publicise these adequately.

4.4 The governing body should provide, and ensure the proper maintenance of any technical facilities necessary for consulting the records and appropriate to their types and quantity.

4.5 The governing body should make public the regulations for access to the records. These should conform to any statutory or official requirements concerning records for which the repository is officially approved.

4.5.1 Details should be given of regular opening hours. In setting these, archive services should endeavour to take account of the needs of their users.

4.5.2 Conditions for the issue of readers' tickets (if applicable) should be stated.

4.5.3 It is highly desirable that readers be required to produce written evidence of identity before being given access to unique archival documents.

4.5.4 General restrictions on access, such as any statutory or customary time-limited closure of the records, or any applicable derogations of closure (for example with regard to Freedom of Information or Data Protection), should also be explained in the regulations.

4.5.5 Readers should not take coats and bags to their study places.

4.5.6 Readers should write with pencils only, and not write on or trace directly from any records.

4.5.7 Provisions for the protection of the records from theft or damage during public inspection and for the prevention of unauthorised access to the records should be laid down.

4.6 The governing body should, through such visitor registration processes as are in operation, make users aware of rules, regulations and other codes of conduct which apply to the use of the archive service.

4.7 All records which are open to inspection by the public should be clearly described, in publicly available finding aids. All newly created finding aids should be compatible with approved national and international standards.

4.8 The governing body should provide efficient means of delivering records for public inspection in the designated study areas without undue delay and without damage to the records.

4.9 When in use the study area should be constantly supervised by sufficient staff to provide an effective level of invigilation of the whole area, under the direction of a professionally qualified archivist.

4.10 It is desirable, and in the case of Public Records mandatory, that facilities be provided, either in the repository or by appropriate arrangement elsewhere, for making photographic or other copies of the records, with due regard to copyright. Copying should not, however, be carried out if in the opinion of the professional staff the records in question are too fragile to withstand copying. Suitable arrangements should also be made for the authentication of copies for legal and other purposes.

4. *Explanation of finding aids and document ordering systems.* At this stage your user's 'frequently asked questions', for example about genealogical sources, can be answered via a range of 'how to' guides and some will find other secondary sources useful too. Even practised researchers are likely to need help as despite increasing standardisation, different archives still have idiosyncratic finding aids, and written (or verbal) instructions are necessary. Your system for ordering documents from the strong rooms might involve the user either entering requests on a computer terminal or completing duplicate or triplicate paper slips. You may need to restrict the numbers of documents that may be ordered at any one time (though exceptions may be made at the discretion of the staff). Production staff will retrieve the requested items, and after use return them to storage, once they have been checked back in. You should keep records of production for a set period of time so that missing items can be looked for among other items issued at the same time. They also enable you to analyse user research interests and most frequently used classes of records.

5. Instructions for ordering copies, use of laptops and cameras, and any charges that might apply should also be available. Like much guidance you can issue this in leaflet form.

6. *Exit interviews.* These are still fairly commonly held, especially in America. Whatever form the interview takes, it is important to get feedback on your service so that you can make improvements. Areas covered might include a description of which collections the user accessed, the value or otherwise of the finding aids, their view of their experience of the search room, and the attitude and helpfulness of staff. Users should also have access to a complaints system if they wish to give a more formal voice to their concerns. Evaluation and impact studies are being seen as an increasingly important aspect of service provision and this is where raw data for these can be generated.

Users of archives are often our greatest supporters and their interests should remain at the forefront of our minds. Some archives have dedicated 'Friends of the Record Office' that help it in fighting for services, providing volunteers or in raising funds. Others are involved in generating interest in new ways and in reaching new audiences. We all need to learn how to advertise what we do in effective and measurable ways.

Advocacy and outreach

We know that government objectives to increase access to nations' archives are currently driving many agenda. These can only properly be achieved when the necessary infrastructure, legislation and funding are in place. However, there is also a need for a cultural change about the perception within communities, whether large or small, of the place of archives.

We might believe that '... archives ... belong at the very heart of people's lives – contributing to their enjoyment and inspiration, cultural values, learning potential, economic prosperity and social equity'[31], but if you consider the following quotes:

> Archivists, like the archives in their care, have an image problem[32]
> Archives need to be brought out of the shade[33]

it would seem that we still have some persuading to do.

Although stories regarding record-keeping are in the news almost daily there is not much public awareness of its value. How can we make the existence of records and archives services a natural part of people's consciousness in the way that other services – such as citizen's advice, waste disposal or libraries – are? So that although people may not need or want to use them at the moment they know they are there for when they do? Successfully publicising what we do involves archival advocacy both at the individual and at the national strategic level. When asked informally what we do, we should be able to take the opportunity to discuss our archival role with enthusiasm. At a national level archival bodies, national archives and professional associations will take every opportunity to 'plead, support, champion, intercede for'[34] archives and demonstrate the contribution that proper record and archive keeping can make to society. Adopting advocacy and marketing techniques can help achieve promotion of such access objectives as social inclusion and life-long learning in the archival sector.

> Advocacy comprises the mindset and infrastructural tools which are applied to develop comprehensive public programs with an array of outreach activities. It describes the attitudes and techniques essential for defining important 'publics', developing strategies/tactics, nurturing important relationships and identifying promotional opportunities which are prerequisites to undertaking activities and projects.[35]

In this statement Ann Pederson considers how organisations should approach their promotional activities: not by undertaking outreach activities in an *ad hoc* or reactive way ('heavens! we haven't had an open day for three years') but in a planned and systematic manner, with a clear view of the objectives to be achieved in the short, medium and long term. She argues that while strategic co-ordinated public programmes are better than *ad hoc* 'outreach' activities, advocacy adds a new dimension in which you concentrate on the *user* of records in the broadest sense. It also involves a commitment to behavioural change – viewing *all* activities through the lens of promotion and inclusion – and identifying 'publics', those stakeholders who need to be targeted. If this sounds a bit go-getting and brash then may be you are in the wrong job. Working in archives is not about hanging back and waiting for things to happen.

The benefits of successful advocacy from the most basic to the broadest level are:

- survival: in order to avoid being the target of budget cuts or rationalisation programmes you need to demonstrate that you are doing something useful in a proactive way;
- generation of funding: available via demonstration of programmes showing compliance with government and other access agenda;
- increased funding leads to development of services and broadening of your user base: in the UK this fits in with the government's customer-centred service delivery policies.
- increased use leads to generation of wider support and appreciation of archives and contributes benefits to the wider society;
- and – it is to be hoped – the fuller realisation that 'archives belong at the very heart of people's lives'.

Pederson also emphasises that advocacy is 'about people not things'.

> In advocacy people skills and issues are paramount ... For many years, archivists have focused their attention upon the records and their importance as research resources to the neglect of the raison d'être for record-keeping – people and their acts. Understanding how people feel and behave, their roles in organised activity and what they need in terms of documentation – is vital.[36]

Stakeholders

Who are we trying to persuade? The answer is anybody who has an interest, whether direct or indirect, in our service. We might remind ourselves (see Chapter 7) that stakeholders are

> persons, corporate bodies or defined groups with an interest in the present and future activities of the archive service. Stakeholders include those with a financial interest (including tax payers in relation to a public service), office holders (e.g. politicians, committee members), executives, employees, suppliers, customers and the local community. In archive services there are two important additional groups: depositors – the donors or lenders of records; future users: the purpose of the preservation of records.[37]

The tendency is only to see our researchers as our stakeholders. In fact there are a number of other groups too. Defining the nature of the interest that each group of stakeholders has in your service is the first step in planning how to satisfy it. Your own senior management has an interest in seeing that you perform in line with your stated mission within the permitted budget. Office holders, those elected representatives who have responsibilities beyond the organisation to an electorate, board of directors or shareholders, need to be able to justify your service to their particular constituency. Those with other financial interests might include funding agencies – which you certainly need to persuade to support you. Colleagues within the organisation and within and beyond the profession take an interest in your performance, as do inspecting bodies – you need to demonstrate that you are meeting performance targets. The media are (you should ensure they are) important stakeholders: if you can get into the routine of supplying information to local newspapers, radio and television you can enter the wider community's consciousness. And then of course are the diverse groups of direct users of the service: the internal clients, the scholarly researchers, the teachers, students, genealogists, local historians and other professionals, and the general public. Finally, remember that stakeholders may be transient: this year's board member might become next year's exhibition viewer or donor.

Most difficult to define (for obvious reasons) are the non-users of archives. MLA recognises that the main barriers preventing people from accessing archives are physical and sensory, intellectual, cultural, attitudinal and financial. In 2003 it commissioned a MORI (Market &

Opinion Research International) poll into non-users of archives, which interviewed a sample of 1953 people of all ages across the UK. This poll found that 10% had visited an archives in the past 12 months. Of those who had not (1759) the main reasons given for not using or visiting archives were a lack of perceived relevance (16%), time (14%) and interest (13%) but that a further 30% had no particular reason for not doing so. When asked what might encourage them to use archives they said being able to access/find out about archives on the Internet (26%), archives being available nearby (21%), being able to see examples of the records they hold (20%), and making information available about what there is and where to start looking (20%); but 24% still said 'nothing – I will not visit an archives'.[38] It may be politically and professionally uncomfortable to acknowledge that nearly one-quarter of the population *will not* have an interest in archives (just as I shall never have an interest in sky-diving) but information such as this does provide us with a basis from which to start our promotional activities.

Current initiatives to develop community archives are recognising that advocacy is about reaching people where they are. In the UK attempts to reach non-users include the Community Access Development Group and the Community Access to Archives Project that looked at the practicalities of developing community-based online archive projects. Members of the latter project recognised that these can 'contribute to community development, skills development and the preservation of "unofficial" history, and are a means of encouraging non-traditional users to become involved with archives.'[39] Another community archive website Commanet states: 'community archives are where the community creates its own archive, has editorial control over its archive and owns the copyright in its archive.' This redefines the notion of an archive to something that is far more flexible than the traditional perception permits.[40]

Selling your service

When businesses want to extend their customer base they resort to tried and tested marketing techniques. There is no reason why archives should not do the same in their quest to reach new groups and potential users.

Marketing, according to the Institute of Marketing, is 'the management process responsible for identifying, anticipating and satisfying consumers' requirements profitably' and can be undertaken by following a well-recognised marketing cycle. Although the profit we seek for our customers may not be of the financial kind, the process can provide a framework for our activities.

The marketing cycle in relation to archives is as follows:

1. *Formulate a mission* for your archive/museum/information service/library (where do we want to be?). Refer to Chapter 7 for how to define a mission and objectives. Your 'advocacy' objectives might be part of your broader organisational aims: for example 'to make the service more widely known to actual and potential stakeholders'.

2. *Review current position* (where are we now?), and identify opportunities, using techniques such as SWOT and PEST. Chapter 7 provides some guidance on these techniques. You should look at your service in terms of its resources, personnel, specialist expertise, current services, competitors and external influences. Your analysis will help you to think realistically about what objectives you are likely to be able to meet.

3. *Formulate marketing objectives.* Decide what you can set as achievable objectives within your current resources. For example: Year 1: design a marketing framework; develop a relationship with local media and museums and libraries; increase talks to local societies by 20%; Year 2: apply for lottery funding for digitisation project; publish a glossy illustrated guide to holdings.

4. *Undertake market research.* This involves the systematic gathering, recording and analysis of data about the issues relating to the marketing of your services. You need to analyse the existing market place to identify:

   – who the customers are/might be in the future;

   – what services they currently want or need and what future ones might be required;

   – what benefits they will derive from the provision of these services.

   This means collecting information about the people and areas you want to target, which you will already have defined to some extent in formulating your objectives: at whom are you targeting the digitisation project, or guide to holdings? Marketing research specifies the information required to address these issues, designs the method for collecting information, manages and implements the data collection process, analyses the results, and communicates the findings and their implications.

5. *Modify marketing objectives.* The results of your market research might require you to alter your objectives. For example, you discover that what your current users *really* want, rather than the digitisation of the gas works photo collection, is increased opening hours to include evening and weekend opening. (This seems an entirely reasonable request: but your problem is that although you are fairly sure of receiving funding for the digitisation scheme from lottery project sources, is your employing authority likely to pay for the extra staffing needed to support longer opening hours?) You might discover that people in large urban areas have no convenient access to an archive service: might this be an area of untapped potential users?

6. *Formulate marketing strategies* (how do we get there?), balancing various components of the 'marketing mix'.

   You should now be ready to consider how you will deliver your revised objectives in line with marketing's '4 Cs'

   – *customer* needs and wants;

   – *convenience* of the user;

   – *cost* to the user;

   – appropriate *communication* with and promotion to the user.

   If you get the balance of this marketing mix right you will be able to sell your 'product' successfully. To take one example: if you have identified during your research that you might gain new users from distant urban areas by having some kind of outlet in the local library (perhaps with microfilms and other secondary materials), provision of this will be an obvious response to what potential customers want and is convenient for them. It will succeed if you promote it effectively and keep the cost to the customer low. What it does not take into account is the cost to you, and the other areas of your service that may be jeopardised as a result. This is where the balance *really* lies.

7. *Implement marketing strategies.* As with any other set of objectives you will set up an action plan with a programmed set of targets.

8. *Monitor success* (how do we determine whether we got where we wanted to be at Stage 1?).

   Your findings about how successful you have been in delivering the plan will feed into your future planning – into the next cycle. You might find that the market is changing and that your users are becoming interested in different things. Have your own circumstances changed? Can you meet new demands?

9. *Review strategies* – and objectives and mission if necessary (starting again from the top). This completes the cycle and enables you to start on the next.

Outreach activities

If you take a strategic approach to advocacy you will be planning ahead and thinking about what you are doing rather than reacting. You will also be able to judge which particular type of outreach activity will be best suited to which group of stakeholder. Those most frequently adopted by archives services include:

Publications. These include record office content guides, subject guides, annual reports, education packs for school, books of all kinds, information leaflets, newsletters, postcards and other artwork. All of these meet the needs of certain clientele, and it is important to consider before undertaking such publications (some of which are expensive in terms of staff and production costs) who you are targeting and what the cost benefits are likely to be. You may decide that it is worth making a loss in view of the level of publicity gained: but you will have to find the costs from somewhere. Most repositories produce subject guides and information leaflets as basic publications.

As Figure 5.5 shows, many traditional publications are now also published on websites. You need to decide which publications should

---

Figure 5.5 Intercollegiate athletics subject guide at the University Archives, The University of Iowa Libraries, Iowa City, Iowa

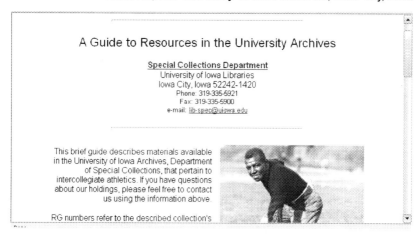

A Guide to Resources in the University Archives

Special Collections Department
University of Iowa Libraries
Iowa City, Iowa 52242-1420
Phone: 319-335-5921
Fax: 319-335-5900
e-mail: lib-spec@uiowa.edu

This brief guide describes materials available in the University of Iowa Archives, Department of Special Collections, that pertain to intercollegiate athletics. If you have questions about our holdings, please feel free to contact us using the information above.

RG numbers refer to the described collection's

only be created online and which should be published in traditional format. The office guide, the mainstay of an office's products and often a prestigious publication, will be out of date before it is published given an office's rate of acquisition. Is the prestige worth the expense? If you think so you might choose to advertise recent acquisitions in a regular newsletter or annual report. Annual reports can provide a range of stakeholders with details of your performance and provide a useful record of developments and progress. Regular newsletters can keep people informed at little cost: you can include a section for readers' queries and contributions. Education packs can be costly, and good liaison with schools is necessary. Some archives bring in children to help compile a pack for their area: this is a good way of involving the local community. Posters, postcards and other items, developed to generate income and provide souvenirs, are probably only viable for larger services, but act as good advertisement.

Web pages are now the prime means of mass communication for archives, and these now need particular consideration. Web pages have some obvious advantages over traditional publications and exhibitions: you can reach a far wider audience much more speedily, it is easy to update text, and there are no printing and distribution costs. However, you risk disenfranchising potential readers who do not have internet access and you may have problems of version control if you also produce material both in hard copy and for web distribution. You do need to plan your web presence and be clear about what you want it to achieve. Do you want your web pages to:

- Be an extension of your existing services, providing the same information in digital form as you currently do non-digitally?
- Provide added value to existing services, perhaps by enabling e-mail advance ordering of documents or sale of goods by e-commerce?
- To reach new users by encouraging people both to visit your archive and to use your site as the chief means of access?
- To provide access to archival networks?
- To provide an international 24/7 service even though the office closes at 5pm?

When you know the answer to these questions you will have some idea of what the content of your website will be. It is not sufficient just to add quantities of material for the sake of it: a mass of text on a screen is a turn-off and people will avoid sites that are unattractive, difficult to navigate and poorly planned. It is best to use short pages with plenty of links to others, both within your own site and to other relevant sites. Bear in mind that the web is dynamic and will need constantly updating: ensure that you have the help of a good designer and web manager and that you do not need to give several weeks' notice of any changes you want to make.[41]

An added benefit of the web for the user is the participation of archive services in national networks. We have seen how programmes such as Access to Archives, involved in the retrospective conversion of catalogues from a wide range of repositories, provide access to catalogue data across different archives. In addition, the amount of high-quality material such as standards and guidelines available on the sites of national archives and professional and other bodies provides excellent tools for the professional.

Finally, consider archiving your web pages. Because the web is now an important means by which people undertake their public and personal business and interact with all kinds of organisations, it is important that web content and context be preserved, and, where appropriate, retained for the long term. The National Archives Government Web Archive, through the Internet Archive, is collecting and preserving websites as evidence of the changing nature of the interaction between government bodies, business and the citizen (e.g. Figure 5.6). This initiative collects and preserves 50 government websites as weekly or 6-monthly

Figure 5.6 UK Government Web Archive: 10 Downing Street website the day before the General Election of 7 June 2001

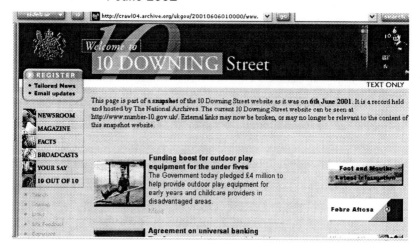

snapshots, using a specially modified version of the Internet Archive's web crawler. The complete archive is being made available on the web and in TNA's public search rooms.[42]

Talks, visits and open days. Public speaking is an important tool for advocacy. Well-delivered illustrated talks to various groups and societies is a tried and tested method of spreading the word about your service. Talks need to be appropriately targeted at their audience, professionally presented and persuasive. You have to give a positive image of archives and archivists: it might be the first exposure that members of the group have to the subject and you do not want it to be the last. However, talks may be costly in terms of preparation and presentation time, and travelling costs in relation to the number of people in the audience. Should you respond to every invitation from every Ladies' Rural Circle? Or should you pre-select those organisations you wish to target? If you allocate a specific budget to this particular activity you will be better able to prioritise your spending in a proactive way.

Inviting specific groups to visit is arguably a better way of enabling you to explain how an archive works: people are often captivated by watching conservators at work and at seeing original documents *in situ*. Even greater audiences are efficiently reached through open days: if well advertised these can be excellent publicity.

Education and learning. The potential for getting the message across to schools and colleges is enormous, given the size of the audience. It introduces the idea of archives to children at an early age, supports the curriculum and offers new methods of teaching to teachers. However, the nature of archival material and the need for its interpretation for students and schoolchildren means that partnerships between teachers and archivists are necessary for this form of outreach to be successful. This can be very resource-intensive and requires equal commitment from each side. At a local level websites offer such services to schools as class visits from students and pupils, the production of curriculum-based resource packs and training sessions for teachers.

Archives are increasingly providing online educational facilities. For example, the Royal Bank of Scotland targets teachers and pupils studying the Scottish and English & Welsh curricula and J. Sainsbury's Virtual Museum includes sections aimed at schools (Figure 5.7).[43]

National archives have greater capacity to do this. TNA offers a range of resources to teachers, parents and children, such as on-site and video-conference workshops, an on-site museum and online virtual museums and exhibitions, the 'Pathways to the Past' site and the curriculum-based Learning Curve, as well as puzzles and games for children.[44]

Figure 5.7 Sainsbury's Virtual Museum

Government drivers continue to have an impact on the wider 'learning' agenda. The Inspiring Learning for All programme, developed by MLA, claims that it 'will transform the way in which museums, archives and libraries deliver and engage users in learning'. It aims to have an impact beyond the formal education setting and focuses on users, and on museums, archives and libraries as organisations and how they can help people to achieve certain learning outcomes through their experiences.[45]

This kind of approach is becoming central to application for funding for many projects at local, regional and national levels in the UK.

Supporters' groups. Many archives find that a 'Friends of the Archives' or other such group is helpful in promoting their cause and supporting their activities. These may become involved in fundraising, volunteering or acting as a pressure group on its behalf. Where the balance is right these work well – although there have been instances where office policy and practice have been unduly influenced by such groups to the disadvantage of other users.

Exhibitions. It has always been a challenge to make exhibitions of archives on their own interesting, and far too tempting to accompany copies of dense looking documents with long explanatory labels. The public is increasingly sophisticated and expects a product that reflects investment and the expertise of professional designers. Artefacts often capture the imagination more readily than documents, and partnership with museums can be useful, where documents can be displayed alongside contemporary objects. Original documents give a unique sense of verisimilitude, but must be exhibited in accordance with their preservation needs. Copies today can be very convincing and can often be presented more attractively. Venues for exhibitions should be chosen for maximum accessibility: exhibitions within the archive itself are fine, but are preaching to the converted. Alternatively, it can be effective to create all-purpose panels on the role and purpose of the archive that can be transported from location to location. These can be used for history fairs, placed in libraries and museums, shopping centres, for example.

An original (and probably very expensive) exhibition put on by HSBC in their London headquarters is the History Wall (Figure 5.8): you can see nearly 4000 images on site and also on the website.[46]

You will find increasingly that archives are turning to online exhibitions for displaying their wares and promoting their services; there are many excellent examples. The British Library's 'Turning the Pages' is an interactive program that allows museums and libraries to give members of the public access to precious books while keeping the originals safely under glass. It allows visitors on site and online to virtually 'turn' the pages of manuscripts in a realistic way and you can access such items as Leonardo's sketches, Jane Austen's History of England, the Lindisfarne Gospels and many others.[47]

The media. Sensational stories about records or archives are more likely to attract media interest than the trivial – but we are unlikely to be able to offer them an Enron (shredding of key records) or the James

---

Figure 5.8 HSBC's History Wall

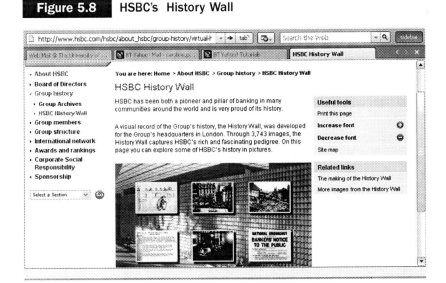

Cameron story, nor would we want to. But you might consider developing a strategy that uses the newspapers, radio and television to promote a positive image of public archives. Local newspapers are often glad to have regular copy from a credible source and you might offer a monthly 'Does anyone recognise the photograph?' competition or a 'tales from the archives' column. This will keep the service in the public eye so that subsequent initiatives such as open days, fundraising and requests for volunteers should receive a good response.

There are a number of articles on and guides to media management. One argues that the skill is to find an angle or 'hook' to hang a story on.[48] How would you try to get a press release for an exhibition published simultaneously in the *Springfield Gardeners Weekly*, *Aromatherapy Today* and the local press?

Press release

Solve your health problems with cheap and safe grow-your-own remedies!

Local resident and botanist Florence Gardner, mother of ten and grandmother of 40, is to open the Springfield Archives latest exhibition 'Come into the Garden Maud: Herbs and Herbal Remedies from the Archives' in Springfield Town Hall at 3 o'clock on Saturday October 10 2006. Florence, (75) who swears that use of the natural plant hellebore (helleborus niger) helped her to limit the size of her family, uses as medicines only plants and herbs recommended in the medieval herbals that are the focal point of this fascinating exhibition.

Come and see Florence open the exhibition; try - and buy - some of the (safest) remedies; and look at the colourful illustrated medieval herbals with their extraordinary remedies: 'ete garlick and it will cure ye wormes'! At a preview the Mayor of Springfield said 'I have never seen anything like this in my life!' The exhibition will run until 30 April 2007.

Find out what other fascinating things are to be found in the archives! The staff will be there to answer any questions (they are experts on family history and advising you on the care of your own archives too.) Springfield Archives in Bank Street is open every day except Sunday and bank holidays 10am -7.30pm.

To find out more contact Hyacinth Flowerdew,
Springfield Archives, Tel 01234 5678,
E-mail archives@springfield.gov.uk

You can probably tell that I am not an expert at this. Your organisation may well require any public notices to pass the desk of the public relations officer, who will know how best to phrase and place this kind of publicity material.

There may be the occasional opportunity to speak on local radio: if someone in your office has the knack of speaking (well and accurately) off-the-cuff, you might get a regular slot. Television again provides good publicity for archives: the recent BBC series 'Who do you think you are?', which used archives to trace the history of celebrities' families, had enormous impact. A word of warning: having television cameras in your archive causes enormous disruption and is best accommodated out of office hours. If producers tell you that filming will only take an hour, expect to be there for four.

Evaluating the impact of access services

Your archive service should, as with all services (and particularly public ones), be able to demonstrate that they are meeting required standards and achieving their objectives on time and within given resources. In Chapter 7 I consider some ways of auditing or measuring performance, in particular quantifying facts and figures through the application of performance indicators. These provide useful data for statistical analysis and for comparison with other services.[49] Increasingly, services are being asked to provide evidence of the quality of the experience received by their users, so measuring access provision and outreach activities and *responses to them* becomes an important part of the overall strategy. You might find the guidance from the PSQG's *Standard for Access* shown in Table 5.1. useful.[50]

If you follow this type of framework you will be able to compare your practices against policies in an evidence-based way and to analyse the outcomes of your service. Measuring outcomes, the *quality* of services provided, is another way of judging the impact that they have. Impact measurement is a familiar tool in some library and museum sectors where social and educational impact (identified as community identity, lifelong learning, quality of life, confidence, work ability and skills) is measured by responses to such questions as:

- Did we create greater awareness (i.e. what new information was received)?

Table 5.1   PSQG audit of access objectives

Objective	Audit method: how to check that the service has been achieving the objective
7.1 The archive service is aiming to satisfy users throughout its community	Check awareness of relevant legislation Documentary evidence of policies and of review Evidence of benchmarking and adoption of best practice in terms of equality of opportunity and dealing with diversity Evidence of analysis of the community and of service take-up, with appropriate action plans and implementation
8.1 The archive service has open, effective two-way communications with its community	Check existence, currency, variety of user communications Check evidence of communication to wider community Check evidence of recent inward communication from users and wider community
9.3 The policies of the archive service reflect the views and interests of its stakeholders	Evidence of identification of stakeholder groups – staff, users, potential users, funders, local community, other archive services and information providers, etc. Evidence of engagement with stakeholders and understanding of their requirements, e.g. minutes of meetings Evidence of action
14.1 The archive service is known by the community it exists to serve	Existence of material to publicise and promote the service and its holdings to a diverse community Evidence of evaluation of publicity methods and reorientation of promotion, where necessary, in the light of feedback and findings
16.6 Community benefits from the content in ways other than direct access	Evidence of activities undertaken in response to community needs

- Did our audience comprehend what we were communicating (i.e. did their level of understanding increase above what it was before)?

- Did we change attitudes (i.e. what do they believe and feel that they did not before we began communicating)?

- Did our target audience change their behaviour as a result of our communication (i.e. what did they actually do that was different from before)?

This type of approach introduces – or enhances – the importance of the idea that how people *think and feel* as a result of an experience, as well as what they do, is important in judging the quality of that experience too. It is given increased emphasis in the UK Government's Inspiring Learning for All policy described earlier, which defines learning thus:

> Learning is a process of active engagement with experience. It is what people do when they want to make sense of the world. It may involve increase in or deepening of skills, knowledge, understanding, values, feelings, attitudes and the capacity to reflect. Effective learning leads to change, development and the desire to learn more.[51]

Developed by MLA the policy is intended to improve services in museums, archives and libraries, and to measure the impact of these on people's learning. Its Learning Impact Research Project (LIRP) team contends that

> not all museums, archives and libraries see themselves as places that should primarily focus on the learning experiences of their users. In many cases the emphasis has been on service targets. As a result, attitudes towards learning vary enormously across organisations as well as across the sector as a whole. Common concepts of learning and a language to describe the experiences that users have are also lacking.[52]

They have therefore developed a set of generic learning outcomes (GLOs) that services can use to assess their impact upon the learning experiences of their users. They appreciate the difficulty of measuring learning in informal environments such as cultural organisations because it includes 'soft outcomes' such as attitudes, values, emotions and beliefs, which are often not seen as evidence of learning in the way that 'hard' facts and demonstrable skills are. LIRP argues that learning is not separate from emotions, and that emotions can actually help people to learn more and that 'enjoyment, amazement or inspiration can provide the motivation to acquire facts and knowledge'.

These GLOs are not dissimilar from early impact measurements. They seek to measure:

- an increase in knowledge and understanding;
- an increase in skills;
- a change in attitudes or values;
- evidence of enjoyment, inspiration and creativity;
- evidence of activity, behaviour and progression.

Guidance is given on how to use these in any environment and how to use the data generated. A pilot project in 15 services showed that you can generate:

- Quantitative data by counting the occurrence of each GLO and producing tables or charts in order to make comparisons. Thus, '25% of our sample said they now understood that you can use archives in researching your family tree.'

- Qualitative data by describing the range and depth of evidence from each GLO, often using quotes from users. Anecdotal data are valuable here. Thus, 'I nearly cried when I saw the photo of my grandmother's house in Rosamund Street after it had been bombed in the War'.

Measuring the performance of an archive service is becoming an increasingly sophisticated affair. It may be inappropriate for every service to measure itself in this way, but if we are going to understand the impact of what we do and to increase the influence of our services we need to engage proactively with all those who have an interest in them – as well as with those who do not yet, but will do soon, if we have any choice in the matter.

Notes

1. The Twenty-eighth Report of the Royal Commission on Historical Manuscripts, 1991–1999, *Archives at the millennium* (1999) Historical Manuscripts Commission. London: The Stationery Office, p. 4.
2. Council of Europe Committee of Ministers (2000) *Recommendation No. R (2000) 13 of the Committee of Ministers to Member States on a European Policy on Access to Archives.*
3. International Council on Archives *Code of Ethics*, 1996, *http://www.ica.org*
4. For example, Society of American Archivists *Code of Ethics for Archivists*, *http://www.archivists.org/governance/handbook/app_ethics.asp*; Australian

Society of Archivists *Code of Ethics*, *http://www.archivists.org.au/about/ethics.html* [accessed 25 August 2005].

5. UK Government Policy on Archives, 1999, *http://www.nationalarchives.gov.uk/policy/idac/government.htm* [accessed 25 August 2005].

6. Resource (MLA) (2001) *Developing the 21st century archive: an action plan for United Kingdom Archives*, p. 4, *http://www.mla.gov.uk/documents/21centarc.pdf* [accessed 30 October 2005].

7. Archives Task Force (2004) *Listening to the past, speaking to the future*, *http://www.mla.gov.uk/documents/atf_report.pdf*

8. National Council on Archives (2001) *Taking part: an audit of social inclusion work in archives*, *http://nca.archives.org.uk/takepart.pdf*

9. *Government Policy on Archives*, *http://www.nationalarchives.gov.uk/policy/idac/government.htm* [accessed 6 January 2006] Section 4.3, and p. 7.

10. Information Commissioner's Office, *http://www.informationcommissioner.gov.uk/eventual.aspx* [accessed 30 October 2005].

11. Freedom of Information Act (Great Britain. 2000 c.36), *http://www.hmso.gov.uk/acts/acts2000.htm* [accessed 30 October 2005].

12. Codes of Practice under sections 45 and 46, *http://www.nationalarchives.gov.uk/policy/* [accessed 30 October 2005].

13. Data Protection Act, 1998, *http://www.opsi.gov.uk/acts/acts1998/19980029.htm* [accessed 30 October 2005].

14. Leppard, D. (2004) 'Foreign Office doubts on a visa witch hunt', *Sunday Times* 12 September, *http://www.timesonline.co.uk/newspaper/0,,176-1257934,00.html* [accessed 30 October 2005].

15. Public Record Office, Society of Archivists and Records Management Society (2002) *Code of practice for archivists and records managers under section 51(4) of the Data Protection Act 1998*, *http://www.archives.org.uk/publications/soacodev2.pdf*; Public Record Office (2000) *Data Protection Act: a guide for archivists and records managers*, *http://www.nationalarchives.gov.uk/policy/dp/* [accessed 25 October 2005]

16. Padfield, T. (2004) *Copyright for archivists*, 2nd edn. London: Facet Publishing.

17. Standard for Provision of Access to Public Archives Controlled by Archives New Zealand, November 2001, *http://www.archives.govt.nz/continuum/dls/HTMLDocs/S4-access-standard/S4-access-standard-contents.shtml*; ALA-SAA Joint Statement on Access: Guidelines for Access to Original Research Materials, August 1994, *http://www.archivists.org/statements/alasaa.asp* [accessed 30 October 2005].

18. Public Services Quality Group (PSQG) *Standard for Access to Archives*, September 2003, *http://www.nationalarchives.gov.uk/archives/psqg/access.htm* [accessed 30 October 2005].

19. National Archives *Standard for Record Repositories*, (2004) 1st edn, *http://www.nationalarchives.gov.uk/archives/framework/* [accessed 30 October 2005].

20. Jenkinson, H. (1966) *Manual of archive administration*, 2nd edn. London: Lund Humphries, p. 124.

21. Hedstrom, M. (1998) 'How do archivists make electronic archives usable and accessible?' *Archives and Manuscripts* 26:1, 6–22.

22. Tavistock Institute (1997) *JISC Archives Sub-Committee: a project to develop measures of user satisfaction for university archive and manuscript repositories*. London: Tavistock Institute.

23. Survey of Visitors to British Archives, 2001, *http://www.nationalarchives .gov.uk/archives/psqg/survey.htm* [accessed 30 October 2005].

24. Hill, A. (2004) 'Serving the invisible researcher: meeting the needs of the online users', *Journal of the Society of Archivists* 25:2, 139–48; Sexton, A., Turner, C., Yeo, G. and Hockey, S. (2004) 'Understanding users: a prerequisite for developing new technologies', *Journal of the Society of Archivists* 25:1, 33–49; Sexton, A., Turner, C., Yeo, G. and Hockey, S. (2004) 'Testing the LEADERS demonstrator application', *Journal of the Society of Archivists* 25:2, 189–208; Economou, M. (2002) *User evaluation: report of findings*. London: Museums, Libraries and Archives Council.

25. Sexton, A. *et al.*, *op. cit.*, pp. 192–202.

26. Access to Archives (A2A), *http://www.a2a.org.uk/* [accessed 30 October 2005].

27. Directory of Archives in Australia, *http://www.archivenet.gov.au/archives .html* [accessed 30 October 2005].

28. Archives Canada, *http://www.archivescanada.ca/index2.html* [accessed 30 October 2005].

29. ARCHON Directory, *http://www.nationalarchives.gov.uk/searchthearchives/* [accessed 30 October 2005].

30. National Archives *Standard for Record Repositories*, *http://www .nationalarchives.gov.uk/archives/framework/pdf/standard2005.pdf*

31. Resource (MLA) (2001) *Developing the 21st century archive: an action plan for United Kingdom Archives*, p. 4, *http://www.mla.gov.uk/documents/ 21centarc.pdf* [accessed 30 October 2005].

32. The Twenty-eighth Report of the Royal Commission on Historical Manuscripts, 1991–1999, *Archives at the millennium*. London: The Stationery Office, p. 6.

33. Lord Evans, Chair of Resource, Speech at the Society of Archivists AGM, April 2001.

34. *Oxford English Dictionary* definition for 'advocacy'.

35. Pederson, A. (1997) 'Educating for advocacy', *Janus* 1, 7–15.

36. Pederson, A., *op. cit.*, p. 9.

37. PSQG *Standard for Access to Archives*, 3.3.5.

38. Archives Task Force (2004) *Listening to the past, speaking to the future: the report of the Archives Task Force*, Annex D: Non-Archive Users Survey: Omnibus Study, MORI, June 2003, p. 3.

39. Community Access to Archives Project, *http://www.nationalarchives.gov.uk/ partnerprojects/caap/team.htm* [accessed 30 October 2005].

40. Commanet, *http://www.commanet.org/* [accessed 30 October 2005].

41. Shenton, C. (2002) *Archival websites*. London: Society of Archivists: Best Practice Guideline.

42. National Archives Digital Preservation, *http://www.nationalarchives.gov.uk/ preservation/* [accessed 30 October 2005].

43. Royal Bank of Scotland 'our Teaching Resources', *http://www.rbs.co.uk/ Group_Information/Memory_Bank/Our_Teaching_Resources/default.htm*;

J. Sainsbury Virtual Museum, *http://www.j-sainsbury.co.uk/museum/ museum.htm* [accessed 30 October 2005].

44. The National Archives, Teachers Parents and Children, *http://www .nationalarchives.gov.uk/teachers/?source=ddmenu_research9* [accessed 30 October 2005].

45. Museums, Libraries and Archives Council, *Inspiring Learning for All, http:// www.inspiringlearningforall.gov.uk/introduction/default.aspx* [accessed 30 October 2005].

46. HSBC The History Wall, *http://www.hsbc.com/hsbc/about_hsbc/group-history/ virtual-history-wall* [accessed 30 October 2005].

47. British Library Turning the Pages, *http://www.bl.uk/onlinegallery/ ttp/digitisation5.html* [accessed 30 October 2005].

48. Black, P. (1997) *Manipulating the media: a handbook for librarians.* London: Library Association.

49. Collated for UK local authority services in England and Wales in *Chartered Institute of Public Finance and Standard for Access Accountancy Archives Services Statistics, 2003–4.*

50. PSQG *Standard for Access, http://www.nationalarchives.gov.uk/archives/ psqg/pdf/access_standard.rtf* [accessed 30 October 2005].

51. Museums, Libraries and Archives Council, *Measuring the Outcomes and Impact of Learning in Museums Archives and Libraries: The Learning Impact Research Project End of Project Paper*, 1 May 2003, p. 8, *www.mla.gov.uk/action/learnacc/lirp.asp* [accessed 8 January 2006].

52. *Measuring the Outcomes and Impact of Learning in Museums Archives and Libraries*, p. 4.

6

Preservation

Introduction

The third in our triad of core aims, alongside the selection of archives and the provision of access, is the preservation and maintenance of the material in our care in the long term. Although the majority of current records have built-in retention periods and will be disposed of in a planned manner, those deemed archival need to be kept for posterity. This is a real challenge given the external and internal threats that face archival material. Unlike other functions, preservation underpins every activity that takes place in the archive, is the responsibility of every member of staff and should be explicitly incorporated in the daily routine. It is central to collections management.

This chapter will enable you to:

- define the preservation function;
- develop and implement preservation policies, strategies and standards;
- assess preservation needs through surveys, audits and bench-marking;
- recognise the attributes of and threats to diverse media and formats;
- undertake preservation activities: appropriate and secure buildings, environmental management, storage and packaging, handling and use;
- compile an emergency plan;
- understand the role of conservation;
- reformat materials and create surrogates, from paper to digital records;
- plan a digitisation programme.

Defining the preservation function

Definitions of preservation vary, depending on the standpoint of whoever is making the statement. TNA provides a definition of preservation that is intended to provide for the longevity of materials of future archives, especially electronic, as well as those already in their care:

> Preservation is defined as all actions that can be taken with the aim of ensuring the current and long-term survival and accessibility of the physical form, informational content and relevant metadata of archival records, including actions taken to influence records creators prior to acquisition or selection.[1]

The Museums Libraries and Archives Council emphasises the wider managerial and curatorial aspects in its definition:

> All managerial, financial and technical considerations applied to retard deterioration that prevent damage and extend the useful life of material and objects in collections to ensure their continued availability. These considerations include monitoring and controlling appropriate environmental conditions; providing adequate storage and physical protection; establishing exhibition and loan policies and proper handling procedures; providing for conservation treatment, emergency planning and the creation of surrogates.[2]

This definition makes clear just how much is involved in the preservation function. It also demonstrates that preservation is an activity that takes place at all levels of the organisation. At the macro level are the development of policies and strategic planning, while at the ground or micro level hands-on decisions and treatment practices are needed to deal with those records delivered on the doorstep or found in a basement that are already in a mouldy, faded and rodent-nibbled state.

Preservation is neither *conservation* nor *restoration*. Restoration is the reconstruction of a document or artefact, through processes that cannot be reversed, so that it looks like the original. Conservation refers to the specific hands-on techniques that set out to stabilise individual documents to prevent further deterioration and where processes are reversible. The document may *look* as if it has been repaired or conserved. Conservation is an important resource within the preservation function. Whereas conservation provides solutions for individual documents, preservation offers large-scale solutions: for example, maintaining the right temperature and humidity affects *all* the documents in storage.

Development and implementation of preservation policies, strategies and standards

As with any other core function, the first job is to establish the necessary policies and strategies to provide a framework for practice in your particular organisation, however large or small.[3] While you are doing this (and bearing in mind that you may be developing other policies at the same time) you will be trying to gain an overview of the scope of your particular preservation problem, through the type of surveys and audits discussed in the next section. You will find that one of the central tensions here is to strike the right balance between the demand for access now and the need for preservation of archives for future generations. The decision that is reached on how this is achieved in each archive needs to be transparent and clearly articulated, because it is likely to be challenged.

A 'policy' is a set of coherent decisions with a common long-term aim(s) and which relate to a specific organisational purpose. It describes the 'what' and 'why' of the policy.

A 'strategy' is the action path the organisation has chosen to realise goals. Strategies establish broad themes for future actions. It articulates 'how' and 'in what order' actions are taken.

As with other policies, you may find it useful first to review the kinds of preservation policies that are already in the public domain. You might track down one from an organisation similar to your own that you can adapt to suit your own purposes. Take care not to plagiarise too blatantly, however – if you borrow extensively you should acknowledge your sources in order to satisfy the demands of copyright and courtesy. Developing policies will certainly be time-consuming at the start, although you will feel the benefit in the long run.[4]

Alternatively, you can seek out existing models and templates (rather than actual policies) on which to base your own policy. One such is that of the UK National Preservation Office (NPO) based in the British Library. This body has a range of extremely useful publications, many available on its website.[5] Their *Building Blocks for a Preservation Policy* is a brief and useful document that suggests what elements should be included in a preservation policy and provides a checklist against which to measure your own. For example, it suggests that the document should state the rationale and scope of the policy, contain a statement of preservation philosophy, be based on the purpose and function of the organisation and be supported by appropriate financial and human resources.[6] It is important to show in your policy that you strive to comply with the industry standards, whether international, national or professional, although you should not set yourself standards that it is beyond your resources to achieve.

Most policies will open with a general statement of aims and objectives. At its core will be a summary of the organisation's approach to the various elements of preservation in which it is involved, noting where separate policies exist for each. In implementing the policy staff will need to develop a set of standards and processes for each activity. Traditional activities include:

- acquisition and retention
- security and environment
- accommodation and storage
- access
- emergency planning
- reprographics
- conservation
- document loan and exhibition

Thus, for example, the section of the preservation policy statement from the State Records Office of Western Australia on storage states:

> Housing materials for the collection (the containers, boxes, file folders and wallets in which the archives are kept) should be chemically inert, and of a structure and size to ensure protection of the material from damage from handling and storage.[7]

Larger organisations have broader policies. Library and Archives Canada and the UK National Archives have adopted a similar framework.[8] In these the contents page outlines the sections included;

that of the Libraries and Archives Canada Preservation Policy is as follows:

1. PURPOSE
2. CONTEXT
3. AUTHORITIES
4. DEFINITIONS
5. ROLES AND RESPONSIBILITIES
6. POLICY STATEMENTS
7. POLICY REQUIREMENTS

   7.1 Preservation Planning and Strategy

   7.2 Acquisition, Selection and Disposal

   7.3 Preservation Management of Collections

   7.4 Accommodation, Security and Environment

   7.5 Disaster and Emergency Preparedness

   7.6 Copying

   7.7 Conservation Treatment

   7.8 Access

   7.9 Preservation Research and Training

   7.10 Stakeholders, Partnerships and Professional Connections

   7.11 Preservation in the Federal Records Centres

   7.12 Public Awareness of Preservation

8. MONITORING
9. OTHER DEPARTMENTAL POLICIES
10. DATE OF EFFECT
11. COMMUNICATION OF THE POLICY

Here, under Section 1, Purpose, Library and Archives Canada states:

> The purpose of this policy is to state the principles that guide the preservation activities of the National Archives of Canada (NA) in fulfilling all aspects of its mandate. It gives direction to staff for carrying out their responsibilities regarding the preservation function and communicates to those outside the institution the principles which guide preservation in the NA.[9]

Some places have separate policies for digital and non-digital resources. The British Library has a separate digital preservation policy on the basis that digital media require active and continued intervention to ensure their survival, and that preservation decisions need to be made at the beginning of the life cycle management of the digital object. Thus, it 'intends to record information specifically for preservation purposes (preservation metadata) at the point when the material is deposited, acquired or created by the Library and make preservation decisions at that point.'[10] There is also an increasing number of preservation policies issued by organisations whose sole remit is digital preservation. Here, too, templates and models are available as are actual policies created by specific organisations, and are comparable in structure with those for non-digital archives. The international ERPANET's (Electronic Resource Preservation and Access Network) template is particularly good at outlining the benefits of such a policy and defining its scope and objectives, providing guidance on how to make it fit *your* organisation. Its coverage for digital resources includes the need to have policies for conversion, reformatting and technical infrastructure.[11]

Similarly, audio-visual archives will also highlight their specialist area of concern. ScreenSound Australia has direct responsibility for the national collection of sound and moving image material. So its preservation policy has sections on ethics; multiplicity of copies and storage; stable formats and media; transfer, digitisation, conversion; virtual preservation and staff training.[12] Thus, although there are common elements that should be included in all policies, there will also be a need to provide for any specialist areas.

A long-term strategy should be developed from the preservation policy, and its content will depend on the priorities set by the organisation through its stated aims and objectives. It will include a number of aims and will set specific measurable objectives. The NPO argues for a strategy for the preservation of library and archive collections in the UK and Ireland, but most are at an organisational level.[13] The British Library's strategy promotes collaboration, developing preservation solutions alongside others, offering itself as a test site for preservation projects and contributing to the development of international standards. There appear to be more strategies for digital preservation than for the preservation of traditional materials: this is probably because without early active intervention these materials will not survive.

Standards and benchmarks

The importance of compliance with standards has been noted in previous chapters. Preservation policies and strategies also need to note which preservation standards they aim to comply with. Numerous bodies generate standards, from the International Standards Organisation (ISO) through national standards bodies such as the British Standards Institute (BSI) to professional associations and organisations. Some of the following standards are quite specialised whereas others are intended for general application (Table 6.1).

I shall be referring most frequently to BS 5454:2000, *Recommendations for the storage and exhibition of archival documents*, which is the standard to which archival repositories in the UK aspire. It is a useful and detailed document, contains a list of further relevant standards and a reading list, and provides all-round guidance. Guidance is included on:

- site of the building
- building construction and protection
- fire protection
- the storage environment for paper and parchment
- lighting
- storage and production equipment
- packaging for storage
- modern media and other materials
- exhibition

The annexes to it cover:

- environmental conditions for the storage of modern media
- ancillary equipment
- packaging materials and applications

The BSI has published a guide to the interpretation of BS5454.[14] Although the BSI is particularly strict in enforcing copyright (no photocopying) it is certainly worth getting sight of a copy – or even buying one.

Table 6.1   Some preservation standards

International standards	
ISO 11799:2003	Document storage requirements for archive and library materials
ISO 15686-1:2000	Buildings – Part 1, Service life planning
ISO 11108:1996	Information and documentation. Archival paper. Requirements for permanence and durability
ISO 14523:1999	Photography. Processed photographic material. Photographic activity test for enclosure materials
ISO 14721:2003	Space data and information transfer systems – Open archival information system reference model
ISO 23081:2004	Information and documentation – Records management processes – Metadata for records – Part 1: Principles
British standards	
BS 5444:1983	Specifications for preparation for microfilming
BS 1153:1992	Recommendations for the processing of silver gelatin-type microfilm
BS 5454:2000	Recommendations for the storage and exhibition of archival documents
BS 4971:2002	Repair and allied processes for the conservation of documents
BS 7799:2000	Code of Practice for Information Security Management
BS ISO 12606	Cinematography – Care and preservation of magnetic audio recordings for motion-pictures and television
DISC PD0013:1999	Records Management: a guide to disaster prevention and recovery
ICA	Guidelines on Disaster Prevention and Control in Archives, 1997
Archival bodies	
UK National Archives	*Standard for Record Repositories*, 2004

Finally, TNA's *Framework of Standards* lists all the standards and best practice guidance that informs the National Archives Standard for Record Repositories.[15]

Assessment of preservation needs through surveys, audits and benchmarking

While developing policies and strategies you should also be assessing your organisation's preservation needs by undertaking a survey or audit of your collections. Although you might be only too well aware of the problems, until you can actually quantify them you will not be able prioritise your resources. Surveys can be undertaken of the condition of the building, its environment, security and storage provision as well as of the condition of one or more collections of the archives.

A survey will:

- provide you with a range of useful statistics about levels of preservation provision and the condition of collections;
- alert you to specific areas and collections that need attention;
- assess causes of deterioration;
- enable you to prioritise actions towards improved practice;
- allow the estimation of necessary costs of improvements;
- enable you to make comparisons with other parts of *this* collection, with other collections in the repository and with collections held elsewhere that use the same methodology;
- provide basic data required when applying for funding.

Surveys can be used to measure preservation provision against the standards noted above. Another way of measuring what you do is to compare – or benchmark – your organisation's performance in specific areas with that of similar organisations. This is considered further in Chapters 5 and 7.

> Benchmarks are standards of practice that have developed from a review of a wide range of institutions and then codified to provide others with an indication of what can be achieved at various levels.[16]

By assessing your current resources you will determine which level of practice you might aim to achieve:

- *Basic practice*: the minimum level.

- *Good practice*: a consensus of current professional good practice, tempered by realistic expectations.

- *Best practice*: the highest standard to which you can aspire, much of which is enshrined in published standards.

The UK Museums, Libraries and Archives Council's *Benchmarks for Collection Care* provides a series of benchmarks that describe the quality and breadth of collection care activities across the three domains. It can be used as a self-assessment checklist that helps determine at which of the three levels of practice a service is currently placed. The three levels are used to evaluate the quality of practice in broadly the same areas as those outlined in BS5454 above. Table 6.2 provides an example.

Table 6.2 Benchmarks for preservation practice

Element	Basic practice	Good practice	Best practice
Buildings: fabric A suitably constructed, well-maintained building is fundamental to the protection of collections	The building is of robust construction and all floors, especially in storage areas, can safely support the load	The building in which the collection is housed is wind-proof and watertight, and can provide basic protection for the collection	A building management plan has been drawn up and is frequently reviewed to update priorities and track progress on implementing recommendations

What comprises basic, good and best practice is open to discussion. In the example above best practice for a UK archive service would include explicit compliance with BS5454: the existence of a management plan is not sufficient on its own to demonstrate compliance with specified standards, although it might indicate that certain processes are taking place.

The NPO's Preservation Audit offers another methodology. This enables a snapshot to be taken of practice in such areas as condition, use, value and environmental condition in a 400-item sample of the institution's holdings. Assistance is provided by the NPO, which will manage the data to provide a number of reports. Although this service is paid for by the individual institution it does mean that where a number of institutions use the same methodology comparisons can be made across different institutions and in different regions, to gain a more strategic picture of practice.[17]

These two models may not suit your particular needs. If you plan to devise your own survey form consider the following suggestions. The survey form should:

- be clear about its objectives from the outset;
- keep questions to the minimum required to achieve its objectives (its very tempting to gather masses of data 'while you're at it' that will confuse, and that you will never use);
- be simple enough to allow any member of staff to complete;
- require the completion of each section in a consistent manner;
- be accompanied by guidance notes on the completion of each section;
- present data in a way that can be easily quantified and added to a database;
- be based around a clear view of what reports it will generate;
- be clear about the level of detail required (no more than necessary);
- aim to enable the setting of objectives once all forms have been analysed.

Recognising the attributes of and threats to diverse media and formats

Preservation activities must encompass all media and formats on which information can be stored and presented. 'Media' and 'format' are quite difficult to separate in our minds but these definitions, from the *Concise Oxford Dictionary* might help.

> Medium = 'the means by or through which something is communicated'. For example: parchment; paper; film (emulsion); video/audio tape (image/sounds on magnetic tape); digital and optical (binary digits, non-magnetic, read by laser).
>
> Format = 'the shape, size of' for example, a book or periodical; the style or manner of an arrangement or procedure. For example: rolls, books, folded (deeds), single sheets, files, volumes, photographs, films, microfilm, cassette, disks, CD-ROM, electronic records held electronically in computer system.

Remember: film, video and audio tapes (as well as electronic records) are 'machine-readable'.

There are two basic types of hazard that can cause damage or deterioration to archives: extrinsic and intrinsic.

Extrinisic threats include fire, flood, atmospheric pollution, insect and mould infestation, theft, vandalism and poor handling. The risk of these occurring can be mitigated through the application at the organisational level of proper building standards, environmental controls, and security and handling procedures. I shall consider these in some detail.

Intrinsic threats are those that are inherent in the media themselves. Although the longevity of parchment and paper is understood, that of photographs, microfilm, audio-visual material and electronic records has yet to be fully catered for.

> As a generalisation, the greater the storage density of the medium, the more sophisticated is the equipment needed to access the information stored, and the shorter the life of that medium. The implications for preservation are that either a museum of obsolete equipment in working order needs to be maintained or an ongoing program of data conversion from one medium to a more current medium is required. The first of these solutions is not now longer seriously mooted and attention is being directed towards the latter.[18]

Thus, although our information resources are increasing vastly in quantity they are also becoming increasingly physically vulnerable. Early records are written on parchment, which is a relatively tough material. However, paper is less resilient. Before the mid-nineteenth century paper was made from rags derived from cotton or flax often of good quality. Around 1850 cheaper wood pulp replaced cotton as the main component of paper, resulting in a substance that is intrinsically acidic, is liable to mould growth in damp conditions, and becomes yellowed and brittle in dry conditions. You can see this happening almost before your eyes to a newspaper left on a windowsill. The use of acidic iron gall inks can also eat into the fabric of paper.

Most repositories hold archival material in other intrinsically delicate media too. Photographs are liable to chemical decomposition and fading, particularly if exposed to prolonged light, dust or pollutants. Too high a temperature and relative humidity causes the emulsion layer to become sticky and cause mould growth, while too low a temperature and humidity causes the emulsion to become brittle and crack. Glass plate negatives and positives are easily broken and need individual packaging. Cinematic film, and audio-visual and sound recordings are also vulnerable not only because of their composition but also because of issues surrounding access to fragile originals and the availability of appropriate technology to do so. Film made before 1950 is particularly susceptible: its nitrocellulose base will decompose and blister and may even spontaneously combust. Nitrate film therefore needs early identification and dealing with by experts. Magnetic and optical media have very specific problems. The longevity of these media is not yet known, they are fragile and easily corrupted and so strategies for their preservation and migration must be explicit from an early stage.

Electronic records

There is no doubt that the digital information revolution is having a tremendous effect on the way that most organisations manage information. In practical terms, as described on the National Archives of Australia website,

> corporate information has moved from paper memoranda and letters, to email messages. Reports, books, leaflets and publications of government agencies are now more likely to be accessed through websites. A shared folder on an agency's intranet replaces the correspondence file, and relational database systems replace paper forms and case files.[19]

All this has enormous implications for preservation. Preservation of digital media means the management in the short, medium and long term of electronic data whether born-digital or subsequently digitised and converted to e-media: of office systems, including e-mail and databases, websites and digital images. If their content is archival, then archival repositories must be able to receive and support them in the long term.

What is the implication of having records in such media in an archive? They may be on 'non-traditional' media but still be integral to a collection. Any archive may include photographs, videos, CDs, databases, websites, e-office data, for example. To detach them from the main collection on the grounds of their non-textual media would be to destroy evidence of the business processes of the organisation. However, many archives do not have the resources properly to care for these special formats. Film, sound, internet archives and so on have the expertise to help out: should you deposit them where they can be properly cared for? These kinds of archives prioritise 'film', 'sound' or 'websites' as a medium, which means that items in their collections may be removed from their context of creation. It is a less integrated approach. However, depositing material with these bodies is certainly a solution, provided you can still access it and make clear its place in a collection in your finding aid. The issue of electronic archives is perhaps the most vexed. Although some archives currently use the Internet Archive to store and maintain their websites, in the long term all organisations will have to decide whether they are going to opt for a non-custodial solution such as this or a custodial solution, in which these media are managed in-house.[20] Although national archives are certainly beginning to cater for the digital archive, smaller archives have yet to provide for them.

Preservation activities: buildings, environmental management, storage and packaging, handling and use

Archives may be housed in a variety of locations, whether purpose-built, an adapted building or a room in a cellar. Where they are kept is largely a resource issue, but whether you are aiming at the luxury model or the bargain basement there are some fundamental elements that must be provided.

Buildings

Chapter 7 considers the layout of an archival building in relation to the various functions that it has to accommodate, encompassing public, staff and storage functions, and work flow. It also states that a primary goal is 'to protect the archives against all forces which might otherwise harm them: in particular fire and water, physical or chemical change resulting from a polluted or under-regulated environment; dust, mould and vermin; theft and vandalism.' Although there are certain precautions that all archives should take to counter these, the level of intervention necessary will vary. A risk assessment should be undertaken in order to gauge the degree of potential hazard so that realistic and appropriate measures can be put in place.

Security

First it is necessary to ensure that archives are kept secure from unauthorised access. Strong rooms or stacks where they are located should be kept locked, and accessible to a limited number of keyholders. Where possible storage areas should be windowless and have a single point of entry, not accessible to non-authorised staff or members of the public. Well-resourced services will have an intruder alarm system linked to the emergency services set outside office hours. A record of productions of archives to researchers should be maintained so that the issue of any item can be tracked. Systems for this vary: a typical method is for researchers (and, of course, staff) to complete a request form in triplicate that notes their name, the date, a description and reference number of the document required. One copy of the form will be put in the document's location when it is retrieved, the second will be kept by the production staff, while the third is retained by the researcher. On the return of the document to storage the office copies of the form are reunited and retained as a record that the retrieval process is complete. Increasingly, computerised production systems are operated, with the user keying their document requests. It is quite easy to misplace documents: this system enables you to see what is out at any one time, and to check for example whether a missing item has been mistakenly put back with another item produced at the same time. Details of the storage location of documents should be available only to staff: and although there have been cases of dishonest staff, they are rare.

Archives are most vulnerable when in use. Details of researchers should be registered so that access is monitored. Use should be supervised at all times to ensure that documents are not mishandled or, in the worst case, stolen. It is a constant surprise how ingenious the determined thief can be, and equally the kind of material they seek to steal. A famous case in the UK was of a man who stole archive photographs of girls' schools' sports teams: not considered to be of great cultural or monetary value by staff, so perhaps supervision of this person was less rigorous than it might have been. Loans of archives should only be contemplated where their security can be assured and the exhibition of originals is best avoided.

Environment

Specific environmental conditions need to be in place to ensure the protection and longevity of archives. The most important of these are temperature and relative humidity (RH) of the storage areas. The optimum temperature will vary, depending on the nature of the materials: the basic rule of thumb is that paper and parchment should be stored in conditions that are cooler than that of a normal office, and that photographic, magnetic and optical media should be kept even cooler than that. The BSI recommends that paper and parchment be kept at a fixed point between 16 and 19 °C with 1 °C tolerance above or below; for photographic material between 2 and 18 °C depending on whether it is black and white, colour, moving image, safety or nitrate film.'[21]

RH refers to the amount of water that is suspended in a given volume of air, expressed as a percentage of the maximum amount that that volume of air could hold at the same temperature. Humid climates, where this percentage is high, have an enervating effect on people and documents. Where humidity is high mould can very quickly develop – you will soon recognise the musty smell. Where it is low paper becomes brittle. Mould is active at an RH of 70–75% and spreads very quickly. The BSI recommended RH is at a fixed point between 45 and 60% with a tolerance of 5% above or below. Photographic material should generally be held at 30–40% RH.

There are a number of ways in which to manage atmospheric conditions in storage areas. A heating and ventilation system (HVAC) – air-conditioning – will control both temperature and RH. This will heat and cool air, humidify and de-humidify it, and also extract pollutants from it. Not surprisingly, this is the most expensive solution. It needs to be regularly monitored and serviced. Other solutions might be a system for heating and cooling air only, where the RH is stable and at an acceptable level: but altering the temperature alone will of course affect the humidity too. Portable humidifiers and de-humidifiers can be used to add or subtract moisture from the atmosphere, and although not amenable to fine-tuning they can be useful in extreme circumstances. The cheapest option, where the building is solidly constructed and well insulated, is to rely on the high thermal inertia of the building structure, where internal and external ambient temperature and humidity are balanced. Finally, it is important to ensure the circulation of air throughout the repository to prevent pockets of stagnant and potentially polluted or dust-filled air from accumulating.

If you cannot aspire to expensive systems that can ensure the appropriate temperature and RH at all times, you should at least try to maintain a steady, stable environment within the accepted ranges, avoiding the fluctuations that cause real damage to documents. Countries with seasons of cold humid nights and hot dry days have particular problems in this regard. In order to maintain atmospheric stability you need to monitor it regularly and frequently. Get advice regarding the appropriate monitoring equipment for your storage area. RH can be measured with a hygrometer, temperature and humidity with a thermohygrograph: a conservator will advise on what is appropriate and affordable.

Other environmental hazards are fire, flood, mould, insects and light. Fire is a major hazard, so as far as possible:

- the structure of the building should be of fire-resistant materials, as should floors, doors and shelving, particularly in the storage areas;

- smoking should not be allowed anywhere in the building;

- electrical and other plant facilities should be located away from the main building;

- electrical wiring, if unavoidable in storage areas, should be insulated and switches located outside;

- archives should be boxed, not kept loose: this will delay or negate fire damage, and protect them from subsequent drenching by fire services;

- check alarms and fire suppression equipment regularly;

- keep all chemicals in locked cabinets;

- do not store combustible materials in storage areas.

There are a range of approaches to the detection and extinguishment of fires. The best is where a detection system is linked to an extinguishment system. Fire and smoke detectors will alert staff and the emergency services. Opinions vary as to what is the best means of extinguishing a fire: water, gases such as energen or carbon dioxide. However, gas-based systems tend to be harmful to people and to the environment and BS5454 does not make a specific recommendation here. Sprinkler systems are a common solution: these are activated automatically and can release water directed at the location of the fire only. Hand-held fire extinguishers are recommended too: water-based extinguishers should not be used on electrical fires – for these gas-based extinguishers are recommended. Staff need to be continuously trained in how to respond in the event of fire. It is useful to maintain regular contact with the fire service and vital to ensure that equipment is regularly checked.

Sensible precautions against water and flood damage are:

- do not site the archives in a location liable to flood, or near a river;

- avoid storing archives in basements;

- if water pipes run through storage areas ensure that they are lagged or are fitted with trays;

- do not store material on the top shelf;
- if a storage area has a tendency to condensation on walls, keep a space between the wall and the shelving;
- do not store material on the floor or have shelves less than 15 cm from the floor;
- locate drains and check them regularly;
- inspect roofs for signs of leakage.

Occasionally, more damage is inflicted by fire services extinguishing fires with water hoses: again regular communication with the emergency services can highlight such issues.

Mould and insects can also be a problem. Documents should be carefully inspected for insect and fungal damage before being taken into the storage area. Problems in this area can be treated in accordance with BS4971:2002, Repair and allied processes for the conservation of documents and in National Preservation Office publications.[22]

Exposure to light, especially to ultraviolet rays, has a damaging effect on documents. It leads to oxidation that weakens, bleaches or darkens paper and causes inks and dyes to fade. This damage is cumulative and irreversible: depending on how intense is the exposure and the length of time the document is exposed. Therefore, in areas where archives are viewed or stored the sun should be blocked out and ultraviolet filters placed over windows and light fittings. Documents should be kept in folders and boxes and the exhibiting of original documents should be carefully managed, with lights kept off except when the document is actually being viewed. Electric lighting has implications too: in storage areas it is best to have lights triggered by movement sensors, a solution that is also environmentally friendly. Light is measured in lux (lumens per square metre). BS5454 recommends that light levels should be no less than 100 lux and no more than 300 lux, and that for exhibition purposes the level of light falling on a document should not exceed 50 lux for inks, dyes and light-sensitive pigments. You can measure lux levels using a lux meter obtainable from conservation suppliers.

Storage and packaging

In addition to providing security and an appropriate environment, another overarching preservation activity and next line of defence is their storage and packaging in archival-quality materials. These provide a buffer against changes in temperature and humidity and offer protection against dust, pollutants, water, heat and smoke: boxes can protect their contents from flood damage for a number of hours. Envelopes, folders or polyester sleeves can provide secondary packaging within the box. Books and volumes can be placed in phase boxes; maps in map tubes and bags. Linen tape and brass paper clips should be used for tying and securing items. Packaging materials need to be chemically inert – in particular acid-free – so it is important to use a reputable supplier. The acidity of a material is measured as pH. On a scale of 1–10, pH 1 is extremely acidic and pH 10 extremely alkaline. The optimum pH for paper documents and for storage materials is in the middle of the range: pH 7 is neutral.

Good packaging will ensure that not too many items are crammed in a box, nor placed in a box that is too large. Boxes should be stored flat, and not on their sides – even if well packed, you need to avoid as much movement inside the box as possible. Rubber bands, metal fastenings and paper clips should be removed (an endless task!) and acidic tape replaced with pH-neutral tape. Sticky tape should be removed by a conservator.

Handling and use

Proper maintenance of collections includes good housekeeping, and proper handling procedures by staff and users. Priorities here are good cleaning policies and practices. Dust and dirt accumulate in storage areas and encourage mould and insect infestation, so a regular timetable for cleaning activities needs to be in place. Whether you do the cleaning yourself, employ someone to do it or bring in outside contractors, everyone should be clear about the extent of cleaning required, what equipment should be used, and any health and safety issues. Usual practices are to avoid the use of water in the strong rooms (use a damp cloth); dusting should precede vacuuming, and floors, shelves and boxes should be cleaned, but any loose archives or fragments should be noted and staff informed. Many archives are dirty when they are first accessioned. These should not be allowed into the storage area until they have been assessed and cleaned by conservation staff, as there is danger of infecting other materials.

All staff should receive training in good handling practices, and guidelines should be available to users too. It is likely that staff are more guilty of poor handling than users. The main areas of risk are in the search room, during cataloguing and conservation processes and in transit from storage.[23] Some basic rules include:

- never overload trolleys transporting documents;
- single items must always be transported in a folder;
- maps and plans should be carefully rolled, encapsulated or otherwise supported;
- volumes and documents should never be left on the floor;
- books should not be removed from shelves by their spines;
- volumes should be consulted on a book support or cushion;
- maps should be covered by inert transparent polyester sheet when consulted.

In addition, strict rules on reprographics procedures should be applied. Much damage is done by inappropriate copying practices: it may be necessary to prohibit the copying of certain items. The NPO's *Good handling principles and practice for library and archive materials* provides further useful information.[24]

Emergency planning

All archives need to have a risk management framework to guard against significant risks – often of fire or flood. But however hard you work to prevent a disaster, if one does occur you should have plans for prompt, organised action to minimise any damage. Such plans may be termed an 'emergency plan', 'disaster preparedness plan', 'disaster recovery plan', or something similar. Regardless, it needs to encompass four main functions, those involved in the prevention of and preparedness for an emergency or disaster and those involving response to and recovery from it. If you have followed guidance on the appropriate building, environmental and storage requirements for archives you will already have minimised the risk of occurrence of fire, flood and unauthorised access. You should consider identifying vital records (those which the organisation needs in order to function) and keeping copies of these off-site or backed up elsewhere.

There is plenty of guidance and a range of current examples of such plans, such as those provided by Stanford University's Conservation On-line site, and a number of texts are available.[25]

The role of conservation

So far I have considered preservation, an all-pervasive function applicable to every activity in an archive. Conservation has a more specialised remit within that overall function, and should be carried out by qualified conservators.[26] Conservators should take the lead in promoting the preservation function to all staff and also in training them. However, small archives are unlikely to employ a conservator and will need to investigate the local availability of such expertise. Remedial conservation work involves the application of specialist procedures to stabilise and repair damaged or fragile items. This is costly, because of the specialised materials used and the immense amount of staff time involved; it therefore needs to be undertaken as part of a planned and budgeted activity.

There are a number of principles that conservators apply to their work. These mainly derive from the understanding that the document should be interfered with as little as is necessary to stabilise and strengthen it. All conservation activity should be documented; details of all materials and methods used should be recorded; only compatible materials should be used and no process should either remove or conceal writing on the document. Conservators do not try to restore items to their original state, fill in missing bits of text, for example.

In the UK a number of organisations are involved in issues of conservation, and plenty of guidance is available. Early in 2005 the Institute of Conservation was established. This has resulted from the merger of five bodies, including the Institute of Paper Conservation (IPC) and the United Kingdom Institute for Conservation of Historic and Artistic Works (UKIC).[27] The British Library hosts the NPO discussed above. International bodies include the European Commission on Preservation and Access and the International Federation of Library Associations and Institutions Preservation and Conservation section (IFLA-PAC).[28]

Reformatting materials, creating surrogates and managing digital data

The physical vulnerability of records and archives can be arrested or circumvented through the processes of reformatting and the creation of surrogates. Media on to which surrogate copies may be made include photocopies, film, microfilm, disk and digital media. This aspect of preservation serves to protect the original through the provision of copies for viewing and also enables collections to be presented in new and exciting ways, as exhibitions, learning material, and so on. Policies and techniques are needed to manage these kinds of surrogate materials if they are to be maintained in the long term. In addition to those for digitising non-digital collections, implications also surround the preservation of 'born-digital' items. Records and other objects are now normally created in digital media in the day-to-day business of an organisation, in the process of creating digital publications, and so on.

This section discusses two overlapping areas of preservation:

- in relation to items whose secondary capture, or reformatting, is in a new surrogate medium, other than digital;
- preservation of digital media regardless of whether items are created in, or converted to, digital form.

Reformatting in surrogate media

Copying (reformatting) material from one medium to another has a number of benefits. It:

- prolongs the life of the original by protecting it from further handling;
- makes unique material more widely available through the provision of duplicates;
- protects the security of vital records by enabling storage of copies off-site;
- may assist in reducing high storage costs.

However, if the issue is one of space saving and it is proposed to destroy an original you need to be sure of the longevity of the preservation medium: this is more usually a records management issue than an archival one, and today is likely to be achieved by the scanning and digitisation of originals. Whatever the purpose, proper standards need to be applied in terms of both the quality of the process and the methods of preparation and checking – particularly if originals are destroyed and the surrogates are to be maintained as authentic records, admissible in court for example. There are a number of International and British Standards on microfilming and photographic processes, some of which are listed above and in annexes to BS5454.

Photocopies may be provided where few items need copying; however, photocopies are more normally provided on demand for purchase by users than as a strategy for the provision of surrogates. Surrogate copying creates its own preservation challenge, as there are significant risks to the original material. Inexpert handling, the forcing open of volumes, and the heat and light generated by photocopying machines are the primary causes of damage. There is plenty of guidance on the development of policies and good practice available.[29]

Microfilm continues to be a popular and reliable surrogate material despite the increasing popularity of digitisation. In spite of its disadvantages – researching material on microfilm can be awkward – it remains a cost-effective and proven way of providing a long-lasting copy of archival material. It has been used very successfully in the copying of newspapers and registers of vital events (births, deaths, etc.). About 500 reduced-sized images can be stored on one reel of film for viewing through a microfilm reader. It can be produced in film or fiche form: microfilm usually at 35 mm and microfiche at 16 mm. Microfilm is of archival quality in that it is processed to photographic standards, ensuring the removal of residual chemicals by a prolonged washing period. Microfiche is of less than archival quality: it is processed with ammonia, which is aggressive and is less carefully rinsed.[30]

Repositories may operate an in-house microfilming service or contract it out: the latter should only be done once archival, security and processing standards are agreed. The former is only done in larger repositories, as the costs are predictably quite high.[31] Usually, three copies of each film are made: one archival-quality silver halide master negative, which should be stored off-site, a second negative copy from which duplicates can be made and a positive reference copy for access purposes. These last two do not need the archival qualities of silver halide: diazo or vesicular film will suffice.

Born-digital preservation and digitisation programmes

Preservation in the digital environment has generated an enormous amount of literature, and this can be quite overwhelming. In the archival environment it tends to focus either on preservation of digital media created in the business environment and managed via electronic document and records management systems, or where cultural resources are being made available through digital channels, i.e. between those born-digital and those digitised. It has been pointed out that it is much easier to obtain funding for the latter than the former: 'the long term benefits and requirements of preservation seem often to be overshadowed by the immediate benefits of current access initiatives'.[32]

I can only touch upon the main issues here but recommend the following initial reading. Seamus Ross in *Changing Trains at Wigan* provides a thoughtful introduction to the wide-ranging issues. Neil Beagrie and Maggie Jones provide a useful basic online handbook, which is maintained and updated by the Digital Preservation Coalition. The National Library of Australia provides an excellent website 'Preserving Access to Digital Information' (PADI). This well-organised gateway to resources has an international advisory group and looks at issues, standards, resources, strategies, formats and media, a literature guide and much else. For those who do not know where to start it offers a series of 'trails'; for example, the beginners' trail is designed 'for those practitioners and students who are new to the area of digital preservation and would like to familiarise themselves with the major issues'.[33]

Various digital preservation projects have generated guidance of value in their particular fields of digital preservation. There are many examples of these. In the UK, CEDARS (Curl Exemplars in Digital Archives) is aimed at those with responsibility for digital preservation in the further and higher education community, research libraries and computing services.[34] The Arts and Humanities Data Service (AHDS) is a national UK service aiding the discovery, creation and preservation of digital resources in and for research, teaching and learning in the arts and humanities.[35] UKOLN is a university-based centre of expertise in digital information management, providing advice and services to the library, information, education and cultural heritage communities.[36] The Technical Advisory Service for Images (TASI) offers detailed advice on the technical side of digital imaging.[37] The European ERPANET concentrates on disseminating information about best practice and skills development of cultural heritage and scientific objects, bringing together 'memory organisations, ICT and software industries, research institutions, government organisations, entertainment and creative industries, and commercial sectors'.[38] Any one of these will provide links to parallel projects and organisations.

Digital media come in a wide variety of formats: text, database, audio, film and image. Born-digital material, produced in all areas of human activity, is only ever intended to be viewed by computer: and because the hardware on which it is viewed becomes obsolescent so quickly and the software formats that carry the data are so easily corrupted and superseded, policies need to be in place at the time the record is created if its longevity, and continued accessibility and functionality are to be assured. Born-digital items are more vulnerable than those created as a result of digitising analog materials because if they are lost there is no original to return to. However, both born-digital items and digital surrogates will ultimately pose similar preservation challenges in the long term. Electronic document and records management systems cater for born-digital data, as well as for documents scanned and digitised for business processes, in organisational office systems. These systems are usually selected only after rigorous testing to ensure that they can undertake the required functions while supporting authenticity, reliability and accessibility requirements. Records managers should be involved in this selection process.

Much of the literature agrees on what are the main issues to be faced. In simple terms the nature of the media gives rise to specific problems, whether in the electronic records management or the cultural heritage resource environments. As David Levy says,

> Here is the problem in a nutshell: In the world of paper documents are realized as stable, bounded physical objects. Once a paper document comes into being, it loses its dependence on the technologies that were used to manufacture it. The photocopied memo takes leave of the photocopier, and never looks back: the printed book takes leave of the printer and bindery, and never looks back. But a digital document, because its perceptible form is *always being manufactured just-in-time, on the spot*, can't ever sever its relationship to a set of manufacturing technologies. It requires an elaborate set of technological conditions – hardware and software – in order to maintain a visible and useful presence.[39]

Table 6.3 highlights some of the attributes of digital media that have preservation implications. In the (over-simplistic) 'solutions' column reference is made to the use of metadata, preservation technologies such as migration and emulation, bitstreams and open formats. These need some explanation. The bitstream is the continuous stream of binary digits (0 and 1) ('bits' for short – 8 bits in a byte) stored on the hard drive, memory stick or file server that digitally represent the content being created or stored. Bits are stored in different file formats, depending on what the function of the digital object is, and file names

Table 6.3 Attributes of digital media

Issue	Problem	Solution
Electronic (digital) records are composed of binary digits (bits)	Machine dependency: need interpretative tool to access	Buy/upgrade hardware and software
The message is independent of the medium on which it is stored	Machine dependency: possibility of corruption or loss	Buy/upgrade hardware and software. Encapsulate message in robust metadata
Message can easily be altered	Continued integrity, authenticity and history of the item	Encapsulate message in robust metadata
Media/software fragility means it is inherently unstable	Impermanence of message, speedy deterioration	Regularly migrate, refresh, emulate using stable storage and management
Hardware obsolescence	Old formats inaccessible	Robust regular migration to new formats
Proprietary software	Constraints on use and migration	Save original bit stream, move to open format
General instability and speed of change	Inaction will lead to loss	Continual programme of active management from creation through life cycle

contain an extension that identifies the format of the document. Thus, a textual document might be in Microsoft Word format (.doc) or portable document format (.pdf), a scanned photograph in .tiff or .jpg file format, animated graphics in Java Script, and a web document in hypertext mark up language HTML (.htm), etc. You cannot see the bits, only the way they are represented on-screen. Preserving the bitstream in an open format (one that is not constrained by the requirements of commercial providers such as Microsoft) makes it easier to progress them to new technologies when their current one becomes outdated.

Preservation technologies

As in the preservation of traditional materials, the physical environment of digital media affects their longevity – so careful handling, controlled temperature and humidity, and proper storage should be ensured.

In addition, there are a number of technologies available for preserving digital materials that aim to keep their content accessible in the face of technological obsolescence and media corruption: which one is the most appropriate will depend on the type of data to be preserved and available resources. Technologies include:

- *Technical preservation*: this involves preserving the original technical environment that ran the system, such as the operating system hardware and the original application software. It is a kind of 'computer museum' solution. Keeping all the necessary dated equipment to do this is expensive and unrealistic as an ongoing solution – obsolete technology cannot keep going forever. It is more of a disaster recovery strategy.

- *Refreshing*: here data are copied to a new carrier of the same type. Thus, digital information is carried from one long-term storage medium to another of the same type, with no change in the bitstream (e.g. an older CD-RW to a new CD-RW) so the appearance of the content remains the same.

- *Migration*: here the data are copied or converted from one hardware/software configuration to another, possibly one that is software-independent (i.e. you are not bound by the proprietary restrictions of a specific commercial supplier in how you use the software). This preserves the essential characteristics of the data, although the 'look and feel' might change. It means you can periodically transfer data to a new generation of computer technology while preserving their integrity and enabling users to retrieve and display the data in the face of constantly changing technology.

- *Emulation*: here software and hardware are used to reproduce the essential characteristics and performance of a specific type of computer of a different design. Thus, it allows programs or media designed for one environment to operate in a different one, but to look the same.

If all else fails 'digital archaeology' might help. This is where content from damaged media or from obsolete or damaged hardware and software environments is rescued. It is really an emergency recovery strategy and may involve specialised techniques to recover bitstreams from media that have been rendered unreadable, for example due to physical damage or hardware failure. Specialist commercial services exist for this – and it is very expensive.

Metadata to support preservation technologies

Whatever preservation technology is chosen, the longevity of digital information also depends on the production and maintenance of data *about* the resource that is being preserved so that it can continue to be supported and accessed. Metadata, often referred to as 'data about data', are 'structured information that describes and/or allows us to find, manage, control, understand or preserve other information over time'.[40] If you think of examples of metadata in a paper archival environment you might come up with such things as indexes, catalogues and file covers – even the printed headers on letters. These support, describe and package the information content – and can exist intrinsically (e.g. letter heads, which are contemporaneous) or be constructed extrinsically and subsequently (e.g. an archival catalogue). Without such metadata – or contextual descriptors – the content cannot readily be understood.

Table 6.4   Types of metadata[41]

Type	Definition
Administrative	Metadata used in managing and administering information resources, e.g. copyright, acquisition information, date of digitisation, name of operator, history of actions performed on the digital object, version control
Descriptive	Metadata used to describe or identify information resources, so that users can search, retrieve and interpret the item. e.g. cataloguing records, titles, subject content via controlled vocabularies, user annotations
Structural	Metadata used to describe the internal contexts and relationships between images, e.g. of pages of a book; letters in a correspondence series
Technical	Metadata related to how a system functions, e.g. digitisation information such as formats, compression, equipment used, image specifications, scanner settings
Use	Metadata related to the level and type of use of information resources, e.g. use and user tracking
Preservation	Metadata related to the preservation management of information resources. Might include physical condition, preservation actions taken, technical details on the format, structure and use of the digital content, authenticity information (e.g. technical features, migration, custody history), and the responsibilities and rights information applicable to preservation actions

Proper use of metadata helps end-users, managers and administrators. Users can discover information (title, date of creation, creator, subject matter, for example) and ascertain and evaluate its content. Those managing and preserving the data will use technical and administrative metadata (such as collection details, copyright information, details of the scanning process, file format and resolution) to enable them to manage, maintain and preserve the digital resource. There are different types of metadata that can be used to describe different aspects or functions of the data content. The main ones are shown in Table 6.4.

However, this table should not be seen as a rigid classification: many metadata schemes support multiple functions, so the categories will overlap. The simplest metadata standard, which forms the basis of descriptive standards in most information services, is the Dublin Core Metadata Element Set (DC). Dublin Core defines 15 elements to support simple cross-domain resource discovery: title, creator, subject, description, publisher, contributor, date, type, format, identifier, source, language, relation, coverage and rights.[42] This may remind you of some of the data elements required for archival description in the ISAD(G): that standard could also be viewed as a set of required and optional metadata elements for describing archives.

Preservation metadata are our main concern here, however. Because virtually any metadata element can be seen as having value for preservation purposes, preservation metadata are less a separate category than an amalgam of other types. An international digital preservation standard to support the long-term preservation of digital information is becoming increasingly accepted. Although it does not prescribe a set of preservation metadata *per se*, it does provide a framework and a common language for practice across a wide range of communites concerned with digital preservation. It first started in the space and earth observation communities, but has relevance for many others, including libraries and archives. The aim of ISO 14721:2003, known as the Open Archival Information System reference model, is to establish a system for archiving information that addresses the full range of archival information preservation functions. These include ingest, archival storage, data management, access and dissemination. In addition, it 'addresses the migration of digital information to new media and forms, the data models used to represent the information, the role of software in information preservation, and the exchange of digital information among archives.'[43] This model has been used by many initiatives developing preservation metadata sets and provides a useful reference point to ensure all relevant information has been included.

Digital archives

Whether archive services should store their own 'machine-readable' archives or buy in the services of specialist organisations has already been considered. For large-scale and ongoing projects, accessing specialist services can offer the best solution. TNA is using the Internet Archive's web crawler technology to archive a selection of government websites for its UK Government Web Archive (Figure 6.1). For example, you can look at sites for the Privy Council, 10 Downing Street and the Northern Ireland Office dating back to 2003. The US-based Internet Archive aims to 'build an "Internet library," with the purpose of offering permanent access for researchers, historians, and scholars to historical collections that exist in digital format.'

TNA also uses the National Digital Archive of Datasets for the specialist preservation and provision of online access to archived digital datasets. These comprise statistical data and documents from UK central government departments, the earliest available being generated in 1963. You can access data about the condition of English houses from 1967, attitudes to and experience of crime since 1982, and even information about bats, their roosts and interactions with humans.[44]

Figure 6.1   UK Government Web Archive

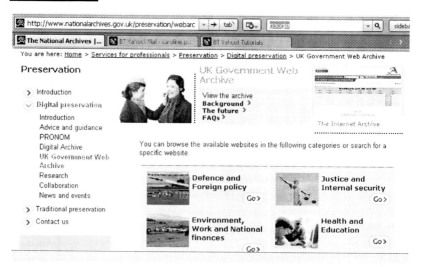

Digitisation projects

For cultural institutions that have the responsibility of collecting and preserving cultural heritage, the creation of digital exhibitions and the digitising of archival collections are more likely to involve the use of digitised surrogates than born-digital objects, but preservation concerns are similar. Preservation is an important aspect in digitisation projects, but unlike for born-digital materials longevity of the surrogate is less of an issue because the intention is not usually to replace or discard the original object.

The NPO suggests the actual digitisation process can be divided into three areas, each with its own activities:

1. *Data capture and creation*: the images are digitised, any associated text (metadata) that describes the images and their content is added and the data (i.e. the digital records: image plus associated text) are stored or archived for future re-use. Activities include: image handling and preparation; image capture; hardware and software; file formats and compression; copyright, intellectual property rights (IPR), ethics and data protection; metadata: image description, indexing and cataloguing.

2. *Data access and delivery*: the image archive owners must plan and implement a delivery mechanism that will ensure the user communities can access the image archive. Activities include: search and retrieval; user issues and access management.

3. *Managing the digital collection*: the production of a high-quality digital image collection that adheres to standards and good practice will be ensured by the co-ordination of 1 and 2. Activities include: database creation and system design; workflow and procedures management; quality assurance; project management; digital preservation and storage.[45]

As indicated, these central activities and processes should be supported by a project management framework to enable you to see the project through successfully from start to finish. There is plenty of guidance available on the different stages to be gone through, managing resources, the types of equipment to use, making technical decisions, and how to ensure quality control and to keep the project on track.[46]

Preservation is an all-encompassing function, and it is incumbent on all of us rigorously to apply appropriate policies and strategies in the care of the material we are responsible for. The development of new media and formats makes it an increasingly complex matter; and increasing demands for access coupled with the need to be proactive from the earliest stages of the life of the born-digital or digitised object means it is a huge responsibility too.

Notes

1. The National Archives (2004) *Preservation Policy*, p. 16, *http://www .nationalarchives.gov.uk/about/pdf/preservation_policy.pdf*
2. Resource (2002) *Benchmarks in collection care*. London: Resource, p. 16.
3. See also Chapter 7 for more guidance on setting policies and strategies.
4. Forde, H. (1997) 'Preservation policies – who needs them?', *Journal of the Society of Archivists* 18: 2, 165–73.
5. National Preservation Office, *http://www.bl.uk/services/npo/npo.html* [accessed 30 October 2005].
6. Foot, M. (2001) *Building blocks for a preservation policy*. National Preservation Office, *http://www.bl.uk/services/npo/npo8.pdf* [accessed 30 October 2005].
7. State Records Office of Western Australia *Policy on preservation of state records*, c.1991, *http://www.sro.wa.gov.au/government/preservation-policy.html* [accessed 30 October 2005].
8. National Archives of Canada (2002) *Preservation Policy*, *http://www .collectionscanada.ca/preservation/1304_e.html*; The National Archives, *Preservation Policy*, 2004, *http://www.nationalarchives.gov.uk/about/ pdf/preservation_policy.pdf* [accessed 30 October 2005].
9. National Archives of Canada (2002) *Preservation policy*, p. 1.
10. The British Library (2002) *Digital preservation policy*, *http://www .bl.uk/about/collectioncare/bldppolicy1102.pdf*
11. ERPANET (2003) *Digital preservation policy*, *http://www.erpanet.org/ guidance/docs/ERPANETPolicyTool.pdf* [accessed 30 October 2005].
12. ScreenSound Australia (2005) *Preservation policy*, *http://www.screensound .gov.au/AboutUs.nsf/Sub+Pages/Publications+Corporate+Policy+Preservation/* [accessed 30 October 2005].
13. National Preservation Office (2001) *A national preservation strategy for library and archive collections in the United Kingdom and Ireland: principles and prospects*, *http://www.bl.uk/services/npo/npo9.pdf* [accessed 30 October 2005].
14. Kitching, C., Edgar, H. and Milford, I. (2001) *Archival documents: guide to the interpretation of BS5454:2000, Storage and exhibition of archival documents*. BSI PD 0024.
15. The National Archives (2003) *Framework of standards*, *http://www .nationalarchives.gov.uk/archives/framework/standards.htm* [accessed 30 October 2005].
16. Resource, *op. cit.*, p. ii.

17. National Preservation Office *Preservation assessment survey: library and archives module*, *http://www.bl.uk/services/npo/paslib.html* [accessed 30 October 2005].

18. Harvey, R. (1993) 'Preservation', In *Keeping archives*. Edited by Ellis, J. Port Melbourne, Australia: Australian Society of Archivists, pp. 74–107.

19. National Archives of Australia, *http://www.naa.gov.au* [accessed 30 October 2005].

20. Internet Archive, *http://www.archive.org/* [accessed 30 October 2005].

21. BS5454:2000 *Recommendations for the storage and exhibition of archival documents*, Section 7.3 and Annex A.

22. National Preservation Office, *The prevention and treatment of mould outbreaks in collections*, *http://www.bl.uk/services/npo/mould.pdf* [accessed 30 October 2005].

23. Rhys-Lewis, J. (2004) *Preservation management*, Version 1.3. University of Liverpool.

24. Available online at The National Preservation Office, *http://www.bl.uk/ services/npo/practice.pdf* [accessed 30 October 2005].

25. Conservation On-Line, *http://palimpsest.stanford.edu/bytopic/disasters/ plans/*; Matthews, G. and Feather, J. (eds) (2003) *Disaster management for libraries and archives*. Aldershot: Ashgate Publishing; Smithsonian Institution, National Archives and Records Administration, Library of Congress, and National Park Service (1993) *A primer on disaster preparedness, management, and response: paper-based materials*, *http://sulserver-2.stanford.edu/bytopic/disasters/primer/* [accessed 30 October 2005].

26. Pickford, C., Rhys-Lewis, J. and Weber, J. (1997) *Preservation and conservation*. Society of Archivists Best Practice Guideline no. 4.

27. Institute of Conservation, *http://www.instituteofconservation.org.uk/ index.html* [accessed 30 October 2005].

28. European Commission on Preservation and Access, *http://www .knaw.nl/ecpa/*; International Federation of Library Associations Preservation and Conservation section (IFLA-PAC), *http://www.ifla.org/ VI/4/pac.htm* [accessed 30 October 2005].

29. National Preservation Office (2000) *Photocopying of library and archive materials*, *http://www.bl.uk/services/npo/pcopy.pdf*

30. National Preservation Office (2000) *Guide to preservation microfilming*. London: The Office.

31. Roberts, D. (1993) 'Using computers and document imaging'. In *Keeping archives*. Edited by Ellis, J. Port Melbourne, Australia: Australian Society of Archivists, pp. 350–84.

32. Beagrie, N. (2003) *National digital preservation initiatives: an overview of developments in Australia, France, the Netherlands, and the United Kingdom and of related international activity*. Washington, DC: Council on Library and Information Resources and Library of Congress, p. 2.

33. Ross, S. (2000) *Changing trains at Wigan: digital preservation and the future of scholarship*. National Preservation Office, *http://www.bl.uk/ services/npo/occpaper.pdf*; Beagrie, N. and Jones, M. *The handbook*, *http://www.dpconline.org/graphics/handbook/*; National Library of

Australia 'Preserving access to digital information', *http://www.nla.gov.au/padi/* [accessed 30 October 2005].

34. CURL Exemplars in Digital Archives, *http://www.leeds.ac.uk/cedars/indexold.htm* [accessed 30 October 2005].

35. Arts and Humanities Data Service, *http://www.ahds.ac.uk/* [accessed 30 October 2005].

36. UK Office for Library and Information Networking, *http://www.ukoln.ac.uk/* [accessed 30 October 2005].

37. Technical Advisory Service for Imaging, *http://www.tasi.ac.uk* [accessed 30 October 2005].

38. Electronic Resource Preservation and Access Network, *http://www.erpanet.org/* [accessed 30 October 2005].

39. Levy, D. (2001) *Scrolling forward: making sense of documents in the digital age.* New York: Arcade Publishing, p. 152.

40. Cunningham, A. (2001) 'Recent developments in standards for archival description and metadata', presented at the International Seminar on Archival Descriptive Standards, University of Toronto, *http://www.archivists.org.au/cds/cunningham.html* [accessed 30 October 2005].

41. Gilliland-Swetland, A.J. (1998) 'Defining metadata', In *Introduction to metadata pathways to digital information.* Ed Baca, M. USA: Getty Information Institute, pp. 1–8.

42. Dublin Core Metadata Initiative, *http://dublincore.org/* [accessed 30 October 2005].

43. ISO 14721:2003 Space data and information transfer systems – Open archival information system – Reference model *http://www.iso.org/iso/en/* [accessed 30 October 2005].

44. The Internet Archive, *http://www.archive.org/*; National Digital Archive of Datasets, *http://www.ndad.nationalarchives.gov.uk/* [accessed 30 October 2005].

45. Young, K. *Managing the digitisation of library, archive and museum materials*, *http://www.bl.uk/services/npo/dig.pdf*, pp. 6–7 [accessed 30 October 2005].

46. UKOLN (2004) *Technical guidelines for digital cultural content creation programmes.* University of Bath, p. 12, *http://www.minervaeurope.org/structure/workinggroups/servprov/documents/techguid1_0.pdf* [accessed 13 January 2006].

7

Managing an archive service

Previous chapters have discussed the attributes of archives and records and considered how we might undertake the core, substantive functions of selecting, describing, preserving and making them available. Now you can move on to considering the strategic and practical issues involved in managing an archive service. This chapter aims to:

- Set out the overall framework for your work. It will consider strategic issues, setting policies and business plans, defining aims and objectives and how you measure your progress towards achieving them.

- Locate these within the context of the range of managerial and archival functions, and consequent activities and processes that you will need to undertake in order to fulfil the stated objectives of your service.

- Discuss tasks related to the facilitative functions of staffing, finance and establishment. Whether you will be engaged in these in a managerial capacity or not, they are an important part of the overall picture.

This chapter will assist you to:

- define your role within your organisation;
- place your organisation in a professional context;
- set organisational missions, goals, aims and objectives;
- establish your own aims and objectives: applying SMART techniques;
- apply project management techniques;
- develop an archives policy;
- take stock of your resources: analysing staffing, finance and accommodation;

- survey your core holdings;
- undertake organisational functions and activities;
- measure progress towards achieving objectives.

Define your own role

You need first to establish your own role and responsibilities. What have you been appointed to do? If you are expected to act as an experienced professional your job description and person specification will remind you of these, and should also show where you fit in to the wider organisational framework. If you are a volunteer or have been called in to start a service from scratch then it may well be up to you to formulate your own role description, and to construct broader aims and objectives.

You also need to have a good understanding of your own position within the administration. Which department do you belong to? Who is your line manager and what authority does he or she have? Which committee do you/your line manager report to? It is a good idea, if you can, to find a 'champion' – someone who has some standing and will support you in achieving some of your goals: making friends and influencing people can be very useful.

The organisational context

In Chapter 2 I considered the factors that helped define the different models of archival authority or service. These are: the source of its authority, the legislative and regulatory environment in which it operates, its sources of funding, its overall mission or goal, its stakeholders, its acquisitions remit and its access remit. Knowledge about all these will enable you to focus your work appropriately and so before you can do much in the way of planning you need to be clear about all these in relation to your own organisation. Where will you find out? Its own website, regular publications such as annual reports and financial statements will all be of use. Small archive services or those that are just starting out may have fewer resources from which to discover this information. In this case you will need to look to organisations and archival services in similar situations to your own: indeed, make contact with some of these – it may prevent you re-inventing an already well-running wheel.

Be clear about the nature of the materials in your care. Are you responsible for the records and archives generated by your organisation? For 'orphaned' archives generated by external bodies? A proportion of manuscript, ephemeral, illustrated and printed items? Museum-type artefacts? And in what media? Just paper and parchment? Or film, audio or other video/audio materials? Electronic records, archives and datasets? Digitised images and archived websites? In due course you will need to conduct a survey of all these in order to determine what plans you will need to put in place in order to manage them properly.

Organisational planning

In order to plan effectively and to think strategically it is important to think managerially, and to appreciate the roles of missions, goals, aims and objectives, and strategies and policies. Management involves a whole new area of terminology and if you are to convince people that you mean business you need to be able to speak their language, and to use it properly. Although it may sometimes seem like jargon, terms such as those described below do have specific meanings and in using them you will demonstrate your understanding of your chosen environment.

A '*mission*' is what an organisation sets out to do: it expresses its purpose, business and values at the highest level. Who are we? What do we do? For whom do we do it? Why do we do it? This is often expressed in a 'mission statement'. A mission statement is useful to have because it can encapsulate in a very few words the basic aims and ethos of an organisation.

A '*goal*' or '*aim*' is directed towards a broad ideal and is consistent with the overall mission of the organisation. It is something the organisation wants and aims to accomplish in the future and is drawn down from the mission statement. It offers a bit more detail than the mission statement, but you cannot measure it: an organisation might have three or four broad aims.

An '*objective*' is a specific and measurable target, with a result expected within a particular time period, and is consistent with a goal or aim. It is a clear 'milepost' along the strategically chosen path to the goal. So goals/aims are broad, general intentions; objectives are narrow and precise. Goals/aims are abstract and cannot be measured; objectives are concrete and can be measured and validated.

A '*policy*' is a set of coherent decisions with a common long-term aim(s) that relate to a specific organisational purpose. You will find it useful to develop a policy for most of the archival functions you identify. This articulates *what* has to be done and *why*.

A '*strategy*' is the action path the organisation has chosen to realise its goals. Strategies establish broad themes for future actions and should reflect reasoned choices among alternative paths. It describes *how* something has to be done and *in what order*. The '*business*' or '*action plan*' is the instrument that forces you to clarify your thoughts and intentions and helps you to achieve the objectives outlined in your strategy.

Developing mission statements

A *mission* statement should explain briefly why the archive exists and what it sets out to achieve: it has to be succinct and to persuade its stakeholders of its values and ethics. It is a high-level statement from which flow all further objectives and activities. The mission statement for the International Red Cross, for example, is 'To serve the most vulnerable', which is very short and to the point, and most importantly is free of jargon. The mission statement of the archives of the British Red Cross might be more precise – perhaps to 'record the history and activities of the British Red Cross'.

Now consider an example I downloaded from the Dilbert website as an object-lesson in what *not* to aim at. In fact there is a mission-statement 'generator' on this website that simply re-arranges the jargon into a meaningless phrase or sentence:

> The customer can count on us to seamlessly revolutionize business meta-services and professionally simplify market-driven solutions for 100% customer satisfaction.[1]

This means very little, shows confused thinking and does not put whatever organisation it is meant to represent in a good light.

Mission statements need to articulate the organisation's purpose, business and value. Below are two from within the archives and library sector that do this quite successfully.

If your archives does not have a mission statement you might find it useful to construct one before going on to consider your aims (or goals) and objectives. Working in this way from the top down will help you focus your long-, medium- and short-term targets appropriately.

Mission statements

The National Archives of Australia:

'The National Archives of Australia promotes good government recordkeeping and encourages community awareness and use of valuable Commonwealth records in its care.'[2]

The Anarchist Librarians Web:

'We are a network of radical and anarchist librarians who are working towards a better world and socially responsible libraries. We get together at library conventions, anarchist conferences, and radical book fairs to put on protests, raise awareness, or simply drink beers together.'[3]

Defining an archive's aims (goals) and objectives

Aims

The *aims* of your archive service, or of the section of it that you are most directly involved with, will be more explicit than its over-arching mission statement (if it has one) and more long term and less detailed than its stated objectives. According to the UK's Government Policy on Archives:

> The three key aims of any archive are **to select** the most important records for long-term safekeeping, to ensure that they are then safely **preserved and stored** and properly managed and to ensure that everyone who needs to can have **ready access** to them.[4]

This makes quite clear the general aims of a service and you might choose to incorporate this quote if it is appropriate in your own situation. Another, from the UK Business Archives Council, again highlights *three* overarching areas of action:

> The objects of the Council are to promote the preservation of business records of historical importance, to supply advice and information on the administration and management of both archives and modern records, and to encourage interest in the history of business in Britain.[5]

Objectives

As discussed, an *objective* is a specific step, a milestone, which helps you to accomplish an aim or goal. You should define a number of objectives that will enable you to achieve a specific goal; these are likely to be ongoing and renewable. If the *aims* of an archives service are to 'select', 'preserve' and 'make accessible' you can see that it is a fairly straightforward intellectual task to derive from these some specific measurable objectives that can be achieved by carrying out specific activities. For example, the 'acquisition' function will have a number of specific objectives ranging from the short, medium to long term and these are represented by a specific activity. Table 7.1 shows a selection of these.

However you describe your objectives, it is obviously crucial that they dovetail in to any wider mission and aims.

Your objectives will clearly depend on your individual circumstances, but planning is always easier if you have a few 'hooks' to hang things on. One way of thinking about this is to remember that:

- the difference between *where we are* (current status)
- and *where we want to be* (mission and aims)
- is *what we do* [target objectives and business (or action) plans].

Objectives seek to answer the question 'where do we want to go?' They also:

- enable an organisation to control its planning;
- help to motivate individuals and teams to reach a common goal;
- provide an agreed, consistent focus for all functions of an organisation.

Table 7.1 Achieving short-, medium- and long-term objectives

Function	Aim	Activity: short-term objective	Activity: medium-term	Activity: long-term
Acquisition	Select the most important records for long-term safekeeping	Publish acquisition policy: December 2006	Approach first tranche of donor organisations January 2007– June 2008	Publish a guide to collections December 2009

Another hook on which to hang your objectives-setting is the widely recommended SMART technique.[6] In order to work properly objectives have to be:

- *Specific*: describe a precise action, behaviour or achievement that is also linked to a measurable rate, number, percentage or frequency.

- *Measurable*: include a system that allows the tracking and recording of the progress made in the action that is the focus of the objective.

- *Achievable*: capable of being reached; i.e. there is a likelihood of success – but that does not necessarily mean easy or simple.

- *Realistic* and have sufficient resources to make it happen (people, money, materials, time); must also be important to the organisation.

- *Timed*: have a date for when the task has to be started (if it is ongoing) and/or completed (if it is short term or project related). Put simply: no date = no good.

Is my objective, to write an acquisitions policy, a SMART one?

- *Specific*: I know precisely what an acquisitions policy must encompass – I have examples from other organisations and have read appropriate guidance.

- *Measurable*: My stepping-stones will include a draft completed in August; to be sent (and returned) for corporate approval by end September; received quotes for the cost of publication also by end September; and have it returned by my selected printer by end November for distribution in December.

- *Achievable*: This is achievable – it is within my competence to do it and is not difficult, but very important to get right.

- *Realistic*: It is not resource-intensive except in terms of time and my dependence on other people delivering. I do not have to get it formally printed, if that proves too expensive. It is a basic plank in my acquisitions platform.

- *Timed*: I have set start and finish dates, as well as interim targets.

I think it is SMART.

Project management

It is quite possible to consider a specific objective as an individual project and to achieve it through the application of project management techniques. A project is 'a unique set of co-ordinated activities, with definite starting and finishing points, undertaken by an individual or team to meet specific objectives within defined time, cost and performance parameters.'[7] In archival terms project management is the methodology used to undertake finite projects that are set up, perhaps as a result of short-term funding – to digitise a collection, conserve a particular series of archives or catalogue a new deposit for example. It could also be a project to change a system: for example, to automate a manual document request system or introduce a new staff post to undertake paid research for enquirers living at a distance.

There is an immense and easily accessible literature on project management. Some of the guidelines I provide here are taken from the Joint Information Systems Sub-Committee (JISC) InfoNet website, but you might prefer to look for others.[8]

When planning a project we must first answer the following questions:

- What are we trying to do?
- When will we start?
- What do we need?
- Can we do it alone, or do we need help?
- How long will it take?
- How much will it cost?

The answers to these will clarify your required outcomes and available resources and will enable you to plan the management of the project in a logical, organised way, following defined steps. This is often called the project life-cycle. If a project fails it is likely to do so because one or more of its component stages was not well managed: timescales were unrealistic, the budget was insufficient, the staff doing the work were not up to speed, for example (Table 7.2).

Table 7.2 Why projects fail[9]

What the user wanted	A tricycle
What the budget allowed for	A bicycle
What the timescale allowed for	A unicycle
What the technician designed	A pogo stick
What the user finally got	A wheelbarrow

There are four main stages in the project life-cycle:

Stage 1: initiation

The principal participants, probably at senior management level, identify the need for a project, decide on what its outcomes should be and determine whether it is feasible. The project team and its leader are identified and any necessary training provided. Documents required include a business case, feasibility study, terms of reference and project scope.

Stage 2: planning

The scope, goals and necessary resources are further defined. Realistic project milestones are established and performance measurement criteria articulated. Documents required include detailed project, financial, quality and risk management plans to ensure that all project phases, activities and tasks have been clearly identified and adequate resources and finances have been allocated.

Stage 3: execution

The project is underway. This phase involves the execution of each activity and task listed in the project plan. While this is happening systematic evaluation and monitoring should ensure that the project is continuing on schedule and within budget and that the predefined stages are reached. Any changes, risks or other issues that might affect the final outcome should be identified and dealt with.

Stage 4: closure

The project is nearing completion. This stage involves releasing the final results and communicating them to all stakeholders, and evaluating the project's success. Decisions about the maintenance of the outcome or system need to be made, and how many improvements might be made in an ongoing or similar project. The project terminates.

A project plan should be in place by the end of Stage 2. This should provide the following details:

- *Identity/name of project.*
- *Project manager*: name the person responsible for the project.

- *Project description*: short description of the project, explanation of business needs and customer requirements and how the project outcomes will meet these.

- *Major tasks/stages*: list the main tasks (usually 5–8) that need to be achieved for the successful completion of the project. Identify team members and who will be responsible for each stage or task. Supply dates for completion of each stage.

- *Resource requirements*: estimate the costs of equipment, supplies, training and person-hours required, and the sources of funding for these.

- *Risk management plan*: identify all possible risks that might affect the project's timetable and budget, and assess the likelihood of any of them occurring.

- *Strategies*: explain the rationale behind the chosen approach to the project and tasks, outlining alternative strategies should risks identified in the risk management plan surface.[10]

With such a logical approach you might think a project could hardly fail. You have a clear mandate, appropriate resources and explicit and timetabled goals. However, some of the greatest stumbling blocks often centre on intangible things such as communication, consultation, leadership and interpersonal skills. The project leader while 'leading' must also actively communicate and consult with stakeholders and team members. Team members also need training in effective communication, recognising that lack of regular and honest interaction can spell disaster. Mutual confidence is probably the most important element in team success, and needs careful nurturing – perhaps not only in office hours.

Developing an archives policy

The instrument that more than any other encapsulates your mission, aims and objectives is your archives policy. This is 'a broad written statement outlining the purpose, objectives and conditions which define the scope of archival activities, the authority under which they operate and the services offered to clients.'[11] It is not the only written policy that you will need to develop – you will need separate acquisitions, preservation and access policies too, as discussed in earlier chapters – but is a high-level and strategic document, and is best kept brief.

Below is a model archives policy, appropriate for a university archives service.

University of Christminster
Christminster University Archives Policy

Status and Authority

The constitution and functions of the University Archives, first approved by Senate in 1965, are set out in the Statutes, Ordinances and Regulations (2004 edition, p. 360). This includes the statement that the Archives Committee 'shall have broad control of the affairs of the University Archives'. The University Archives forms part of the University Library and Special Collections Department. The University Archivist reports directly to the Director of Library Services.

Mission

Christminster University Archives is the guardian of the University's collective memory and acts as a central research facility for the wider community.

Aims

Its aims are: to advise the University on records management and archival issues; to select, preserve and maintain the University's own archives and those externally acquired; and to advance the University's research agenda through the promotion of its archives as an accessible research resource.

Acquisition policy

The University Archives is the place of deposit for the records of the University, its predecessors and affiliated bodies. It seeks to acquire such records of individual students, staff members, groups and societies as will support and illuminate the official administrative record. In addition, it seeks, as a research resource, the archives generated by national and local textile business organisations and associated bodies.

Maintenance and preservation

The University Archives are stored in compliance with the requirements of British Standard 5454:2000 and the National Archives Standard for Records Repositories and in accordance with its own preservation policy. Archives will be arranged, described and catalogued to recognised professional standards.

Access

Unless otherwise agreed at time of acquisition and subject to any legislative exemptions that may apply, archives acquired by Christminster

> University Archives will be made available for use by researchers, including staff, students and members of the public, in conformity with standard access policies, and in accordance with its own access policy. Information contained in accessible archives may be copied at the request of users without restriction subject to standard reprographic procedures and in conformity with copyright legislation.
>
> ### Revisions
>
> Christminster University Archives policy is subject to an annual review cycle. January 2005.

Stocktaking: the survey or environmental analysis[12]

Before you will able to set yourself useful aims and objectives, with specific measurable outcomes, you will have to take stock of your current situation in terms of the resources you have, the job you anticipate having to do and what further resources you will need in order to do it. This is what we need to discuss next, because the results of your stock-taking, or what you might more grandly call your 'environmental analysis', will inform the objectives that you set yourself. Clearly, you will not be able to set 'making archives available to the public' as an objective until you have at best a reading or search room and at worst a table somewhere in the office for people to use.

So at the same time that you are developing your own broad mission, aims and policy documents (more on these below) you will need to spend some time taking stock of your current situation. When you have a clear picture of your resources, assets and liabilities you will be able to write some detailed, and timed, objectives.

Macro- and micro-environments

You have already taken some account of the situation and context of your organisation and of your position within it – thus, you have touched on what in marketing terms are called the 'macro-' and the 'micro-' environments. If you want to analyse these in more detail you can follow recognised analytical models. PEST analysis, applied to the macro-environment, is a methodology used to gauge the political, economic, socio-cultural and technological issues that might affect you from outside, but which you have no power to control. For example, new legislation might require action, or a change in the political leadership of your public authority might mean swingeing cuts across all services: not a lot you can do about it, but it needs to be taken account of in your plans.

You do have a little more capacity to influence your micro-environment. This is the environment beyond your immediate internal setting that affects you directly – it describes the relationship between your service and the factors that influence it and concerns your relationship with your stakeholders. As part of your early environmental analysis you need to consider who your stakeholders are because they can help – or hinder – what you do.

A *stakeholder* is anyone who has, or may have in the future, an interest of any kind in what you do. Stakeholders can come in a variety of guises, external and internal. The UK Public Services Quality Group, which develops standards for application in the records and archives environment, describes them thus:

> persons, corporate bodies or defined groups with an interest in the present and future activities of the archive service. Stakeholders include those with a financial interest (including tax payers in relation to a public service), office holders (e.g. politicians, committee members), executives, employees, suppliers, customers and the local community. In archive services there are two important additional groups: depositors – the donors or lenders of records; future users: the purpose of the preservation of the records.[13]

You might make a list of the stakeholders – those groups of people you are likely to come into contact with on a regular basis – and consider how you might influence their actions to your advantage.[14] To some extent the type of service you work in will define your list, but most of the groups are common (although the titles they have may differ across the corporate, public and charitable sectors). Do not forget that you can make the media a stakeholder too. Nor, as discussed in Chapter 5, that identities can change – a resource allocator might become a user; today's exhibition viewer might become tomorrow's donor or depositor.

Internal environment

What will have an immediate bearing on all your actions is the capacity, or resources, of your third environment – the internal environment. This includes your immediate resources (human, physical, technical and financial) as well as the information resource (the archives) it is your job to manage. You need to obtain detailed information about these. On establishing the range and quantity of resources required you can analyse the strengths and weaknesses of your current situation so that you can plan improvements. You may have come across SWOT (strengths, weaknesses, opportunities and threats) analyses before: an example is shown later in this chapter.

Human resources: staff and volunteers

Probably your most expensive and important resource are the personnel whose job it is to help achieve the objectives of the archives service. It is important to have a clear view of your personnel requirements alongside those of your other resources.

It should be quite easy for you to establish:

- how many staff you have;
- working how many hours;
- at what level: qualified professional, administrative and clerical, volunteer;
- at what annual financial cost
- what proportion of your annual revenue budget are staffing costs.

And for each member of staff:

- what is the defined role of each person;
- what are his or her specific areas of skill and expertise/job description
- what current tasks, in line with objectives, he or she has to achieve.

And for the future:

- what might be the staffing implications of any future planned objectives;
- whether you are in a position to take on more paid staff and/or volunteers;
- what skills will you require staff to have?;
- what you can afford now, and in five years?

Some guidance on staffing is given in the UK National Archives *Standard for Record Repositories*, 2004. It states that 'the number and categories of staff employed in any record repository should be commensurate with the extent and nature of the records held and with the intensity of their use.' And:

> In determining the staff complement of the record repository the governing body should take into account its declared objectives and the following minimum requirements:
>
> (a) to keep the records safe and to make them available for public inspection
>
> (b) to advise the governing body and, where relevant, other owners of the records on their care, and to prepare adequate finding aids to the records
>
> (c) to take all necessary practical steps for the preservation and conservation of the records.
>
> Beyond the very smallest, record repositories accordingly require the services of:
>
> (a) one or more professionally qualified archivists with training or experience relevant to the kind of records held.
>
> (b) one or more professionally qualified conservators
>
> (c) one or more non-professional archivist or records assistants, and appropriate clerical staff
>
> (d) support staff, who may include word processor/keyboard operator(s), porter(s) and cleaner(s).[15]

This may, of course, be beyond your wildest dreams (especially the conservator – these are hard to get at the best of times, and you may need to outsource this activity). But a standard such as this is very useful and you can hold it up in front of your budget holder or resource allocator as an accepted, required standard for reputable repositories. The range of staff and expertise required will depend on the nature of your service. A business archive with few external users will be less concerned with staffing a search room than with promoting the value of the archive to the company itself – so a promotions officer could be a priority. A public archive might employ an education officer to encourage schools' use of archives; or a museum archive might need a photographer in order to improve the quality of exhibition work. A useful rule of thumb is to aim at having:

- more support and administrative staff than professionally qualified;
- no more volunteers than you have the capacity to plan for and supervise properly.

Managing staff is, and should be, time consuming. Whether they are paid or volunteers, staff will need a description of the duties expected of them; agreed outcomes; appropriate support in the implementation of their duties – including training; and regular meetings to discuss progress and agree further targets.

Financial resources: the budget – purpose, process, content

Purpose

The budget is the allocation of financial resources you receive in order to achieve particular goals, and deliver specified services. It is essential to have a budget to run a service, and caring for archives must always be considered a long-term investment, given that we seek to secure their indefinite existence and protection. You cannot deliver a good service if you cannot rely on year-on-year (revenue) funding; you can only plan for short-term goals, and there may be conditions attached to the funding which mean you cannot set your own priorities. Services that depend on short-term project funding are bound to be less robust than those that are part of an ongoing sustainable establishment.

> The archivist in charge should be responsible to the governing body for an identifiable budget.[16]

Funding is normally received:

- Directly from a parent body: for example, the Rothschild Archive is funded via a trust, an independent body of family members and advisers committed to securing the future of the collection and to developing its use; Cheshire and Chester City Archives and Local Studies Service is funded by Cheshire County and Chester City Councils.
- From external bodies: grant-making organisations, such as the National Historical Publications and Records Commission (NHPRC) in the US, which helps non-federal institutions to preserve and make records accessible; or the Heritage Lottery Fund in the UK, which

gives grants to a wide range of projects involving the local, regional and national heritage.

- From both these types of sources.

Let us assume that you have some measure of sustainable funding. You are assured of revenue and you know how much it is: you also need to find out how the budgeting process and budgeting cycle is managed and by whom, and what level of responsibility you will have in this. The more influence you can bring to bear, the better.

Case study:
England and Wales local authority archives service

What you do with your budget will need to tie in with your stated policy objectives and be part of the wider business planning process. For example, in a UK local government environment the council will set its broad objectives for the authority as a whole in the light of central government policy themes, such as enabling life-long learning or fostering social inclusion. Each department and service, including the archives service, will then develop its own medium-term objectives and immediate action plans, which identify activities that can contribute to these corporate objectives within their own particular core purpose or function. In the case of an archive service, support for 'life-long learning' might manifest itself in, say, collaboration with the University of 3rd Age for a course on how to use the archives, in retirement.

Process

In the model we are discussing here, where you have an annual budget, this will normally be allocated year by year, although you might receive longer-term settlements in line with government policy. In practice, there is likely to be considerable continuity in budget from year to year, most of which will go on core functions: policy initiatives normally affect only a relatively small part. The budget would normally be prepared by you or your line manager in discussion with the relevant funding committee, during the autumn, to be ready for the start of the financial year the following April.

Budgets are divided into two types of expenditure: capital and revenue

Capital funding is intended essentially for one-off projects, such as new buildings, major purchase of an archival collection, or a new computer

---

system. This kind of funding is sometimes treated almost as internal loan; it can have ongoing revenue consequences (while you are paying it back) for many years. Th UK Government sets limits for local authorities on capital spending and currently encourages them instead to take part in private finance initiatives (PFIs), because its policy is to complete new capital-intensive projects without increasing public spending.

Revenue is the normal recurring expenditure that you get and spend year-on-year. Below is an example of the kind of budget that is operated by UK archive services in the local authority public sector. You might find it useful as a checklist in your own case and tick off items of expenditure that you will have to consider making provision for. Your overall budget may be divided under a number of budget heads according to the staff, supplies and services and other facilities you need to buy in, and it will take skilful planning to allocate the appropriate funds to each, and to stay within your target limits. This gets easier with experience: price your commodities carefully, and keep auditable records of all transactions so that you can provide a sound end-of-year financial report. You need to know how much if any you can carry over until the next year – there is no point in under-spending if you cannot use it later.

Revenue expenditure

Staff

- salaries; oncosts (pensions superannuation , National Insurance, etc.)
- travel, subsistence
- training

Premises

- heat, light, rates, water, maintenance, rent
- furniture, cleaning
- telephones, computer maintenance

Central charges (your contribution to services provided by the organisation, but outside your specific service)

- IT, financial and legal services, personnel, accountancy, administration costs

Capital charges

- revenue effects of capital expenditure – a form of interest on the capital sum

Staff, premises, central and capital charges are costs over which the archivist may have limited control. Salaries usually take up by far the largest part of any budget.

Supplies and services

- transport
- conservation/storage materials (e.g. boxes, shelving, trolleys, conservation materials)
- document purchase
- stationery, reference books
- office equipment, photocopiers, etc.
- exhibition equipment

Supplies and services are costs that you may have direct control over.

Income

Sales

- photocopies, publications, photographs

Services

- archive services to other authorities
- research consultancy
- records management
- talks and exhibitions

Charges

- donors' and depositors' contributions
- admission

Grants

- Lottery or other grant funding

One analysis of local authority services in England and Wales showed that, overall, 52% of costs went on staff, 13% on premises, 25% on central charges and only 8% on supplies and services.[17]

You may well be working in a much smaller and less well-established operating environment. It is possible, though, to extrapolate from the above example to suit your own purposes.

Table 7.3   Archives service budget

Blankshire Archive Service	
Budget head	£ 000
Expenditure	
Salaries and staff-related	460
Premises-related	76
Central and support charges	91
Capital charges	23
Supplies and services	75
Total expenditure	£725,000
Income	
Other authorities	184
Publications and reprographics	27
Research consultancy	8
Total income	£219,000
Revenue expenditure	£506,000

Financial and personnel management are, as you will recall, facilitative functions: you need to be able to do these well in order to carry out your service's core, or substantive, functions satisfactorily.

Physical and technical: accommodation, equipment and facilities

Buildings and accommodation

The archive service's accommodation needs to be able to cater for the successful implementation of its three core aims of selecting, preserving and making available archives for the long term. However large or small your provision, the space you occupy must serve the disparate needs of staff and administration, internal clients and/or public users accessing material, and of the archives themselves. Beyond this it is difficult to generalise because the type of provision will depend on a variety of factors such as the size and nature of the collections, their media, the kind of use it is anticipated they will get, and – above all – what resources are available over what time period to cater for them.

Three reference works used particularly by UK archivists as benchmarks in the provision of archival accommodation are the British Standard BS5454:2000, Christopher Kitching's *Archive buildings in the United Kingdom, 1977–1992* (which is currently being updated) and the National Archives *Standard for record repositories*, the last being available from the National Archives website.[18] Although these supply essential information about the construction and conversion of buildings, they also offer much practical advice where smaller scale solutions have been decided on. Kitching states:

> There are ... two fundamental keys to success: and they are more a matter of objectives than bricks and mortar ... (1) to protect the archives against all forces which might otherwise harm them: in particular fire and water, physical or chemical change resulting from a polluted or under-regulated environment; dust, mould and vermin; theft and vandalism; and (2) to promote also the work and well-being of everyone (staff and public alike) going about their business there.[19]

Accommodation solutions might vary from a purpose-built archival facility; a conversion of an existing building to archival use; shared use, for example with a library or museum; to the provision of one or two rooms. There is much good advice available elsewhere but the following checklist might be useful (Table 7.4).

Ask yourself:

- What materials do I want to store?
- What are their particular storage needs?
- What is their quantity?
- What rate of accessions, and therefore growth in storage capacity do I need?
- What level of access will be required; how many users?
- Supported by how many staff?

Within the building or rooms allocated to the service it is important to be able to segregate the archive services functions depending on their different required levels of security, environmental control, access, human comfort, and so on.[20] These are usually divided into:

Table 7.4 Accommodation options

	Select	Avoid
Purpose built	Free-standing design; constructed of brick, stone or concrete; protection against intruders, fire, flood, pests; room for expansion	Floodplains; proximity to potentially hazardous neighbouring properties; poor transport links
Conversion	Check construction materials; load-bearing capacity of floors	Buildings which will not enable separation of functions
Shared use	Capable of being isolated. Choose neighbours with similar access, storage and security requirements	Situations where you have no control over other parts of building or activities in it
Rooms	Choose adjacent rather than separated rooms that can be secured and access controlled	Basements; shared access; storage with water pipes; heating or air conditioning plant

- storage
- staff offices and processing areas
- public areas
- technical services (e.g. conservation, reprographics)
- plant

The last two are probably confined to larger archives. The smallest service might store archives, provide access to them and undertake administrative work all in the same room. But it is better if areas can be divided so that they reflect and support the needs of the archives themselves. Allocation of space in relation to these functions requires careful planning. Storage typically takes up more space than processing, administrative and public areas together: one formula suggests that 60-70% of space is allocated to storage, the remaining 30–40% being divided among the public and staff areas.[21]

Archive storage areas need to be kept secure from unauthorised access, and to have a stable environment in terms of temperature and relative humidity. This will mean a cooler environment than public and working areas, ideally within the range 16–19°C and with a constant relative humidity within the range 45–60%. Audio-visual and digital materials need to be kept even cooler. As the security of archives is paramount, the public should not have unauthorised access to staff or storage areas and all use of the archives themselves should take place in the public search room where use and users can be logged and supervised.

The other balancing act relates to work flow. While maintaining separate staff, public and storage areas might work well in terms of environmental, access and security requirements, you still have to maintain good lines of communication between them. What routes will the records, staff and people need to take within the building? Archival storage at the opposite end of the building from the public search room, or that is located in a basement with no lift to a search room two floors above, or where you can only access a public lecture room through the search room or a secure staff area do not make for smooth and efficient functioning of the service.[22]

Surveying the archives

Having considered infrastructure – staff, finance and accommodation – we should now turn our attention to the actual and potential content of our strong rooms, the archives and other materials that will be our job to manage.

Surveys are regularly undertaken for a range of reasons: as part of a records management programme; to determine preservation requirements; to allocate archival cataloguing priorities, for example.[23] A survey is one of a range of ways in which data can be gathered, and it provides information on which you can base your future activities. The best surveys are those that are clearly focused on collecting data for a stated purpose, with defined outcomes established in advance; the worst are those that are insufficiently planned and that collect large amounts of data much of which are subsequently unused or unusable.

We want this basic survey to enable us to collect raw data about our collections on a survey form that we can enter into a database and that we can interrogate in a number of ways. If databases are not for you, you can present your findings in the form of a tabulated analysis. What fields should your survey form include? Here there is some difficulty in being prescriptive because so much depends on individual situations. Will you be surveying current records, in files and series, as well as archival? Will they include printed book materials, video, audio and/or digital materials as well as paper-based ones? Will the materials be located in one or more places? Will they be 'in-house' materials, collected from sites around your organisation? Or will they be 'orphaned' archives that you have to go and collect from external bodies, of widely varying provenance?

Example of survey

A quantity of material in a former caretaker's basement of my organisation has come to my attention. He is known to have hoarded old departmental files, and it is suspected that friends of his passed on some 'archival' material rescued from a library that had subsequently been demolished. The intended outcome of my survey is to transfer to archives those that have some continuing value. I therefore need to identify for each identifiable block of material that appears to 'belong' together [this might be a run (series) of files or volumes or individual files; a 'collection' of archives, etc.] specific characteristics or attributes to be fed into relevant fields on the survey form.

About the survey

Date of survey
Name of surveyor
Name/tel./e-mail details of contact at record location

About the records

Location
Nature and description of content (title, if supplied)
Source (if known)
Owner or custodian (if known)
Quantity (linear or cubic feet or metres)
Covering dates
Medium
Format
Physical condition

Decision

Destroy (with permission, if available)
Sample
Transfer to archives
Remove for further appraisal

You will find you often have undertake surveys in less than perfect conditions, and need to be prepared for this. I have spent many hours in dark, previously flooded basements trying to peel files off the floor, or in freezing church vestries with no kettle or toilet in sight. So as well as taking the usual necessary equipment, boxes, archival tape, chalk, pens, pencils, rubbish sacks, etc., remember to dress appropriately and bring your own refreshments.

The final analysis

Once you have identified your stakeholders, defined some overall goals or aims and measured your resources, you are in a position to evaluate your current circumstances and key issues in an informed way. One method of doing this is via a SWOT analysis (see Table 7.5). This will enable you to identify the strengths and weaknesses, opportunities and threats that are relevant to your situation. You can then concentrate on formulating some more detailed, timed, objectives based on what you have discovered. Complete each section to fit your own situation.

Strengths and weaknesses are generally considered to be internal whereas opportunities and threats are perceived as coming from outside (but different from PEST analysis discussed earlier, and which is to be more concerned with external environments). Weaknesses are often the downsides of your strengths – for example, you do have an annual budget, but it is half what you needed. So you have to choose between fitting out a conservation unit and racking for one of the stacks or strongrooms, versus a filing cabinet for yourself or a desk and chair for your users, depending on your situation. Or, your colleague is brilliant with the public but is computer-illiterate. Opportunities might include

Table 7.5   SWOT analysis

STRENGTHS	WEAKNESSES
OPPORTUNITIES	THREATS

making a friend on your governing board or committee, or a new grant aid scheme aimed at smaller archive services; while a threat might result from cost-cutting exercises beyond your control. A word of warning: SWOT analysis can be a very subjective exercise. Try doing it with a colleague and compare notes.

Measuring your performance

There are all kinds of reasons why it is important to measure your progress towards achieving your objectives and judging your performance on a regular basis. It:

- improves the quality of your service;
- assists with the decisions that have to be made about the allocation of resources;
- shows that you are accountable to your stakeholders in your actions;
- enables you to plan realistically, based on past performance;
- and involves measuring, evaluating, and monitoring your progress systematically.[24]

An example of some objectives, set in relation to specific activities within the acquisition function, was given earlier in this chapter. The targets set there were quite specific and you would be able to assess whether you have achieved them on time or not. You might include some interim targets, and introduce some further measures. For example, in order to fulfil your medium-term objective, of approaching the first tranch or section of donor organisations (e.g. local businesses or schools) you would need to have determined how many of these there were; their contact details and so on. Your operational plan will be made up of such objectives, which will include measurable performance targets.

As well as measuring performance against specific objectives with internally set targets, there are other ways of assessing 'performance' using it to assess products and services on an ongoing basis.

If you are required to do this in a formal way you should seek further information on performance measurement.[25] Even if you are doing this for no more than an end-of-year review, it is useful to understand how it works. The first stage is to measure how you are doing against your own targets. But it makes sense to look beyond your own institution and consider how others are operating in the same area or sector, locally and nationally and using the best of these as a 'benchmark' with which to compare. The basic plan or cycle is: set objectives, identify performance standards, and compare results against standards, than make corrections and alterations.

You can measure your success through the application of 'performance indicators' – these measure your actions in achieving a given objective. Performance indicators can measure:

- *Input*: what resources you used (staff time; money; equipment).

- *Output*: how much work was completed, or service delivered over a period of time (number of collections catalogued; researchers through the door; enquiries answered).

- *Outcomes*: the quality of work accomplished or service provided (researcher experience; range of collections acquired or catalogued).

- *Efficiency*: the cost per unit of output or outcome (cost per researcher visit; cost per volume conserved).

Using these indicators you can both count statistics (we had 600 remote users accessing our website) as well as determine the nature or quality of your service provision (85% found our service to be excellent), i.e. perform quantitative and qualitative analyses. It is much easier to count statistics than gauge the quality of a service, but currently organisations and funders also want to know what is the quality or 'impact' of your service – so you need to be able to measure it.

The Public Sector Quality Group is developing performance indicators for the archive sector in the UK, and a small sample of these will help to show what I mean. The area that is being measured here is that of the level of provision of access to and use of the archives, and within that, information about individual visits and satisfaction ratings (Figure 7.1):

With each of these are details of the purpose of the indicator (*what* it measures), rationale (*why* the measure is needed) and definition (*how* to measure it). Information derived from these will satisfy questions about statistical provision as well as its quality. It is primarily aimed at public local authority services, although there is plenty here also of relevance to other types of services. If used widely it will enable a comprehensive comparative picture of archive provision in the UK to be made. Further suggestions on evaluating your service are provided in Chapter 5.

Figure 7.1   Sample of performance indicators from the UK National Council on Archives: Public Sector Quality Group Performance Indicators: Towards generic and universal PIs for archives, August 2003

Phase 1: Access and Usage (front of house)

1. SERVICE DELIVERY OUTCOMES[26]

1.1. Usage – Visits (individual)

    1.1.1.   Visitor numbers

    1.1.2.   Purpose of visit

    1.1.3.   Subject of enquiry

    1.1.4.   User familiarity with services

    1.1.5.   Length of visit / dwell time

    1.1.6.   Services / facilities used

    1.1.7.   Material consulted

2. QUALITY

2.1. Overall satisfaction ratings of service users

    2.1.1.   Service satisfaction ratings of service users

    2.1.2.   Value of archives services as perceived by users

---

Moving on

You are now equipped to apply your knowledge and skills in a wide range of practical situations in the workplace. You understand your role within the organisation, and the general aims to which it, and you, aspire. You know what your resources are in terms of staff, money and facilities, and the strengths and weaknesses of these. Your objectives will be planned and undertaken within these parameters, and centred on the core archival functions and activities described in earlier chapters. You will also be able to measure the degree to which you have achieved your objectives, because you will have set yourself clear targets. You will be aiming to succeed.

Notes

1. The Dilbert website is available at *http://www.dilbert.com* [accessed 14 February 2005].
2. National Archives of Australia, *http://www.naa.gov.au/* [accessed 14 February 2005].
3. Anarchist Librarian's Web, *http://www.infoshop.org/alibrarians/public _html/* [accessed 14 February 2005].
4. Lord Chancellor's Department (1999) *Government policy on archives*, *http://www.nationalarchives.gov.uk/policy/idac/government.htm* [accessed 11 January 2006]
5. Business Archives Council, *http://www.businessarchivescouncil.com/* [accessed 14 February 2005].
6. For example in the Dorling Kindersley Essential Managers series such as: Hayward, A. (2001) *Essential managers: do it now!* London: Dorling Kindersley.
7. Office of Government Commerce, *http://www.ogc.gov.uk* [accessed 30 October 2005].
8. Joint Information Systems Sub-Committee, *http://www.jiscinfonet.ac.uk/ InfoKits/project-management/pm-intro-1.4* [accessed 30 October 2005].
9. Adapted from JISC, *http://www.jiscinfonet.ac.uk/InfoKits/project-management/pm-intro-1.2* [accessed 30 October 2005].
10. Kurtz, M.J. (2004) *Managing archival & manuscript repositories*. Chicago: Society of American Archivists, pp. 89–100.
11. Schwirtlich, A-M. (1993) 'Getting organised', In *Keeping archives*. Edited by Ellis, J. Port Melbourne, Australia: Australian Society of Archivists, p. 26.
12. One of many websites dealing with these issues is *http://www .marketingteacher.com/Lessons/lesson_marketing_environment.htm* [accessed 15 February 2005].
13. Public Services Quality Group (2003) *Standard for access to archives*, available from the website of the UK National Archives, *http://www .nationalarchives.gov.uk/archives/psqg/* [accessed 30 October 2005].
14. Arrowsmith, A. (1999) 'Talking with hedgehogs: archival profile and communications', *Journal of the Society of Archivists*, 20:1 93–7 provides a useful list: she calls her stakeholders 'hedgehogs'.
15. The National Archives (2004) *National archives standard for record repositories*, *http://www.nationalarchives.gov.uk/archives/framework/ repositories.htm*, Section 2 [accessed 11 January 2006].
16. National Archives (2004) *op. cit.*, Section 1.6.
17. Published details are available from the Chartered Institute of Public Finance and Accountancy Archives Services Statistics 2003–4.
18. BS 5454:2000 *Recommendations for the storage and exhibition of archival documents*; Kitching, C. (1992) *Archive buildings in the United Kingdom, 1977–1992*. London: HMSO; The National Archives *Standard* (2004), *op. cit.*
19. Kitching, C., *op. cit.*, p. 10.

20. Kitching, C., *op. cit.*, p. 11.
21. Schwirtlich, A.-M., *op. cit.*, pp. 50–2.
22. Kitching, C., *op. cit.*, p. 61.
23. Preservation audits and surveys are discussed in Chapter 6.
24. Evaluation of access provision is discussed in Chapter 5.
25. NARA National Archives and Records Administration Archives Library Information Center annotated Bibliography on Performance Measurement, *http://www.archives.gov/research_room/alic/index.html*; UK Audit Commission Library of Performance Indicators, *http://www.audit-commission.gov.uk/performance/*; UK National Council on Archives: Public Sector Quality Group Performance Indicators: Towards generic and universal PIs for archives, August 2003, *http://www.nationalarchives.gov.uk/archives/psqg/* [accessed 30 October 2005]; Williams, C. (2003) 'Data collection and management in the archival domain', *Journal of the Society of Archivists*, 24:1, 65–81.
26. These are more like 'outputs' according to my definition.

Bibliography

Details of the publications referred to in the text are brought together below. General standards, reference books and articles on archives and records management are supplied in the first section. Many of the general works listed there include chapters on the specific core archival functions that form the basis of this volume. Items relating to these specific functions follow thereafter.

Archives and Records Management: general

ARLIS/UK & Ireland Visual Archives Committee (2003) *First steps in archives: a practical guide.* Art Libraries Society.

Arrowsmith, A. (1999) 'Talking with hedgehogs: archival profile and communications', *Journal of the Society of Archivists*, 20:1 93–7.

AS 4390.1-1996, *Records Management*, Standards Australia, Australian Standard Homebush, NSW.

Best, D. (2002) *Effective records management – Part 1: a management guide to BS ISO 15489-1*, BSI DISC PD0025-1: 2002. London: British Standards Institute.

Bradsher, J.G. (1988) *Managing archives and archival institutions,* London: Mansell.

Cook, M. (1999) *The management of information from archives*, 2nd edn. Aldershot: Gower.

Cox, R.J. (1992) *Managing institutional archives: foundational principles and practices.* New York: Greenwood Press.

Cox, R.J. (2001) *Managing records as evidence and information.* Westport: Quorum Books.

Duchein, M. (1992) 'The history of European archives and the development of the archival profession in Europe', *American Archivist* 55: winter, 14–25.

Ellis, J. (ed.) (1993) *Keeping archives*. Port Melbourne: Australian Society of Archivists.

Erlandssohn, A. (1997) *Electronic records management: a literature review.* Paris: International Council on Archives, Committee on Electronic Records.

Hunter, G.S. (2004) *Developing and maintaining practical archives*. New York: Neil-Schumann Publishers.

ISO 15489-1: 2001. *Information and documentation - records management – part 1: general.* International Standards Organization.

Jenkinson, H. (1966) *Manual of archive administration*, 2nd edn. London: Lund Humphries.

Jimerson, R.C. (ed.) (2000) *American archival studies: readings in theory and practice.* Chicago: Society of American Archivists.

Ketelaar, E. (1997) 'The difference best postponed', *Archivaria* 44: Fall, 142–8.

Kurtz, M.J. (2004) *Managing archival & manuscript repositories.* Chicago: Society of American Archivists.

McKemmish, S., Piggott, M., Reed, B. and Upward, F. (2005) *Archives: recordkeeping in society.* Wagga Wagga, NSW: Centre for Information Studies, Charles Sturt University.

Mackenzie, G. (1999) 'Archives the global picture', *Archives* XXIV:101, 2–15.

Mcleod, J. (2002) *Effective records management – Part 2: Practical implementation of BS ISO 15489-1,* BSI DISC PD0025-2. London: British Standards Institution.

MacNeil, H. (2000) *Trusting records.* Dordrecht: Kluwer.

Nesmith, T. (1999) 'Still fuzzy, but more accurate: some thoughts on the "ghosts" of archival theory', *Archivaria* 47: Spring, 136–50.

O'Toole, J. (2002) *Understanding archives and manuscripts.* Chicago: Society of American Archivists.

Parker, E. (1999) *Managing your organization's records.* London: Library Association.

Posner, E. (1972) *Archives in the ancient world.* Reprinted (2003). Chicago: Society of American Archivists.

Schellenberg, T.R. (1956) *Modern archives.* Chicago: University of Chicago Press.

Schellenberg, T.R. (1965) *The management of archives.* New York: Columbia University Press.

Shepherd, E. and Yeo, G. (2003) *Managing records: a handbook of principles and practice.* London: Facet Publishing.

Statistical Information Service (2005) *Archive services statistics 2004–5.* London: Chartered Institute of Public Finance and Accountancy.

The National Archives (2003) *Framework of standards. http://www .nationalarchives.gov.uk/archives/framework/standards.htm*

Turton, A. (ed.) (1991) *Managing business archives.* Oxford: Butterworth Heinemann.

UK National Council on Archives (2003) *Public Sector Quality Group Performance indicators: towards generic and universal PIs for archives,* available at *http://www.nationalarchives.gov.uk/archives/psqg/*

Williams, C. (2003) 'Data collection and management in the archival domain', *Journal of the Society of Archivists,* 24:1, 65–81.

Appraisal

Abraham, T. (1995) 'Documentation strategies: a decade (or more) later', paper presented at the annual meeting of the Society of American Archivists, August 1995.

Booms, H. (1987) 'Society and the formation of a documentary heritage: issues in the appraisal of archival sources', *Archivaria* 24: Summer, 69–107.

Cook, T. (1992) 'Mind over matter: towards a new theory of archival appraisal', In *The archival imagination: essays in honour of Hugh Taylor.* Edited by Craig, B.L. Ottawa: Association of Canadian Archivists, 38–70.

Cook, T. (2004) 'Macro-appraisal and functional analysis', *Journal of the Society of Archivists* 25:1, 5–18.

Cox, R.J. (1994) 'The documentation strategy and archival appraisal principles: a different perspective', *Archivaria* 38: Fall, 11–36.

Cox, R.J. (1995) 'Archival documentation strategy, a brief intellectual history 1984–1994, and practical description', *Janus* 3: 76–93.

Cox, R.J. (1996) *Documenting localities.* Lanham, MD: Scarecrow Press.

Cox, R.J (2004) *No innocent deposits: forming archives by rethinking appraisal.* Lanham, MD: Scarecrow Press.

Craig, B. (2004) *Archival appraisal: theory and practice.* Munich: KG Saur.

Duranti, L. (1994) 'The concept of appraisal and archival theory', *American Archivist* 57: Spring, 328–44.

Ericson, T.L. (1991–2) 'At the "rim of creative dissatisfaction": archivists and acquisition development', In *American archival studies:*

readings in theory and practice (2000). Edited by Jimerson, R. Chicago: Society of American Archivists, 177–92.

Golder, H. (1994) *Documenting a nation: Australian Archives: the first fifty years*. Canberra: Australian Archives.

Greene, M. (1998) '"The surest proof": a utilitarian approach to appraisal', In *American archival studies: readings in theory and practice* (2000). Edited by Jimerson, R.C. Chicago: Society of American Archivists, 301–44.

Ham, F.G. (1975) 'The archival edge', *American Archivist* 38: January, 5–13.

Honer, E. and Graham, S. (2001) 'Should users have a role in documenting the future archive?', *Liber Quarterly* 11: 382–99.

Kitching, C.J. and Hart, I. (1995) 'Collection policy statements', *Journal of the Society of Archivists* 16:1, 7–14.

Menne-Haritz, A. (1994) 'Appraisal or documentation: can we appraise archives by selecting content?', *American Archivist* 57: Summer, 528–43.

Raspin, G.E.A. (1988) 'The transfer of private papers to repositories', *Society of Archivists Information Leaflet no 5*.

The National Archives (2004) *Appraisal policy*; also available at *http://www.nationalarchives.gov.uk/recordsmanagement/selection/pdf/appraisal_policy.pdf*

The National Archives, *Acquisition policy*; also available at *http://www.nationalarchives.gov.uk/recordsmanagement/selection/acquisition.htm*

The National Archives (2004) *Terms of loan (deposit) for privately owned archives: guidance note for record repositories*; also available at *http://www.nationalarchives.gov.uk/archives/advice/*

Willa Samuels, H. (1992) *Varsity letters: documenting modern colleges and universities*. Lanham, MD: Scarecrow Press Inc.

Willa Samuels, H. (1992) 'Who controls the past', *American Archivist* 55: Winter, 109–24.

Yorke, S. (2000) 'Great expectations or none at all: the role and significance of community expectations in the appraisal function', *Archives and Manuscripts* 28:1, 25–37.

Arrangement and description

Canadian Council of Archives (2003) *Rules for archival description*, Ottawa. Available at *http://www.cdncouncilarchives.ca/archdesrules.html*

Encoded Archival Description Application Guidelines. Available at *http://www.loc.gov/ead/ag/agcontxt.html*

Hensen, S.L. (1989) *Archives, personal papers and manuscripts: a cataloging manual for archival repositories, historical societies and manuscript libraries.* Chicago: Society of American Archivists.

Gorman, M. (ed.) (1989) *Anglo-American cataloguing rules.* ALA Editions, US.

Holmes, O.W. (1984) 'Archival arrangement – five different operations at five different levels', In *A modern archives reader: basic readings on archival theory and practice.* Edited by Daniels, M.F. and Walch, T. Washington: National Archives Trust Board, 162–80. First published in *The American Archivist* 27: January, 21–41.

International Council on Archives (1996) *International standard archival authority record for corporate bodies, persons and families* (ISAAR (CPF)), 2nd edn. Ottawa. Also available at *www.ica.org*

International Council on Archives (2000) *General international standard archival description* (ISAD(G)), 2nd edn. Ottawa. Also available at *www.ica.org*

Library of Congress Subject Headings, 29th edn. 2006.

National Council on Archives (1997) *Rules for the construction of personal, place and corporate names* (NCA Rules). London: National Council on Archives. Also available at *http://www.ncaonline.org.uk/materials/namingrules.pdf*

Procter, M. and Cook, M. (2000) *Manual of archival description*, 3rd edn. Aldershot: Gower.

Roper, M. (1992) 'Provenance', In *The archival imagination: essays in honour of Hugh A. Taylor.* Edited by Craig, B.L. Ottawa: Association of Canadian Archivists, 134–53.

Scott, P.J. (1981) 'Archives and administrative change – some methods and approaches. *Archives and Manuscripts* 9:1, 3–18.

Society of American Archivists (2004) *Describing archives: a content standard.* Chicago: Society of American Archivists.

UK Archival Thesaurus (UKAT). Available at *http://www.ukat.org.uk/*

UNESCO Thesaurus. Also available at *http://databases.unesco.org/thesaurus/*;

Access

Access to Archives (A2A). Available at *http://www.a2a.org.uk*

Archives Task Force (2004) *Listening to the past, speaking to the future.* Also available at *http://www.mla.gov.uk/documents/atf_report.pdf*

Australian Society of Archivists *Code of Ethics*. Available at *http://www.archivists.org.au/about/ethics.html*

Black, P. (1997) *Manipulating the media: a handbook for librarians*. London: Library Association.

Council of Europe Committee of Ministers (Recommendation No. R (2000) 13 of the Committee of Ministers to Member States on a European Policy on Access to Archives), 2000. Available at *http://www.archives.gov.ua/Eng/Law-base/Recommendations.php*

Data Protection Act (Great Britain, 1998, c.29). Available at *http://www.opsi.gov.uk/acts/acts1998/19980029.htm*

Economou, M. (2002) *User evaluation: report of findings*. London: Museums, Libraries and Archives Council.

Freedom of Information Act (Great Britain. 2000 c.36). Available at *http://www.hmso.gov.uk/acts/acts2000.htm*

International Council on Archives (1996) *Code of ethics*. Available at *www.ica.org*

Hedstrom, M. (1998) 'How do archivists make electronic archives usable and accessible?' *Archives and Manuscripts* 26:1, 6–22.

Hill, A. (2004) 'Serving the invisible researcher: meeting the needs of online users', *Journal of the Society of Archivists* 25:2, 139–48.

Historical Manuscripts Commission (1999) *The Twenty-eighth Report of the Royal Commission on Historical Manuscripts, 1991–1999, Archives at the millennium*. London: The Stationery Office.

Lord Chancellor's Department, *Code of practice on the discharge of public authorities functions under Part 1 of the Freedom of Information Act 2000 Section 45*. Available at *http://www.dca.gov.uk/foi/codesprac.htm*

Lord Chancellor's Department, *Code of practice on the management of records issued under the Freedom of Information Act Section 46*. Available at *http://www.dca.gov.uk/foi/codesprac.htm*

Lord Chancellor's Department, *Government policy on archives*, 1999. Also available at *http://www.nationalarchives.gov.uk/policy/idac/government.htm*

Museums, Libraries and Archives Council (2003) *Measuring the outcomes and impact of learning in museums archives and libraries: the learning impact research project end of project paper*. Available at *www.mla.gov.uk/action/learnacc/lirp.asp*

Museums, Libraries and Archives Council (2004) *Inspiring learning for all*. Available at *http://www.inspiringlearningforall.gov.uk/introduction/*

National Council on Archives (2001) *Taking part: an audit of social inclusion work in archives.* Available at *http://nca.archives.org.uk/takepart.pdf*

Padfield, T. (2004) *Copyright for archivists*, 2nd edn. London: Facet Publishing.

Pederson, A. (1997) 'Educating for advocacy', *Janus* 1, 7–15.

Public Record Office (2000) *Data Protection Act: a guide for archivists and records managers.* Available at *http://www.nationalarchives.gov.uk/policy/dp/*

Public Record Office (2002) Society of Archivists and Records Management Society, *Code of practice for archivists and records managers under Section 51(4) of the Data Protection Act 1998.* Version 3 (2005) available at *http://www.archives.org.uk/publications/bestpracticeguidelines.html*

Public Services Quality Group (PSQG) (2001) *Survey of visitors to British archives, 2001.* Available at *http://www.nationalarchives.gov.uk/archives/psqg/pdf/nationalresults2001.pdf*

Public Services Quality Group (PSQG) (2003) *Standard for access to archives.* Also available at *http://www.nationalarchives.gov.uk/archives/psqg/access.htm*

Resource (2001) *Developing the 21st century archive: an action plan for United Kingdom Archives.* Also available at *http://www.mla.gov.uk/documents/21centarc.pdf*

Sexton, A., Turner, C., Yeo, G. and Hockey, S. (2004) 'Understanding users: a prerequisite for developing new technologies', *Journal of the Society of Archivists* 25:1, 33–49.

Sexton, A., Turner, C., Yeo, G. and Hockey, S. (2004) 'Testing the LEADERS demonstrator application', *Journal of the Society of Archivists* 25:2, 189–208.

Shenton, C. (2002) *Archival websites*, Society of Archivists Best practice guideline no 7. Also available at *http://www.archives.org.uk/publications/bestpracticeguidelines.html*

Society of American Archivists *Code of ethics for archivists.* Available at *http://www.archivists.org/governance/handbook/app_ethics.asp*

Tavistock Institute (1997) *JISC Archives Sub-committee: a project to develop measures of user satisfaction for university archive and manuscript repositories.* London: Tavistock Institute.

The National Archives (2004) *The National Archives standard for record repositories.* Also available at *http://www.nationalarchives.gov.uk/archives/framework/repositories.htm*

Preservation

Beagrie, N. (2003) *National digital preservation initiatives: an overview of developments in Australia, France, the Netherlands, and the United Kingdom and of related international activity.* Washington, DC: Council on Library and Information Resources, and Library of Congress.

Beagrie, N. and Jones, M. *The handbook.* Available at *http://www.dpconline.org/graphics/handbook/;*

BS 5454:2000 *Recommendations for the storage and exhibition of archival documents.*

Cunningham, A. (2001) 'Recent developments in standards for archival description and metadata', presented at the International Seminar on Archival Descriptive Standards, University of Toronto. Available at *http://www.archivists.org.au/cds/cunningham.html*

Dublin Core Metadata Initiative. Available at *http://dublincore.org.*

ERPANET (2003) *Digital preservation policy.* Available at *http://www.erpanet.org/guidance/docs/ERPANETPolicyTool.pdf*

Foot, M. (2001) *Building blocks for a preservation policy,* National Preservation Office. Also available at *http://www.bl.uk/services/npo/npo8.pdf*

Forde, H. (1997) 'Preservation policies – who needs them?', *Journal of the Society of Archivists* 18:2, 165–73.

Gilliland-Swetland, A.J. (1998) 'Defining metadata', In *Introduction to metadata pathways to digital information.* Edited by Baca, M. USA: Getty Information Institute.

ISO 14721:2003 *Space data and information transfer systems – Open archival information system – Reference model,* *http://www.iso.org/iso/en/*

Kitching, C., Edgar, H. and Milford, I. (2001) *Archival documents: guide to the interpretation of BS5454:2000, Storage and exhibition of archival documents,* BSI PD 0024.

Levy, D. (2001) *Scrolling forward: making sense of documents in the digital age.* New York: Arcade Publishing.

Matthews, G. and Feather, J. (eds) (2003) *Disaster management for libraries and archives.* Aldershot: Ashgate Publishing.

National Archives of Canada (2002) *Preservation policy.* Available at *http://www.collectionscanada.ca/preservation/1304_e.html*

National Preservation Office (2000) *Photocopying of library and archive materials.* Also available at *http://www.bl.uk/services/npo/pdf/photocopy.pdf*

National Preservation Office (2000) *Guide to preservation microfilming.* London: The Office.

National Preservation Office (2001) *A national preservation strategy for library and archive collections in the United Kingdom and Ireland: principles and prospects.* London: The Office.

National Preservation Office *Preservation assessment survey: library and archives module.* Available at *http://www.bl.uk/services/npo/paslib .html*

National Preservation Office (2004) *The prevention and treatment of mould outbreaks in collections.* Also available at *http://www.bl.uk/ services/npo/pdf/mould.pdf*

National Preservation Office *Preservation assessment survey: library and archives module, http://www.bl.uk/services/npo/paslib.html*

Pickford, C., Rhys-Lewis, J. and Weber, J. (1997) *Preservation and conservation,* Society of Archivists Best Practice Guideline no 4. Also available at *http://www.archives.org.uk/publications/ bestpracticeguidelines.html*

Resource (2002) *Benchmarks in collection care.* London: Resource. Also available at *http://www.mla.gov.uk/resources/assets//B/benchmarks_ pdf_6849.pdf*

Rhys-Lewis, J. (2004) *Preservation management,* version 1.3. University of Liverpool.

Ross, S. (2000) *Changing trains at Wigan: digital preservation and the future of scholarship,* National Preservation Office. Also available at *http://www.bl.uk/services/npo/occpaper.pdf*

ScreenSound Australia (2005) *Preservation policy, http://www .screensound.gov.au/AboutUs.nsf/Sub+Pages/Publications+Corporate +Policy+preservation/*

Smithsonian Institution, National Archives and Records Administration, Library of Congress, and National Park Service (1993) *A primer on disaster preparedness, management, and response: paper-based materials.* Also available at *http://sul-server-2.stanford.edu/bytopic/ disasters/primer/*

State Records Office of Western Australia (c.1991) *Policy on preservation of state records.* Available at *http://www.sro.wa.gov.au/ government/preservation-policy.html*

The British Library (2002) *Digital preservation policy.* Available at *http://www.bl.uk/about/collectioncare/bldppolicy1102.pdf*

The National Archives (2004) *Preservation policy.* Available at *http://www.nationalarchives.gov.uk/about/pdf/preservation_policy.pdf*

UKOLN (2004) *Technical guidelines for digital cultural content creation programme.* Bath: University of Bath.

Youngs, K. *Managing the digitisation of library, archive and museum materials.* Available at *http://www.bl.uk/services/npo/pdf/digitisation .pdf*

Index

Printed in the United States
64977LVS00001B/69

9 781843 341123